TAKING ON THE TRADITION

Cultural Memory
in
the
Present

Mieke Bal and Hent de Vries, Editors

TAKING ON THE TRADITION

Jacques Derrida and the
Legacies of Deconstruction

Michael Naas

STANFORD UNIVERSITY PRESS

STANFORD, CALIFORNIA

2003

Stanford University Press
Stanford, California

Printed in the United States of America
on acid-free, archival-quality paper.

Library of Congress Cataloging-in-Publication Data
Naas, Michael.
  Taking on the tradition : Jacques Derrida and the legacies of
deconstruction / Michael Naas.
    p. cm.—(Cultural memory in the present)
  ISBN 0-8047-4421-1 (cloth : alk. paper) — ISBN 0-8047-4422-X
(pbk. : alk. paper)
  1. Derrida, Jacques. I. Title. II. Series.
B2430.D484 N33   2002
194—dc21

                                        2002007736

Original Printing 2003

Last figure below indicates year of this printing:
11   10   09   08   07   06   05   04   03

Typeset by Classic Typography in 11/13.5 Adobe Garamond.

For Jean-Stéphane

Contents

Acknowledgments

This book is the fruit of several years of sustained dialogue with colleagues and students in philosophy at DePaul University. Although I would never dare identify any particular place with what Derrida in "Violence and Metaphysics" once called a "community of the question," DePaul continues to be an exemplary place for pursuing the kinds of questions addressed in this work. I ask my colleagues and students to forgive me the injustice of thanking them here collectively so as to avoid the perhaps greater injustice of failing to mete out my enormous gratitude in due measures. Each will see in these pages the extent to which I am indebted to them.

I am also extremely grateful to the administration at DePaul University for its generous support of this work, particularly Dean Michael Mezey of the College of Liberal Arts and Sciences, along with the Faculty Research and Development Program Committee.

For Pascale-Anne Brault, my first and best reader, not even the hyperbolic "without her this book could not have been written" could begin to do justice to the debt I owe her. May these words help her better believe it.

Finally, my deepest thanks to Jacques Derrida, for years of friendship and hospitality, and for everything he has given so many of us to live and to think.

Abbreviations

The following abbreviations have been used in the text for frequently cited works by Derrida:

A   *Adieu to Emmanuel Levinas*. Trans. Pascale-Anne Brault and
          Michael Naas. Stanford, Calif.: Stanford University Press, 1999.

"C"   "Cogito and the History of Madness." In *Writing and Differ-
          ence*. Trans. Alan Bass. Chicago: University of Chicago Press,
          1978.

"DRB"   "The Deaths of Roland Barthes." Trans. Pascale-Anne Brault
          and Michael Naas. In *Philosophy and Non-Philosophy Since
          Merleau-Ponty*, ed. Hugh J. Silverman. Continental Philosophy,
          vol. 1. New York: Routledge, 1988.

"FM"   "By Force of Mourning." Trans. Pascale-Anne Brault and
          Michael Naas. *Critical Inquiry* 22, no. 2 (winter 1996).

GL   *Glas*. Trans. John P. Leavey Jr. Lincoln: University of Nebraska
          Press, 1986.

GT   *Given Time. I, Counterfeit Money*. Trans. Peggy Kamuf.
          Chicago: University of Chicago Press, 1992.

H   *Of Hospitality*. Trans. Rachel Bowlby. Stanford, Calif.: Stanford
          University Press, 2000.

"K"   "*Khōra*." Trans. Ian McLeod. In *On the Name*, ed. Thomas
          Dutoit. Stanford, Calif.: Stanford University Press, 1995.

MA   *Mémoires d'aveugle: L'autoportrait et autres ruines*. Paris:
          Editions de la Réunion des Musées Nationaux, 1990.

MB   *Memoirs of the Blind: The Self-Portrait and Other Ruins.* Trans.
        Pascale-Anne Brault and Michael Naas. Chicago: University of
        Chicago Press, 1993.

PC   *The Post Card.* Trans. Alan Bass. Chicago: University of
        Chicago Press, 1987.

PF   *Politics of Friendship.* Trans. George Collins. New York: Verso,
        1997.

"PP"   "Plato's Pharmacy." In *Dissemination.* Trans. Barbara Johnson.
        Chicago: University of Chicago Press, 1981.

RP   *Resistances of Psychoanalysis.* Trans. Peggy Kamuf, Pascale-Anne
        Brault, and Michael Naas. Stanford, Calif.: Stanford University
        Press, 1998.

"T"   "Telepathy." Trans. Nicholas Royle. *Oxford Literary Review* 10,
        nos. 1–2 (1988).

TP   *The Truth in Painting.* Trans. Geoff Bennington and Ian
        McLeod. Chicago: University of Chicago Press, 1987.

"UG"   "Ulysses Gramophone: Hear Say Yes in Joyce." Trans. Tina
        Kendall. Rev. Shari Benstock. In *Acts of Literature*, ed. Derek
        Attridge. London: Routledge, 1991.

"VM"   "Violence and Metaphysics." In *Writing and Difference.* Trans.
        Alan Bass. Chicago: University of Chicago Press, 1978.

"WM"   "White Mythology." In *The Margins of Philosophy.* Trans.
        Alan Bass. Chicago: University of Chicago Press, 1972.

And also:

DR   John Mullins and Sons. *The Divining Rod: Its History,
        Truthfulness, and Practical Utility.* Colerne, Wiltshire:
        J. and H. W. Mullins, 1908.

F   Maurice Blanchot. *Friendship.* Trans. Elizabeth Rottenberg.
        Stanford, Calif.: Stanford University Press, 1997.

HS   Michel Foucault. *The History of Sexuality.* Vol. 1, *An Introduc-
        tion.* Trans. Robert Hurley. New York: Vintage, 1980.

Il.   Homer. *Iliad*. Trans. A. T. Murray. Cambridge, Mass.: Harvard
            University Press, 1924.

"IO"   Jean Starobinski. "The Inside and the Outside." *Hudson
            Review* 28, no. 3 (autumn 1975).

LF   Jean Genet. *Our Lady of the Flowers*. Trans. Bernard Frechtman.
            New York: Bantam, 1964.

"MBTP"   Michel Foucault. "My Body, This Paper, This Fire." Trans.
            Geoffrey Bennington. *Oxford Literary Review* 4 (autumn 1975).

Od.   Homer. *Odyssey*. Trans. A. T. Murray. Cambridge, Mass.:
            Harvard University Press, 1919.

TDR   E. W. Beaven. *Tales of the Divining Rod*. London:
            A. H. Stockwell, 1899.

U   James Joyce. *Ulysses*. New York: Random House, 1961.

Introduction

> It is always necessary that the other sign, and it is always the other who signs last.
> In other words, first.
> —Jacques Derrida, "Force of Law"

By signing on—since it has become a tradition—with an epigraph from the one to whom this book is devoted, I am merely making explicit what is always implicit in any beginning or origin, any reinscription of the tradition, any new chapter in the history of philosophy: it is always the other who signs, who authorizes us or gives us the power to speak, who leaves us a tradition or history to work with or against, who situates us with a name, a place, and a time. It is always the other who signs last, who has the last word, who signs off or does not, and so has in effect the first word, concerning history, tradition, and the very possibility of receiving or taking these on.

All this is to assert nothing more than the seemingly incontestable fact that we are always preceded, that we always think, read, and write within a certain history and from a certain origin, within a unique and irreplaceable tradition that exerts an almost unthinkable and inescapable influence over us. Because our tradition and our history give us not only a set of received views and classic themes but a particular history of the concept of history, a particular tradition of thinking tradition, we are in effect signed into this tradition and history by the mere fact that we *receive* or *recognize* them as our own. We are signed into a tradition and a history not only by agreeing with those who have come before us, that is, by explicitly taking on their tradition or their history, but simply by recognizing or receiving their signature. And this is true even when, and sometimes especially when, we recognize or receive their signature only in order to break away from or repudiate it—that is, only in order to "take it on." For there is a long tradition in philosophy of taking on the tradition, of calling into question certain assumptions, canons, and institutional practices—everything that assumes and supports the values and concepts, even the unity and existence, of a single, monolithic tradition. Whether we are for it or against it, then, it is always in view of a countersignature that we write.

What we receive through the signature of the other is thus not only some determinate tradition, theme, figure, or authority but a certain way of taking on tradition, a certain way of either accepting or rejecting it and its authority. As the tradition itself would tell us, "there is nothing new under the sun," since even our ways of receiving the sun's light or welcoming its arrival have become part of our tradition, illuminated in advance by our history and our concepts.

And yet, each time we receive the tradition, each time we take it on, we are offered a chance to receive something unforeseeable and unprecedented within it. Although all our thinking, all our receptions, are illuminated in advance by the horizon of our tradition, our turning toward that horizon is not. Each day we turn toward the sun blindly; with each reading we receive the tradition anew and so are given the chance of encountering something that escapes the simple duality of "taking on the tradition"— the simple opposition between accepting or rejecting a tradition as our own. With each reception comes the possibility of rethinking what is our own by receiving it before either we or it have been wholly constituted. For although there may indeed be nothing new under the sun, there is no tradition, no sun even, before we have received it.

This book focuses on the way the work of Jacques Derrida has helped us rethink and rework the themes of tradition, legacy, and inheritance in the Western philosophical tradition. It thus concentrates not only on such themes *in* the work of Derrida as tradition, reception, inheritance, legacy, and donation but on Derrida's "own" gestures, his own way of turning toward the sun or the tradition. For even if there is nothing new under the sun, the gesture by or in which a deconstructive reading turns toward the sun or intervenes in the tradition always produces or reproduces, I will argue, a number of wrinkles or disturbances within the chronology and topography of the tradition. By focusing less, then, on what is received from the tradition than on the *moment of reception*, the moment of donation or presentation when time itself is given and received, one begins to catch a glimpse of both the incredible power of the tradition, its way of recuperating the most heterogeneous and marginal elements, *and* its great fragility, its vulnerability to the very gestures of reception that make it—along with our history and our origins—possible in the first place.

Through a series of very focused analyses of Derrida's work I consider how, in a double gesture, this work "takes on" the Western philosophical tradition by at once making it its own and calling it into question so as to locate or reactivate something within it that can be neither simply affirmed nor rejected. Taking on the tradition thus entails neither simply assuming nor jettisoning the notions privileged by the tradition—notions such as presence and permanence, even the notion of a single, uninterrupted Western tradition. For Derrida it is never simply a question of saying "yes" or "no" to what the tradition has given or bequeathed us. But although this is true for all of Derrida's work, "taking on the tradition"—another way of glossing "deconstruction"—takes on an exemplary character when it turns to all those concepts surrounding the very passing on of this tradition, notions such as bequeathing and inheriting, giving and receiving, teaching and learning, writing and reading. Such notions are themselves central to the Western philosophical tradition, as well as to Derrida's reading of it, as many who have followed Derrida have shown. But what has often gone unnoticed in the consideration of Derrida's work is the fact that these notions are not only assumed and contested by Derrida in a critical way but repeated and interrupted, performed and transformed, by Derrida as an inheritor, receiver, learner, or reader of the tradition. Anytime Derrida begins analyzing the notions of reception or legacy within a particular text in the tradition, he ends up, because of the very *necessity* of taking on the tradition, performing and interrupting these gestures in his own reading so as to make possible the coming of "another gesture," one that is neither simply his nor the tradition's.

To take on the tradition, then, and what is most powerful and gripping within it, one must affirm and contest not only the arguments and claims of the tradition but traditional ways of making arguments and claims, of claiming authority, producing evidence, and gaining conviction, traditional modes of receiving and reading the tradition. Hence it is necessary not only to take a critical stance toward the tradition but to adopt a performative strategy with regard to it. Whereas Derrida's texts thus analyze traditional philosophical issues and concepts in order to reveal something untraditional within them, they also perform traditional critical gestures in order to invent other, unprecedented gestures from within them. Each of the readings in this book is thus devoted to what might be called the "performativity" of Derrida's texts, particularly in relationship to the themes of tradition, donation, and inheritance. Because the "performativity" of each of Derrida's texts is context specific and develops always in relationship to particular works in the history of philosophy, each performative gesture must be patiently analyzed. These essays look at the way Derrida's writing tries to mark its indebtedness to traditional philosophical and literary themes and, especially, *gestures* at the same time as it attempts to bring about a displacement within them. In the end we will see that, for Derrida, such a displacement is not at all foreign to this indebtedness, that it is, in fact, the only way of truly affirming it, the only way of truly taking it on.

Throughout his career, from his very early work on the "speech act" theory of John Austin (*How to Do Things with Words*) in the early 1970s to more recent works on the gift, the promise, the secret, perjury, forgiveness, and so on, Derrida has been interested in the ways language is used not only to *say* something but to *do* or *perform* it, in the ways it is used not simply to talk about the world but to engage us in it.[1] Even when a discourse appears to be making a simple statement of fact, Derrida would argue, something is often if not always being performed; for example, even in a statement such as "Jacques Derrida is the founder of deconstruction" or "deconstruction is dead," there is often, depending on the circumstances, an attempt not simply to note some state of affairs, to make claims about the origin or demise of deconstruction, but to elicit or produce certain effects or responses, from tacit agreement or dissent to the production of explicit affirmations or counterclaims. More significant, however, such utterances—which can be found in any number of places today—often aim not simply to provoke some future response but actually to produce or perform something through their very enunciation, in this case, to assign deconstruction an origin by issuing it a birth certificate or to mark its end by pronouncing its death, whether as a solemn proclamation or a triumphant declaration, a word of mourning or a wish fulfillment.

Much of Derrida's work has been devoted to drawing out the implications and consequences of this performativity of language.[2] Although much has been written about the philosophical claims Derrida makes about language, and especially about the performativity of language, what has often been overlooked is the fact that Derrida himself uses language in a highly performative way at the same time that he tries to say something about this performativity. Although such an emphasis on language and style and the way these *work* not simply to note but to *produce* truths is always important in philosophy, it is particularly important in a thinker such as Derrida, who, in writing on the works of others, always ends up employing to some degree the terms, rhetoric, argumentative strategies, and performative gestures of the works he is reading. Only when an understanding of Derrida's philosophical claims is coupled with an attention to such strategies and gestures can we truly understand the deconstructive "practice" of taking on the tradition.

The focus of this book is thus not only *what* Derrida says in the texts I read but the *way* he says it, not only the claims he makes but the rhetoric, language, and strategies he uses to make them. More precisely, the focus is on the fact that the way Derrida says things, the way his texts are performative, is inseparable from *what* he says and the claims he makes. My contention is ultimately that only by taking into account the performativity of Derrida's language will we really be able to understand his claims. To put this hypothesis to the test, the book consists of a series of very different but related studies of particular texts of Derrida—from some of Derrida's earlier readings of Plato and Aristotle on the themes of writing and metaphor to more recent works on Levinas and Blanchot around the themes of hospitality and friendship.

To follow this performativity, I have found it often necessary to pay close attention to the letter of Derrida's texts, and first of all the French text. This way of reading Derrida has no doubt been informed by my work as a translator, which has made me attentive to details or aspects of Derrida's writing that I might otherwise have passed over—sudden shifts in rhetoric, style, or tone, unexpected word choices, all those things that Derrida himself is extremely attentive to in his reading of others. In several chapters I thus reflect on the nature of translation itself, the only way we really have of taking on the tradition and making it our own—or not.

As for the subtitle of this work, there are obviously already many legacies of deconstruction and of the work of Jacques Derrida and many excellent books on various aspects of Derrida's work that bear witness to these legacies. In the English-speaking world alone, where Derrida has found both enthusiastic advocates and fierce detractors, many books offer overviews of

Derrida's work, and many more try to highlight various aspects of it—from its philosophical claims to its aesthetic, political, ethical, and theological implications.[3] If I have dared come forward with—as the rhetorical turn common to introductions would put it—"yet another book on Derrida," it is in part because there are already so many, so many legacies and receptions of Derrida's work, so many attempts to take it on.[4] My intention here is not to assess and evaluate these different legacies but to turn to the modes of reception implied and assumed in them. To do this, I take my lead in each chapter from a very particular text or circumscribed set of texts in Derrida that highlight the themes of legacy and inheritance or that problematize the ways we "take on" the texts of the tradition.

Because Derrida's corpus has grown so large, no work can possibly claim to treat it in its entirety or even to do justice to a set of themes within it. Although I concentrate here on the particular themes of legacy, donation, teaching, learning, and tradition, I have been by no means exhaustive in my analysis. Much more could be said about Derrida's own engagement with issues of pedagogy, with the ways we teach and learn—and thereby sustain if not invent—the tradition.[5] Much more could be said about the ways in which the tradition is always constituted and sustained by "specters" or "ghosts"—terms that have become more and more prevalent in Derrida's work. Much more could be said about the way these ghosts haunt our archives and give us our inheritance.[6] And no matter how well a subject is circumscribed in the work of Derrida, other subjects and themes cannot help but creep in. I have thus tried to follow here a principle of exemplarity, to show in very specific contexts how Derrida's textual practice operates so that similar analyses might be carried out elsewhere.

Because reading is always implicated, compromised even, by what is being read, these readings will not attempt to survey the Derridean corpus from above in order to develop a general theory about it. These readings are, of necessity, *motivated* by Derrida's texts, so that even when they do say something about Derrida's work as a whole, they are marked not only by the conditions and contexts surrounding their production but by the specific "content" they propose to treat. By agreeing to sign on, I could not help but be determined in some sense by the themes, figures, terms, even the rhetoric, of a filiation. Indeed it is only under such a condition that I have the chance of saying anything "new."

Although no rigorous necessity governed my choice of texts to read here, my de facto "canon" was not determined arbitrarily. In almost every chapter I circle round texts that are considered central to the tradition. First, there is a constant return to Greek philosophy, particularly Plato and Aristotle, since there would clearly be no tradition without them. Second, the figures of, among others, Homer and Joyce—figures who, in some sense, mark the beginning and end of the Western epic tradition—run throughout these essays. What I am taking on here is thus perhaps not only the philosophical but the literary tradition that begins in the epic poetry of Homer and ends, it could be argued, in the high modernism of Joyce. From Homer's *Iliad* and *Odyssey* to Joyce's *Ulysses* and *Finnegans Wake*, from Plato and Aristotle to Levinas and Blanchot—it is tempting to treat these as the bookends of a tradition, the beginning and end of the epic story of philosophy and literature in the West. Yet what if we were to suspend or interrupt our reading, our reception, of this epic tale, this more or less linear narrative? What if we were to find resources in this story for reading it against itself, for seeing that it has already from the beginning been other than itself, that its being other than itself was the very condition of its ever becoming itself? Then perhaps we would have to rethink not only our own relationship to the tradition but the very temporality and identity of the tradition itself and, thus, the very identity of those who, as its inheritors or disciples, are given to taking it on.

Part I of this work, "Greek Gifts," treats Derrida's reading of the passing on and inheritance of the philosophical tradition in Greek philosophy. I begin in Chapter I, "A Given Take: The Platonic Reception of Plato in the Pharmacy," with an exemplary scene of giving and receiving, writing and reading, in the history of philosophy, a short passage from Plato's *Phaedrus*, and an exemplary reading of this passage in Derrida's essay "Plato's Pharmacy." By looking at this exemplary scene from the *Phaedrus*, wherein King Thamus receives from Theuth the gift of writing, we will see how Derrida figures within it the reception of the tradition itself. Through Derrida's analysis of Plato we come to understand, I argue, how Plato ultimately became Plato, that is, how philosophical authority is determined in his dialogues, how the authority to evaluate various theories or traditions is actually staged by Plato in the *Phaedrus* so as to legitimate some works, exclude others, and decide what is worthy of being passed on.

For Derrida, Plato's *Phaedrus* is not only a dialogue within the tradition but a dialogue that first gives us a tradition by establishing its own modes of reception, legacy, and inheritance. We encounter there in Thamus and

Theuth, or Socrates and Plato, the first of many father-son, master-disciple pairs to be treated in this work: from Vernant and Derrida in the following chapter to Foucault, Lacan, and Levinas and Derrida in Chapters 4 through 6, to Elijah and Elisha, or Elijah and Dr. John Alexander Dowie, in the Conclusion. In each case the tradition is established *across* generations— and if mothers and daughters are absent here, it is perhaps because they have been for the most part cut out of this inheritance. This absence provides yet another reason to interrupt this testamentary scene and to read Plato, for example, with an eye not only for father figures but for other thoughts of legacy and inheritance, for daughters and mothers like Pharmaceia and Khōra.

In Chapter 2 I turn from a scene of giving and receiving *in* a text to the giving and receiving *of* a text. Having analyzed in the first chapter a scene of giving and receiving between one generation and another, the father-king-master (Thamus) and the son-servant-disciple (Theuth), I consider in "Given Time for a Detour: The Abyssal Gift of '*Khōra*'" the way in which Derrida himself gives, and gives to someone from whom he will have himself received or learned a good deal. After reading *Given Time* to analyze what Derrida *says* about the logic of the gift, I turn to a text that Derrida himself dedicates or *gives* to one of the influences on his work—the classicist Jean-Pierre Vernant—in order to see how Derrida's practice or gesture reflects this logic. For it just so happens that what Derrida gives Vernant is a text concerning Plato's notion of *khōra*, the receptacle or space that itself, according to Plato, *gives* us all our determinations and distinctions. Hence I read Derrida's essay "*Khōra*" in the light of *Given Time* and consider the role played by the context for this work (a Festschrift honoring Jean-Pierre Vernant) in determining the content of it (a reading of the figure of the *khōra* in Plato's *Timaeus*). I read the *khōra* as an exemplary figure of reception and donation in the Western philosophical tradition and Plato's *Timaeus* as an exemplary text of reading and reception. The chapter concludes with consideration of how Derrida's texts relate to those he reads (Plato, Heidegger), as well as to his own past works, works that not only form the backdrop for his writing but come to supplement and haunt it.

Chapter 3, "Stumping the Sun: The Odyssey of Metaphor in 'White Mythology,'" analyzes Derrida's reading of the philosophical accounts of metaphor in the tradition. I attempt here to show that Derrida's own metaphors must be reinterpreted in terms of what is said about metaphor in this essay. I begin by looking at the way Derrida reads the Aristotelian theory of metaphor and other traditional theories in order to show the presuppositions on which they are all based. I then consider a couple of "performative moments" in Derrida's reading of the tradition on metaphor in order to gesture toward the "metaphoricity" that, according to Derrida, makes all metaphor possible. By means of a detour through the *Odyssey* in which I look at Homer's notion of "sure signs," I ultimately argue that Derrida is trying to unearth or uproot a notion of both the sign and metaphor that would rest on a conception of nature or natural resemblance. Questions of identity and language are thus central to this chapter, as they will be again in Chapters 8 and 9 when I return to Homer in order to supplement Derrida's analyses of friendship and hospitality.

Part 2, "French Receptions," looks at several texts in which Derrida reworks, often through a reading of one of his French "teachers" or "predecessors," particular philosophical notions in the tradition (mastery and discipleship, origin and reception, the phenomenon and that which exceeds the phenomenon) so as to remark a performative gesture associated with each.[7] In Chapter 4, "Derrida's Watch/Foucault's Pendulum: A Final Impetus to the Cogito Debate," I consider the infamous debate between Derrida and Foucault during the 1960s and 1970s over a passage of Descartes's *Meditations* concerning the exclusion of madness. I am less interested, however, in assessing the results of this debate, in determining its winners and losers, or even in analyzing its place in French intellectual history, than in following the structure and periodicity of the debate itself, the way certain questions that formed the basis for the debate reconfigure or scan Derrida's very relation to Foucault. I argue that what was at issue from the very beginning of the debate was not simply the question of mastery in the *Meditations* but a struggle for mastery between Derrida and Foucault and, more important, a struggle over the very nature and meaning of mastery itself. Reading Derrida's last text on Foucault, his 1992 essay "'To Do Justice to Freud,'" I conclude that the debate can be most productively thought of not in terms of a master-disciple dialectic but as a nondialectical process of mourning that always exceeds the terms of mastery and discipleship.

As in the preceding chapter, I try to show and, I hope, perform the way in which the subject or theme of Derrida's text—there the gift, here mastery—always comes to haunt or inhabit the situation of the text, its material production and presentation, that is, the way in which confronting or taking on the tradition always entails an appropriation or taking on of its terms and structures. I attempt to demonstrate here, and throughout the book, that the only way to effectively intervene in the tradition—the only way to question its singularity even—is to take it on or appropriate it in this way, to look at the structures of reception and mastery that it hands down to us so as to be able to reflect, reflect on, question, and interrupt them.

In Chapter 5, "Lacunae: Divining Derrida's Sources Through 'Telepathy,'" I argue that philosophical influence and inheritance might be thought of not in terms of a series of privileged themes, concepts, or sources that are passed on to us but as a sort of "telepathy." I thus examine a short text of Derrida's on Freud entitled, precisely, "Telepathy" so as to rethink the very nature and essence of "sources," their location inside or outside that which receives them, their ability to motivate or provoke their very reception. This is the one essay in the volume that analyzes and engages in the kind of lexical play for which Derrida has often been criticized. But the reader must bear in mind that the context for this text rigorously determines the play. I, following Derrida, who is himself following Freud, thus follow certain images and words, certain syllables even, in an attempt to think through or be moved by Freud's shifting views on telepathy. Because Derrida is speaking about Freud's views of the unconscious, he allows himself—and I allow myself in reading him—a greater latitude in the attention to and emphasis on the resonances among words than might otherwise be appropriate. I conclude this chapter on Derrida's "sources"—including that ambivalent source named "Lacan"—by opposing two notions of the future, one determinable by fate and fortune and the other set up and upset by an unforeseeable apocalypse.

Chapter 6, "The Phenomenon in Question: Violence, Metaphysics, and the Levinasian Third," looks at Derrida's long engagement with the work of Emmanuel Levinas by focusing on the relationship between hospitality and the question—a relationship that will be taken up again in Chapter 9. I argue that in light of his 1997 work *Adieu*, an examination of the theme or question of hospitality in the work of Levinas, Derrida's 1964 essay on Levinas, "Violence and Metaphysics," might now also be read as a work on hospitality in Levinas, the possibility of the philosophical logos to "receive" or "welcome" what is radically other or foreign to it. I then demonstrate how *Adieu* can be read as a continuation, some thirty years after the fact, of Derrida's meditations in "Violence and Metaphysics" on the relationship between philosophical language and that which would be beyond or exterior to it. As in Chapter 4 on Foucault, we will see that, more than three decades later, the questions remain more or less the same; even if the master, both masters, will have disappeared in the interim, the questions will still be those of mastery and discipleship, giving and receiving.

In the final three chapters of this work, gathered together in Part 3 under the title "'Our' Legacies," I consider the promises and legacies of Derrida's work in terms of autobiography, friendship, and hospitality, that is, in terms of the self's relation to itself, its relation to the friend, and its relation to other others either as individuals or as members of a community or state. As in Chapter 5, where I try to interpret deconstruction as a kind of "telepathy," I here show how such themes for deconstruction as self-portraiture, friendship, and hospitality come to be received by or reflected in deconstruction itself and, of necessity, in our very understanding of deconstruction. As we will see, the container is always reflected by the contained, the container always contaminated and sometimes even enveloped by what it contains. That helps explain why, at the end of Chapter 9, I will allow myself to claim that deconstruction actually *is* hospitality.

Chapter 7, "Better Believing It: Translating Skepticism in *Memoirs of the Blind*," a text originally written in the form of a dialogue with my co-translator Pascale-Anne Brault, explores the themes of autobiography and self-portraiture in relation to vision and blindness, as well as the relation between Derrida's earlier text on art, *The Truth in Painting*, and his more recent *Memoirs of the Blind*. This chapter asks how Derrida in both of these texts receives and takes on the Judeo-Christian heritage of drawing and painting. Finally, the chapter analyzes what I have assumed throughout to be Derrida's faithfulness and fidelity to the tradition—that is, his endless skepticism with regard to just about everything received in the tradition and his unconditional faith in that which can never be simply received within it, his faith in what might be called the moment of reception or "conversion" itself.

Chapter 8, "Just a Turn Away: Apostrophe and the *Politics of Friendship*," examines the way Derrida reconsiders and reconfigures the Western philosophical tradition on the subject of friendship. I ask about the kind of performativity involved in reading the philosophical tradition on friendship that begins in Plato and Aristotle and comes to a certain end, or so it would seem, in Blanchot. As in Chapters 2 and 9, I attempt to illustrate Derrida's reading of a theme in the tradition by means of a performative supplement of my own. I try to show how, in the *Iliad*, friendship is always related to death, to a proximity interrupted or a presence in withdrawal, to a vocative rather than an accusative modality of thought. I argue that in Homer we can already find the traces of what will become key elements in the philosophical tradition of friendship (presence, resemblance, the friend as another self), as well as the end or interruption of that tradition as we find it in the work of Blanchot, a work that Derrida finds exemplary in its remarking of the discourse on friendship (the friend as always in withdrawal, as infinitely distant, as someone we cannot speak *of* but must only speak *to*).

In Chapter 9, "Hospitality as an Open Question: Deconstruction's Welcome Politics," I look at Derrida's recent work on hospitality and its relationship to the theme of the "question" as a welcoming gesture. Although almost every essay in this collection is, so to speak, an "occasional" piece, originally written for a particular audience and occasion, this fact is particularly important to bear in mind in this chapter. First read in Athens, Greece, to a group of undergraduate students participating in a foreign study program—students who had been for several months the recipients of an exemplary hospitality in a foreign land, and not just any foreign land—the chapter aims to explain Derrida's work in a more accessible and nontechnical manner, using examples from both Homer and Joyce to illustrate what Derrida means in recent works by conditional and unconditional hospitality. In this chapter I try to address certain misconceptions about "deconstruction" in general, a term I do not avoid but also do not emphasize throughout most of the book because of the various polemics surrounding it.

My aim in this chapter on hospitality is not only to be pedagogical in my explanation of Derrida's work but to reexamine questions of learning and pedagogy. Indeed, this is an implicit goal of the entire book. By asking how one receives the tradition, how our notions of reception are already shaped by the tradition, how our traditional notions of reception affect our reception of this tradition, and how these very questions themselves already reveal or betray a certain tradition of questioning, a style of philosophical speculation, I hope also to ask how it is that we learn, how we receive an education, how our notions of learning are already shaped by the tradition, how the history or tradition of learning affects the way we learn or receive this tradition, and how such questions themselves already reveal or betray a certain tradition of questioning, a certain education in philo-

sophical speculation. For what would be the aim of philosophical speculation, of a philosophical education, if not to question and teach others to
question, right up to and including—as Derrida has shown in his readings
of Heidegger and Levinas, and as I investigate in Chapter 6—the very tradition of the question?

The Conclusion, "Passing on the Mantle: Elijah's *Glas* and the Second Coming of Dr. John Alexander Dowie," begins with a short passage
from Derrida's *Glas* on the figure of Elijah in order then to follow this figure throughout Derrida's corpus in its unique relationship to time, tradition, and the future. I look here not simply at the way Derrida understands
two different traditions, namely, Judaism and Christianity, but, more important, at how he brings together two different notions of legacy within
these traditions, one that always determines a horizon for the donation and
reception of any legacy and one that leaves open a radically unknown and
unknowable future for that legacy, what Derrida calls in several more recent texts a "messianicity without messianism." I end the chapter and the
book by invoking the coming of what was, for me, a completely unexpected and unforeseeable Elijah, even if his initials were J. D. and even if
he ended up, as any good messiah should, coming very close to home.

In each of these readings I wish to show how Derrida begins always
with the tradition, with the canon, how he always assumes and confronts
it, that is, "takes it on," so as to locate something within it that the tradition has itself never been able to take on as its own. As Derrida once put
it, "Whatever one ends up doing with it, one must begin by listening to
the canon."[8] One begins by listening to the canon to learn first of all what
the canon says about itself, that is, what it says about reading and writing,
legacy and pedagogy, about itself as the place or giver of all value. One begins by listening the canon because the canon always gives us more than
we imagine, more than we could have expected, because the canon always
gives us, in its folds, something noncanonical, something that can never be
simply included in the curriculum. My hope is that this book will help inform our understanding of Derrida's reading of the canon, his reading of
everything that could be included in a curriculum, with an even greater appreciation for something that could never be so easily included, namely, his
engagement with literary and philosophical writing, his *reenactment* of the
tradition and its gestures.

In other words, I hope to demonstrate in these essays why a text by Derrida is always an *event*. Always contextual, occasional, always written in response to certain conditions—historical, political, philosophical, personal—Derrida's texts try to *invent* new means of reflection and reception from out of these conditions. They attempt to negotiate between conditions and the unconditional, between the tradition and what has not been and can never be received by the tradition, so as to provide another reception for the tradition, another way for it to come into its own. In this sense a text of Derrida's is always an event of reading and reception in which we, as readers, are, like Derrida, *implicated* in the very reception of the tradition. For it is we who ultimately sign off or do not on the tradition, we who give it its ultimate authority, an authority that we will then assume it always already had; it is we who, in receiving the tradition, make it one tradition rather than another, one tradition rather than many.

But by taking on the tradition without simply accepting or rejecting it, we may be better able, in the end, to open it up to what escapes it—expose it both to other traditions, if it is possible to think this, and to what already exceeds the tradition from within. The aim of each chapter, then, is not simply to follow Derrida in his reading of a certain text, or to interpret Derrida and his reading, to provide an exegesis so as to support or contest his claims, but to follow the *event* that Derrida's text is in the hope that, through the supplement of an additional reading—however much it takes from Derrida—*another event* may come to pass.

The last word, the first, is thus always still before us; it, like the tradition, is always still to come. It all depends on whether we sign on and, once we do, on how well it will take. "An abyssal thought of inheritance" if ever there was one.[9]

TAKING ON THE TRADITION

PART ONE

GREEK GIFTS

A Given Take

THE PLATONIC RECEPTION OF PLATO IN THE PHARMACY

> Just to receive in place of everything.
> —Jacques Derrida, "Avances"

As others who have tried to introduce the work of Jacques Derrida will probably attest, there is no natural or self-evident starting point, no privileged point of departure, for understanding this work, only better or worse alternatives depending on the themes one wishes to emphasize and the ends one has for reading. One might thus reasonably begin a work on Derrida by reading the essay "Différance," where the notion of différance as spatial differing and temporal deferring receives its most explicit treatment; or else the first part of *Of Grammatology*, where important themes such as the trace, the proper name, and the supplement are treated in great detail; or else *Speech and Phenomenon*, where the deconstruction of presence and the relationship between speech and thought, expression and intention, is perhaps most clearly articulated; or else a much more recent work, such as *Memoirs of the Blind*, where a reading of drawing and self-portraiture helps illuminate questions of presence and absence, presence to self and the presence of others. Indeed, one could justify almost any point of entry into the enormous and still rapidly expanding corpus of Jacques Derrida. But to say that there is no natural or self-evident starting point does not mean that one should or could begin just anywhere, at random. There are always specific contexts and conditions that suggest some beginnings, some strategic points of departure, rather than others, particular pedagogical takes in accordance with specific pedagogical aims and requirements. Since we are concerned here not only with such important Derridean "themes" as presence, the trace, différance, and so forth but with the very structures of reception, donation, legacy, bequeathing, and, of course, reading and writing, teaching and learning, the question of the pedagogical aims and requirements of beginning becomes particularly relevant and acute. It is thus precisely because no beginning is ever innocent, because each comes with its own risks, that we are obliged to choose our beginning well.

I have taken the risk of beginning with the passage in "Plato's Pharmacy" where Derrida rereads the famous myth recounted by Socrates at the end of the *Phaedrus* concerning the alleged inferiority of writing in relation to speech not only because it has become an almost *canonical* text within the work of Derrida, not only because Derrida himself has referred to it frequently in other places, not only because of its extremely influential reinterpretation of Plato, but because in its staging of the donation, reception, and judgment of writing in the *Phaedrus* it turns our gaze toward both the scene itself and *our reception* of it, our turning toward it, our way of learning from it. It is, thus, an *exemplary* scene—exemplary in Plato of the dangers of a written tradition, of the negative values attached to the passing on of thought in writing rather than speech; exemplary for Derrida, who sees in this scene the organization and hierarchization of values that will dominate an entire philosophical tradition; and, finally, exemplary for us of the way in which these values and this tradition are repeated, reinscribed, given and received, reaffirmed and taken on, exemplary, therefore, of the questions of tradition, pedagogy, and legacy that will be at the center of this work. Even if many of the themes of this "classic" Derrida text have been taken up and analyzed by others, we are, I believe, far from having exhausted its oblique gesture.

*

Himself extremely attentive to the strategies of beginning, Derrida opens "Plato's Pharmacy" with a short, seemingly displaced two-page preface that speaks not so much of Plato but of the nature of writing and of the text more generally. We will return to the necessity of this opening gesture at the end of this chapter. For the moment let us leap ahead to Derrida's reading of Plato "proper," which begins, in imitation of such dialogues as the *Sophist* and *Statesman*, with the injunction or invitation: "Let us begin again."[1] Having just spoken in the preface of the decision involved in every reading, Derrida begins (again) by marking his own incision into what he has just characterized as the textual "web." But rather than cutting into

Plato's corpus at the place in the *Statesman*, for example, where the paradigm of statesmanship is weaving together various dispositions in the city and the paradigm of this paradigm is learning letters, Derrida begins with the *Phaedrus*. Rather than beginning with a Platonic dialogue that explicitly links composition and weaving, Derrida begins with a dialogue whose very composition and organization have often been at issue—particularly the relationship between the various parts of the dialogue and the whole, Plato's capacity or incapacity, we might say, to weave together the various parts into a coherent or organic whole.

Derrida recalls that although Diogenes Laertes and, some seventeen centuries later, Schliermacher both thought the *Phaedrus* to be the work of a young Plato, the reverse was argued in the beginning of this century, when it was claimed that the *Phaedrus* is an inorganic and poorly composed dialogue because Plato, although knowing how to make it into an organic whole, was too old and feeble to accomplish his intention. To counter both of these claims and the assumptions on which they rest, Derrida will try to follow what he calls a "more secret organization of themes" ("PP," 67)—one that would be neither properly organic nor inorganic, an organization that would in fact first orient and organize the whole notion of organization as a relationship among present parts, that is, a notion of organization that judges a dialogue good inasmuch as it is a well-proportioned body whose parts fit together according to some ultimately discoverable order or plan. Derrida is looking for another kind of organization that would explain why, for some two millennia now, this dialogue has appeared so unbalanced and inorganic, particularly because of the myth of writing added on inelegantly or inorganically at the end.

Notice, then, the place Derrida has chosen to mark the supplemental nature of writing: a dialogue that has always been understood as doing the very thing for which Socrates condemns writing in the *Phaedrus*—that is, not respecting the organic order of things but simply putting them together randomly—and then, within this dialogue, a myth about writing that has always been taken to be a supplement, a mere appendix to the body of the dialogue itself, a myth wherein writing is condemned for being supplemental to speech, a mere bodily appendix to the living word. Finally, Derrida begins not simply with this supplemental myth in a somewhat supplemental dialogue about the supplement of writing; he begins not simply with the dialogue *itself* but with the dialogue's *reception* in the tradition. This is Derrida's supplementary thread. Although beginning with these so-called secondary sources on Plato might appear to be a typically scholastic gesture, Derrida ultimately interrupts this gesture by demonstrating how such secondary sources have already been programmed to a large extent by the primary text they are interpreting. For in "Plato's Pharmacy" Derrida is interested not only in the theory of writing presented in the *Phaedrus* but in the way that theory has been assumed in the criticisms of the *Phaedrus*. He begins, therefore, not merely with a description of the supplemental nature of myth and writing as it is given in the *Phaedrus* but with the way this dialogue has itself been thought by the tradition to be a supplementary text in the Platonic corpus, written when Plato was either young and overly ambitious or old and already failing. The suggestion is that the general theory of writing proposed in the *Phaedrus* in some way programs or prescribes its reception in the tradition. Derrida's gesture thus turns out to be a fitting one, for it fits commentary or interpretation to a text that has produced a certain tradition of commentary or interpretation. Such a gesture is, thus, "rigorously called for from one end of the *Phaedrus* to the other" ("PP," 67).

Implicit in all of this, then, is the question of the legacy of writing, the inheritance of a certain tradition and, thus, our relationship to that tradition. If we, as readers, are indeed the heirs of a tradition of Western philosophy, how should we respond to what our "forefathers" have given us— and how should we respond to or read Plato, arguably the forefather of all forefathers, the one for whom the rest of Western philosophy would be but a footnote?[2] This question gives us yet one more reason why Derrida begins with secondary texts on the *Phaedrus*. This secondary literature on Plato, located by Derrida within a certain hermeneutic tradition of interpretation, is emblematic of what Derrida finds already programmed in the *Phaedrus*, where what is at issue is precisely the relationship between writer and reader, or speaker and listener, the one who produces or "fathers" a speech or text and the one who receives or inherits it. What is at issue is the relationship between *primary* and *secondary* texts, the bequeathing of a tradition and its reception. But what is this bequeathing and this reception; what is inheritance or legacy; indeed, what is this filiation? What is the filiation between speaker and listener, writer and reader, giver and receiver? What secret thread—not to be confused with some hidden or secret law— is to be found between them?

In the section of "Plato's Pharmacy" entitled "The Father of Logos" Derrida turns to the moment of the donation of writing. He begins this section with a citation from the *Phaedrus*, with the moment when Theuth presents the *pharmakon* of writing to King Thamus, the moment when the servant gives to the king a gift to be evaluated by the king—the moment, we could say, when the disciple, the inventor of *écriture*, presents his new invention to the master. The servant gives to the king a gift that will then be valued by the king, by the giver of all value, as if this gift had no value before it was received by the king, as if everything logically began with the king, with the sun, under his light, as if, finally, the relationship or filiation between servant and king, speaker and hearer, writer and reader were determined only after the reception of a neutral, valueless gift.

We recall that in the *Phaedrus* it is Socrates, the one who did not write, as Nietzsche called him, who recounts the story of Egyptian Theuth and Thamus to Phaedrus. Theuth was the inventor of numbers, arithmetic, geometry, astronomy, draughts, dice, and, "above all, letters [*grammata*]" (274d), the inventor, it could be said, of grammatology. When Theuth travels from his home in Naucratis to see King Thamus in Ammon, what the Greeks called Egyptian Thebes, Theuth enumerates the uses of each of his inventions and then awaits the praise or blame of Thamus. When it comes to letters, Theuth credits his new invention with being able to improve the memory of the Egyptians and make them wiser. Derrida cites Socrates citing Theuth in the *Phaedrus*: "'This discipline, my King, will make the Egyptians wiser and will improve their memories [*sophōterous kai mnēmonikōterous*]; my invention is a recipe [*pharmakon*] for both memory and wisdom.' But the King said . . ." ("PP," 75/*Phaedrus* 274e).

It is at precisely this point that Derrida interrupts his citation of the *Phaedrus* and writes, "Let us cut the king off here. He is faced with the *pharmakon*. His reply will be incisive" ("PP," 75). With this gesture Derrida seems to suggest that if we rush ahead to the king's response and valuation, we will have missed the crucial moment at which this *pharmakon* called writing is presented—that is, the moment just before it is received and given value by the king. There thus appears to be something extremely radical, politically charged, perhaps even revolutionary, in the injunction "Let us cut the king off here." By cutting the king off at the pass, at the moment he is to pass judgment, by making an incision into the textual web at the very moment that, as we will see, the text is about to become an organized book, written from the very beginning from the point of view and with all the values of the king, Derrida attempts to isolate not simply the oppositional structure of the text but that which orients it and makes it oppositional and hierarchical in the first place. Derrida's strategy is to suspend the action at the moment of this decision, at this moment just before valuation, a moment whose status is difficult to determine since it is the king who, as we will see, by giving value, gives tradition, legacy, inheritance, even time itself. For Thamus is the king of kings, the god of gods, *basileus*, says Derrida, being "the other name for the origin of value" ("P.P.," 76). So Derrida cuts the king off at the moment when he will have to decide, to cut, to be incisive, decisive, at the moment when it is a question of the value of writing and the writing of value, an exemplary intervention in the text at the very moment when intervention is at issue.

By suspending the moment of reception, Derrida suspends not simply one particular valuation within the purview of the king but the very structures of valuation on which the power of the king rests. For the *reception* of the king's authority does not simply *confirm* that authority but actually *confers* it upon him; by suspending this reception, we thus catch a glimpse of what might be called the king's "mystical authority." Derrida writes in "Force of Law":

These moments, supposing we can isolate them, are terrifying moments. . . . This moment of suspense, this epochē, this founding or revolutionary moment of law is, in law, an instance of non-law. But it is also the whole history of law. *This moment always takes place and never takes place in a presence.* It is the moment in which the foundation of law remains suspended in the void or over the abyss, suspended by a pure performative act that would not have to answer to or before anyone.[3]

Although the king himself—like Socrates—does not write, he is the one who will pass judgment on writing, on the *next generation* of inventions. I emphasize "generation" here because Thamus is, as Derrida remarks, not only a king but a father, and the *pharmakon* is presented to him by not only a servant but a son. Whereas Theuth, the son or servant, writes, Thamus, the father or king, speaks—and in speaking determines the relationship and relative valuation of writing and speaking, servitude and kingship, obedience and authority, the son and the father. This association of the origin and power of logos with the paternal position is an indispensable part, says Derrida in one of those large claims that itself cannot be neatly separated from the metaphysical tradition, of "'Platonism,' which sets up the whole of Western metaphysics in its conceptuality" ("P.P.," 76).

Just at the moment, then, when the king is about to decide on the value of writing, Derrida cuts him off, freezes the action. At stake is not simply a particular decision or judgment but the very structures of decision and judgment, not a particular value but the institution of value as such in the name of the king. By cutting the king off in this way, Derrida draws our attention both to a certain philosophical legacy and to the very legacy of this legacy, to the handing down of a particular way of handing down, of orienting a whole matrix of oppositions: speech/writing, life/death, presence/absence, master/servant, father/son, legitimate son/bastard son, and so on. By immobilizing the moment of this passing down, Derrida is able to ask not only about the legacy of the king but about the legacy of Plato's text, a legacy of philosophy that we might all too easily accept—that is, that we might all too easily receive while remaining blind to the structures of our own reception.

Derrida stops the action right at the moment the *pharmakon* is to be received and evaluated—in other words, put into other words, understood and *translated* into other registers or languages by the king. For it is the king who ultimately takes the *pharmakon* in hand so as to evaluate, interpret, and, in some sense, properly translate it. He thus receives Theuth's invention of writing and gives it the opposite value of that assigned to it by Theuth. Writing is not, says the king, a recipe for wisdom, a remedy for memory; in fact, it will actually harm memory. If it is a *pharmakon*, that is, a recipe or remedy, for anything, it is only for "reminding":

But the King said, "Most ingenious Theuth, one man has the ability to beget arts, but the ability to judge of their usefulness or harmfulness to their users belongs to another; and now you, who are the father of letters, have been led by your affection to ascribe to them a power the opposite of that which they really possess. For this invention will produce forgetfulness in the minds of those who learn to use it, because they will not practice their memory. Their trust in writing, produced by external characters which are no part of themselves, will discourage the use of their own memory within them. You have invented a recipe [*pharmakon*] not for memory [*mnēmēs*], but for reminding [*hypomnēseōs*]; and you offer your pupils the appearance of wisdom, not true wisdom." (Phaedrus 274e–75b)

Now, as many have noted before Derrida, the Greek word *pharmakon* can mean not only "remedy" but "poison," not only that which heals but that which destroys; and Plato himself uses the word in various dialogues in both of these senses—that is, in one way or another, *depending on the context*. But can we simply assume that *pharmakon* should be read or understood as *either* remedy *or* poison depending on the context? What are the philosophical assumptions of this either/or and this understanding of context?

The question posed throughout "Plato's Pharmacy" is whether *pharmakon* does indeed mean "remedy" in one place and "poison" in another, depending on the circumstances, on the context, or whether *pharmakon*—as what would escape, yet remain unthinkable outside of, any particular context—can never in fact be mastered in this way, reduced to an either/or. The question is whether *pharmakon* can be mastered by a notion of context where what is important is the meaning and not the process of writing or speaking, or whether *pharmakon* is the name of a fundamental *ambivalence*, being both remedy and poison at once, an antisubstance that would precede the separation of thought and expression, speech and writing. To say straightaway that the meaning of *pharmakon* depends on its syntactical relation in the dialogue would already be, as Derrida shows, to accept the opposition between meaning and expression, signifieds and signifiers, where what is important would be what is *meant* and not what is *said*, what is *thought* and not what is *expressed*. It would be to repeat the very valuation of the king *before* it is fully given, his condemnation of writing as mere expression cut off from live intention. Derrida will thus try to reintroduce the ambivalence of the *pharmakon* back into the body of the dialogue, or, rather, he will try to release or reactivate it from within so that it might be shown to organize the dialogue from beginning to end without ever being present as such.

Because "Plato's Pharmacy" is, as I have argued, as much about the *reception* of Plato's text as about the text "itself," it is appropriate that Derrida underscores the problems of understanding the *pharmakon* through the problem of translation. Indeed, it might be said that it is through the supplement of translation, the reception of Plato's Greek text into another language, that the ambivalence of Plato's text is most clearly revealed—revealed insofar as the *choice* necessitated by translation perpetually highlights the concealing of this ambivalence. Whereas English or French translators often have to choose between "remedy" or "poison" in translating *pharmakon*, Plato did not have to make such a choice—or at least that is how it initially appears.

In speaking, then, of the various translations of the Greek *pharmakon* into English and French, Derrida does not claim that "remedy," "poison," "drug," or "philter" are incorrect or illegitimate translations of this word—assuming that it is, in fact, a word. There is always, as we like to say, something lost in the translation, but when it comes to a word like *pharmakon* the loss is essential and inevitable. For if we simply go ahead and translate this word by making reference to the context in which it is used, we may

be reducing to mere polysemy, to a polysemy regulated by context, something that is fundamentally ambivalent—an antisubstance that cannot be
reduced to one meaning or another. So the problem is not translating *pharmakon* as "poison" when what is meant in a particular instance is "remedy";
the problem is *translating* or *receiving* it at all. Although words such as *drug*,
philter, elixir, or, as the above translation in "Plato's Pharmacy" has it, *recipe*
might better preserve the ambivalence or undecidability of *pharmakon*
than value-laden words such as *remedy* or *poison*, these latter are not simply mistakes in translation (indeed they are in a certain sense correct) but
paradigmatic moments in a Platonic tradition of translation. The French
translation Derrida cites of this passage from the *Phaedrus* makes this even
clearer, dispelling any possible ambiguity and, thus, making *even more evident* the stakes of receiving the *pharmakon*. Theuth claims his invention
to be a *remède*, a remedy—not just a "recipe"—for both memory and wisdom, a translation that appears perfectly legitimate given the context of
Theuth's speech.[4] Curiously, then, the English translation of "Plato's Pharmacy" obscures somewhat Derrida's critique of a certain tradition of interpretation and translation by choosing to use an English translation of Plato's
Phaedrus that is more faithful or at least more open to the kind of ambivalence Derrida is trying to point out. By using an English translation of Plato
that is, in some sense, more in line with Derrida's overall argument in
"Plato's Pharmacy," the English translation of "Plato's Pharmacy" makes it
somewhat more difficult to grasp that overall argument.

Again, the *Phaedrus* programs its own translation; it programs its own
reception, its own essential dispersion, into other languages, into English,
French, but, first of all, into Greek. Indeed we see at the end of the dialogue
that what might be understood as glossing, that is—to gloss—explaining
what is said in a text with other, usually simpler, words, is itself a sort of
translation from Greek to Greek; and in the *Phaedrus* we see that this is always done in the name of interior speech or thought, in other words, in the
name of the king. In Thamus's speech at the end of the *Phaedrus*, *pharmakon* is glossed, translated, in effect, from Greek to Greek as "remedy," as
that which remedies not *memory* but only *reminding* ("You have invented a
recipe or remedy [*pharmakon*] not for memory [*mnēmēs*] but for reminding [*hypomnēseōs*]"), the ambivalence thus being reduced to a regulated
polysemy. This occurs not as a result of the particular translation choice
but by the very fact that *pharmakon* is translated at all, glossed in one way
rather than another. By receiving the word *pharmakon* as a word that is

polysemic—that is, as having different meanings determined by the context or by the intention of the one who uttered it—we, as readers or interpreters, end up repeating the decision of the king, the decision that *will have* in fact already framed the dialogue from the very beginning.

For the *pharmakon* is, in truth, presented and judged *even before* it is presented and judged; it is taken up and received already in the understanding and translation of Theuth's own speech, where Theuth himself already interprets and glosses the value of his gift ("my invention is a recipe or remedy [*pharmakon*] for both memory and wisdom")—even though, from the point of view of the king, he attaches the wrong value to it. It is not, strictly speaking, necessary, therefore, to unfreeze this freeze frame, to restart the film, if you will, in order to watch Thamus receive and then give value to the gift of Theuth. For Theuth *had already* presented the *pharmakon* as something it in fact may not be, misrepresenting not only its worth—claiming it to help memory when it would in fact harm it—but its very nature, presenting it as something nonambivalent, as something that *can be presented*, something that can be accepted *or* rejected, said yes *or* no to. Although Theuth and Thamus disagree about the value and effect of writing, they agree about how to understand the word *pharmakon*: in both cases it means a recipe or elixir that brings benefits, that remedies. But, even more important, they tacitly agree that it is a word that can be unambiguously understood, that can be glossed, said in other words, its meaning repeated in other terms. Theuth had thus already presented the *pharmakon* from the point of view of the sun—that is, from the point of view of all value, the father-king-good who determines the relative values of speech and writing, origin and reception, and who, in deciding, frames the entire dialogue from the very beginning ("PP," 111). The story of the invention of writing is thus already framed by the values of speech; Thamus, who does not write, speaks his judgment to Theuth, but Theuth had already *spoken* of writing to Thamus. All this, recall, takes place in a story told by Socrates to Phaedrus, a story that, even if *written* in a dialogue called the *Phaedrus*, subordinates the values of writing to those of speech—not just in what is said but, more essentially, in how it is said.

This is also why, it should be said in passing, the legitimacy of the father always depends on the son; it is why, as Derrida shows, the phrase "father of logos" can never be considered a mere metaphor because it is the logos that first makes possible the order of the generations and the very meaning of fathers and sons. The son is thus the father of the father, the father already an effect of the son. Because Theuth interprets the *pharmakon* before Thamus does, the son before the father, because the order between fathers and sons had already determined the relative values of all the terms, we begin to see that the immobilization of this scene of donation could only ever have been feigned, simulated, staged.[5]

Yet because the word *pharmakon* is presented, because it makes an appearance, it is given a chance, the chance to be put into play with all the other uses of the word *pharmakon* in the Platonic corpus and beyond. The *pharmakon* is neutralized as soon as it is put into play, but it is still given the chance each time it is neutralized to be received—to be received "as such," as the place or medium of transfer, transition, and translation. Although the sign *pharmakon* marks an ambivalence within the Platonic corpus that is neutralized each time by the decision of reading or translation, this neutralization cannot occur without this decision, reading, or translation, that is, without *our reception*.

Derrida thus begins each of the early sections of "Plato's Pharmacy" with a question not simply about reading Plato but about reading in general, about how to read or receive the tradition. Because the *Phaedrus* gives us, presents to us, a general theory of writing, it is an exemplary place to ask about the relationship between theory and practice, the general and the example. Once again, the status of the example, the relationship between the form or paradigm and the particular—all those things that are at the heart of Plato's metaphysics—turn out to be the guiding threads of "Plato's Pharmacy," even if Derrida is pulling on them all to see what comes undone.

By cutting the king off and immobilizing the scene at the moment of decision, Derrida is able to focus attention not only on the moment of a particular legacy or handing down but on the moment when legacy and filiation are themselves handed down. In so doing he is able to locate or immobilize the unlocatable and unimmobilizable filiation of this legacy, its twisted topology.[6] This is what legitimates and necessitates the move from the legacy in the dialogue to the legacy of the dialogue. By simply stopping the scene just before writing has been put down, before speech has been privileged over writing because it is closer to the breath, to life, to the truth of intention or of speech within the soul, our own decision about how to read or interpret is also momentarily interrupted.

Hence we are justified, I think, to imagine Derrida himself—and eventually *ourselves*—as the inheritors of a tradition in the role of Theuth the servant, waiting for the moment when the tradition will tell us about the value of our writing and reading and, most important, about the value of our legacy. The tradition thus plays the role here, of course, of the king, the tradition, or, as if there is any difference, the Platonic text, which gives itself to us and, in giving itself, determines how we are to value and receive it.

As I have just argued, however, we are, as the disciple Theuth, already the master Thamus, for in waiting for the decision of the king, in accepting to receive it, we have in effect already received it, already given or passed it down to ourselves; we are both the tradition's disciple and—unbeknownst to ourselves and even when we think ourselves most radical—its master. By suspending this moment of donation, of what we now see to be a self-donation or self-bequeathing, Derrida suspends the moment when we will have to decide how to read, how to read ourselves, when we will have to decide what reading and writing—what *we*—are.

We thus catch a glimpse of the twisted topology suggested here: we are in essence reading a text about reading and writing wherein there is a scene depicting and doubling our own reading of writing. We are reading a text that has been handed down to us in which there is a scene that depicts and doubles the handing down of this text and our reading of it. The *Phaedrus* can thus be read as *either* one very small although important and influential moment in the history of Western philosophy *or* as the self-representation and programmation of this entire history. The scene between Theuth and Thamus can be read as *either* a small part of a philosophical tradition on reading and writing *or* as the representation and repetition of our own reception of this tradition.

For the sake of making a claim—and thus of reinscribing the values of pedagogy and mastery—I would argue that this second understanding must be part of any deconstructive reading, for it is the moment when one's reading of a text becomes implicated in what is being read, when one's status as disciple becomes implicated in the structure of the master text, when the homage one is paying to a text, teacher, or tradition becomes implicated in the structures established by that text, teacher, or tradition. And it is also that moment, supposing, as Derrida says, that it is a moment and that it can be located, that the master's authority is not simply interrupted or immobilized but is shown to be self-justifying, which is to say, ultimately unjustified, the result of a "mystical authority" wherein the master—like real life—is always absent.[7]

All this raises, of course, the enormous and no doubt irresolvable question of the relationship between Plato and Platonism, between the origin of a tradition and that tradition, between the origin and its reception. As we have seen through this exemplary scene from the *Phaedrus*, the tradition seems to begin already at its origin, whereas the origin becomes itself only in being received. Plato's text will have been Platonic because it will have programmed its own reception; yet because each reception offers the chance for the groundlessness of the corpus to be reinscribed, Platonism always repeats and represses a gesture of Plato's that always comes before and already goes beyond Platonism.

On the one hand, the "Platonic" reading of Plato, the reading that would subjugate writing to speech, the sensible, exterior world of the body to the intelligible, interior world of the soul, is pro-scribed or pro-grammed in Plato. The ambivalence of all *pharmaka* is arrested, suspended, neutralized by the Platonic text through such textual strategies as metaphor, context, and irony, through a text that wants us to understand what it *means* rather than what it *says*. In other words, whatever might seem to threaten the Platonic corpus from within is, in a first moment, immobilized, frozen, hierarchized and thus solidified into a system that will retain only the appearance of movement because everything will have been answered and determined from the start by means of an inaugural decision or judgment. As soon as one is forced to say "yes" to speech and "no" to writing, or, as we will see in the next chapter, "yes" to logos and "no" to mythos, hierarchies are established. So Platonism, which itself receives the Platonic text as a sensible, exterior corpus of writing that conceals, as its secret, an intelligible, internal speech, that is, the truth of Plato's texts, essentially recapitulates the system of Plato's oppositions. Platonism is thus no accident. It does not simply supervene on a Plato who would have nothing to do with the movement that borrows his name.

On the other hand, Plato's texts are never simply Platonic insofar as they allow for moments and often seem to court notions—the *pharmakon* being just one, *khōra*, as we will see in Chapter 2, being another—that destabilize the entire oppositional matrix we identify with Plato. In Plato there is always this other hand that seems to pull the rug out from beneath the first, a second moment that seems always to disrupt the time and continuity of the first. Hence, Derrida practices throughout his work a double reading, one that works within the corpus, within the Platonic oppositions of a text, and another that works not outside the text or those oppositions but at their limit, intervening within the text in order to produce a displacement.

We thus always begin, Derrida seems to suggest, "within" Platonism. We begin with or within Platonism as the first moment in a deconstructive reading, even if the "within" must ultimately be criticized or rethought and the "second moment" cannot simply be that which sequentially follows the first. The relationship between these two hands will not be that of a binary pair. Yet to produce these displacements within Platonism, we begin with the moment of opposition, structure, and hierarchy—the Platonic moment—because without it there would have never been any philosophy as such and thus no tradition to "take on."

We begin to read where we are, "within" Platonism—but this does not mean that we must receive Plato's text unequivocally. Derrida writes in *Positions*: "When I try to decipher a text I do not constantly ask myself if I will finish by answering *yes* or *no*."[8] Derrida does not constantly ask whether he will, in the end, say "yes" or "no" to Plato or to Platonism, whether he will see it as a remedy or a poison. One can neither simply receive nor refrain from receiving. This is why Derrida speaks so much in "Plato's Pharmacy" of the heritage and transmission of the *Phaedrus*, about the legacy of the text—of this text of legacy—and about our reception of it. Although the king says "yes" to speech and "no" to writing, "yes" to life and "no" to death, *our* reception threatens to repeat these choices by saying "yes" to the thought or intention of the text and "no" to ambivalence, "yes" to the living author now gone and "no" to the text, "yes" to speech and "no" to writing. By interrupting this testamentary scene, by intervening in it, Derrida lets us see both the structure of this scene and the ambivalence that this structure had to suppress: the ambivalence in the reception of both Thamus and Theuth and in the *pharmakon* "itself."

Because the *pharmakon*, as Derrida shows, upsets the economy of the king, it must be suppressed, repressed, or neutralized so that a valued economy between king and servant, father and son, speaking and writing, and so forth might be established. This ambivalent *pharmakon*, neither remedy nor poison, or both remedy and poison, had to be repressed so that the *pharmakon* could be received in one way rather than another—received, that is, *as present*. For the *pharmakon* to enter the economy of the king—or, as we saw, the servant of the king—it had to become present in one way or another, its threat to the principle of noncontradiction neutralized.

Indeed, the *pharmakon* seems to threaten the very matrix of oppositions it ultimately makes possible: speech and writing, life and death, thought and image, living repetition and mechanical repetition, reality and appearance, memory and forgetfulness, interior and exterior, real being and spectrality, maturity and childishness, knowledge and ignorance, property and dispropriation, familiarity and strangeness, legitimacy and illegitimacy, nature and artifice, obedience and rebellion, sovereignty and servitude, and so on. But if the *pharmakon* threatens and eludes the oppositions it makes possible, is there any way to receive the *pharmakon* "as such"? In my emphasis throughout this work on *receiving* the tradition, I will want to ask whether it must always be a *present* that one receives or whether reception can be rethought so as to accommodate something that eludes all presents, something that can never even be recognized as something to be received.

In the *critical reception* of "Plato's Pharmacy" it has been precisely the ambivalence of the middle term, of the *pharmakon*, that has most often been emphasized—yet, curiously, overlooked. In the formula "Thamus receives the *pharmakon* from Theuth," it is easy to assume—as I have assumed thus far—that the *pharmakon* simply comes *between* Thamus and Theuth, the king and his servant. The *pharmakon* would simply "be there"—even if ambivalent—waiting to be given by the servant and valued by the king, even if the servant presents it already from the position of the king. Yet where would this ordering—be it temporal or logical—come from? Might it not be that in order for Thamus and Theuth to become differentiated and hierarchized in the first place (the king over the servant, the father over the son) the threat of the *pharmakon* had *already* to be overcome? Indeed, it would seem that the threat Theuth poses to Thamus, the threat of a servant to his king, of a son to his father, can take place only as the *simulacrum* of the *capital threat* found in the *pharmakon*. In other words, Theuth's parricidal threat can take place only because it follows on, and is the simulacrum of, an even more radical "parricide," one that threatens the very difference and order of master and slave, father and son. The *pharmakon* is the place of this other parricide, this capital threat—a threat not simply to some term within the tradition (some king or father) but to the tradition itself and all the hierarchies it establishes.

By interrupting the family scene between the father and the son, Derrida shows that the scene was itself constituted by an even more originary act of violence. The *pharmakon* of writing is not a mere supplement to an already constituted scene, an external threat to an already established order, but that which threatens from within the very value system of the father-king-sun. The suspension of the scene in the *Phaedrus* thus reveals that the king's authority, and so that of the tradition, is always grounded in a pure performative act, a performative that is no longer pure, however, as soon as something is "actually" performed or instituted, that is, as soon as the king becomes present and identifiable. But what would it mean to receive this scene of legacy as such, to receive not this scene of reception where one says "yes" or "no" to the *pharmakon* or "yes" or "no" to Platonism but the fundamental ambivalence of this scene? How would one prepare for such a reception—for receiving that which interrupts all reception? How would one ever, to cite Derrida, "receive in place of everything"? How would one ever carry out or even recognize a "pure performative act"? Finally, if Platonism—along with anti-Platonism—is the necessity of saying "yes" or "no," of deciding, if it is a place of valued, hierarchized oppositions, how might one understand the relationship between the Platonic scene of legacy and the legacy of the *pharmakon*, between the Platonic house and the pharmacy, between all that is staged by the tradition and what goes on behind the scenes?

Derrida's analysis of the *Phaedrus* demonstrates why and how the tradition exercises such power and control over us. It does so not simply because it furnishes us with our themes and concepts—indeed with just about everything under the sun—but because it gives us the means and resources for our *receiving* all these themes and concepts, for our turning toward the sun. As in the scene from the *Phaedrus*, we are determined as inheritors—as disciples—of a tradition not simply because of the immense power of the past but because of the structures of inheritance and reception that constitute and sustain that power. Since Plato's *Phaedrus* is preoccupied with questions of authorship and authority, legitimation and control, that is, with questions of the canon, it is an exemplary text that would seem to teach us something about the very possibilities of its own reception, the very possibilities for its being read.

We can thus now understand why Derrida begins "Plato's Pharmacy" with a short, two-page preface, or *protokollon*, that initially appears superfluous or misplaced since it gives a very general statement of what writing or a text is and thus seems to belong more properly to the preface of the book *Dissemination* than to the essay on the *Phaedrus* within it. But these two pages help alert us to the fact that the *Phaedrus* is not only a canonical text about authorial intention, that is, about the relationship between thought, what Plato called in the *Sophist* "speech in the soul," and expression, but an exemplary place of its deployment or performance.

The *Phaedrus* is indeed a good place to start in order to analyze what philosophers have said and thought about intention. But to read the *Phaedrus* only to decipher what Plato meant by or thought about thought would already be to understand what is essential about a text as what is meant by it, that is, as what is intended, not what is done or performed *by* the text. One is always obliged to determine as rigorously as possible what Plato meant or meant to say, but meaning or "thought in the soul" can never be the last word; it must be treated as one philosopheme among others in a larger textual network. Although Plato might *say* that everything begins and ends in internal thought, with speech in the soul, we must look at what Plato's text *does* with this thought in those places where it says something about it.

The question here, then, is what it means to read or receive a text. The implicit view of reading or reception that Derrida is calling into question is that reading is external to writing, that the thoughts contained in writing are the internal, essential truths that reading would try to discover. Derrida is in effect asking what would happen if we did not take or receive these notions for granted. What if reading were implicated by writing, if it could not remain outside it like a spectator without becoming caught in the textual web? What if reading were an activity that did not simply analyze or dissect the organism from afar, a merely contingent empirical supplement to a writing that would remain essentially intact before and beyond reading, but a practice that added to, got caught in, and then actually helped constitute the textual web? The point is clearly not to conflate reading and writing, for that is what a certain philosophical tradition has always done—a good reading being defined as one that merely repeats the writing or the intention of the text—but neither can reading and writing be considered completely independently of one another. The reading of a text determines what *will have been* written—including all that will have been written about the nature of reading and writing. To assume we already know what reading and writing are would be to give up the game before it even began. To read Plato already knowing, for example, that reading is the activity through which one uncovers the truth and meaning of what is said would be to have already answered everything in advance. Neither a mere repetition or doubling of what has already been written nor a merely subjective activity external to writing, reading would be the moment of *decision*, the moment when a tradition is taken on—always with the chance for something singular and unprecedented.

In the end "Plato's Pharmacy" is much less about Plato's dialogue than about the possibilities for reading the dialogue, the possibility of turning toward it *without* immediately and irremediably receiving it as it was *meant* to be received, that is, the possibility of receiving it at the limits of a theory of intention. Because reading as the deciphering of intention—or, in Plato, of internal, live speech—is indeed part of our own philosophical tradition, part of our Platonic heritage, it is necessary to begin by deciphering this speech, to discern as rigorously as possible, taking Platonic irony and the dialogical context of Plato as seriously as possible, what Plato meant to say. But this must always be done with an eye to that moment or place wherein the theory of intention is itself given or staged in the Platonic text. Although "Plato's Pharmacy" would thus appear to be a reinterpretation of Plato based on a close reading of the *Phaedrus*, it is concerned more essentially with the reception of Plato in the tradition, with the way the Platonic corpus programs, in some sense, its own reception. Rather than being simply another interpretation or reading of Plato, it is a reading of how we read in the tradition, an interpretation of how we interpret, an analysis not only of what Plato has given us but of how what he has given us has transformed our reception of him. Indeed, Derrida leads us to understand that if his task in "Plato's Pharmacy" had been simply to decipher Plato's intentions concerning speech and writing, life and death, and so on, he would have *already* received—and thus implicitly agreed to, taken on—a certain Platonic understanding of intention and, right along with it, perhaps, an entire tradition.

The power of the tradition should never be underestimated. Yet the tradition is not some immense program that simply unfolds and inscribes us irremediably within it from the beginning. Every time the tradition is handed down, the decision to receive it is at once revealed and concealed. It is concealed insofar as the structures of reception are received without question, in a reception that then reconstitutes the tradition as it will have been, as we will then assume it *always already was*. But this decision to receive the tradition will be revealed insofar as the tradition is shown to depend on its reception—on the structures of reception. It is revealed insofar as it allows us to catch a glimpse of another tradition or history, not another history of what has been received but another, discontinuous history of reception. Such a history would provide not only new analyses and new themes but new places for thinking, for thinking reception and for *thinking as reception*.

I will contend in the chapters to follow that the work of Derrida provides an exemplary place for such thinking. As we will see, Derrida appears always to begin "within" the tradition, that is, with what he has been given and with the ways he has been given it, so as to introduce an almost imperceptible displacement within our traditional terms and concepts, our traditional gestures and modes of reception. It is this displacement, this reinscription, that alone is capable of giving us a history, not the eternal return of the same but a repetition in difference, a tradition that is indeed programmed from the very start, and programmed even in its modes of reception, but that has programmed within it "moments" that escape all programs—in other words, the "possibility" of an *event*. It is this displacement, this reinscription, this question at the limits of the tradition that keeps us in suspense, on both the giving and the receiving end of the tradition, between Socrates and Plato but also between Thamus and Theuth, between Theuth and himself, receiving from the other, but also receiving from ourselves, receiving the chance for reception only at the moment, at the unlocatable moment, when we stand breathless between two breaths, two gestures, or two times, at the moment when we are cut off, frozen, immobilized, having not yet received and yet already ready to sign off on the tradition.

Given Time for a Detour

THE ABYSSAL GIFT OF 'KHŌRA'

> It appears that we are here taking a detour. In the realm of such efforts, however,
> detours are sometimes the nearest ways.
> —Martin Heidegger, *Hölderlin's Hymn "The Ister"*

"Let us take the time for a long detour."

I begin with this suggestion, or invitation, because when it comes to
reading and writing, the shortest distance between two points is not always
a straight line, because when it comes to the topology of texts, the proximity of one text to another, or even to itself, is never simply given but
must be reinvented with every reading and writing. I beg the reader's in-
dulgence, then, in giving me the time for a long detour in order to get to
my point, since, in the end, the detour *will be* the point.

"Let us take the time for a long detour." This line is not mine but
Derrida's, and it comes not from *Given Time*, the text to which my title
would seem to allude, but from *"Khōra,"* a little text of Derrida's published
back in 1993 and translated into English as part of *On the Name*.[1] The line
occurs about a third of the way through the text, opening up a discreet but
all-consuming tear in the textual fabric, a tiny aperture or eyelet through
which several other texts, from "Restitutions" in *The Truth in Painting* to
Given Time, are, one might say, given to one another, allowed to come into
proximity with and to haunt one another in the time of an abyssal detour.
Through this detour in the *"Khōra"* text Derrida does not simply lay the
groundwork for reading or receiving the passage on the *khōra* contained
in Plato's *Timaeus* but allows himself to *give* himself his corpus, to be formed

and marked by a certain part of his corpus—which is itself always marked by the corpus of another. Through this self-marking or donation, this auto-donation, Derrida is able to give us a glimpse not only of this or that text, this or that theme or moment in *The Truth in Painting* or *Given Time*, but of the very logic of the gift at work in both of these texts.

"Let us take the time for a long detour." This line, which now forms the beginning of my own detour, one that is necessitated, I believe, by the very logic of the detour and the gift, is a translation of *Donnons-nous le temps d'un long détour.* The fact that this phrase recalls the title of the book that most explicitly takes up the question of the gift—*Donner le temps* or *Given Time*—is, as I will try to show, more than just a coincidence. It is, as Derrida might say, the chance of thinking, since the implicit or explicit evocation or autodonation of other texts within the *"Khōra"* piece will turn out to be the "true gift" of that work.

Let me begin, then, by noting that the translation of this line from *"Khōra"* as "let us take the time for a long detour" is itself a confirmation of Derrida's claim in *Given Time* that giving can be understood—and thus translated—only from within an economy of exchange, that is, from within an economy where there is always a reciprocity between giving and taking. To give, Derrida argues, is already to take, even when one would appear to get nothing back from one's giving. For the mere recognition that what one is giving *is* a gift and that the one to whom one is giving it *is* a recipient is enough to annul the gift, since one is already beginning to take back—to gain the satisfaction of good conscience, for example, of having given without the expectation of return. It is thus appropriate that *donnons-nous le temps d'un long détour* be translated not as "let us *give* ourselves the time for a long detour" but, rather, as "let us *take* the time for a long detour." As I will try to show, there is in every detour a certain taking—especially in the detour of translation—a taking or self-giving that always aims at some anticipated profit or advantage. But as I will argue by the end of this long detour, the one thing that cannot be taken or self-given in a detour is precisely its time. The time of a detour will be the one thing that cannot be used or capitalized on, the one thing that can be neither given nor received, since it has, as we will see, the structure of a gift.

Whereas we cannot, therefore, take the time *of* a detour, we can—indeed often must—take the time *for* a detour. For example, we take the time for a detour in philosophy, we go out of our way, in the hopes that by taking our time we may receive something in return.[2] We take the time for a detour, for a pause, an explanation, a parenthesis, perhaps even a story or myth, because we hope that it will illuminate the philosophical terrain for ourselves or others. In this sense a detour always has the structure of an annulled gift; just as the gift is always given with the expectation of some return, so the detour is always taken with the expectation of some future taking or taking back, the expectation of getting back on track further down the road or of returning older but wiser, with a greater appreciation for the road already taken. A detour is, thus, always speculative, always bent on some capitalization of time or space. Like the pure gift of *Given Time*, the pure detour—the detour that would really take us out of the way, that would exceed the economy of return—can never be taken, can never simply *present itself.*

"Let us take the time for a long detour." We can now begin to hear this line from Derrida's *"Khōra"* as both an invitation to speculate and invest, a promise for future advantage, and an impossibility, since the pure detour—the detour that does not belong to the economy of expenditure and recompense, loss and gain—is impossible, or, as Derrida says in *Given Time, "the* impossible."[3] If detours in philosophy are thus always to some degree speculative, then Derrida's detour in *"Khōra"* is speculative in an exemplary fashion since it is a detour concerning speculation and, thus, a detour concerning detours. It is not only a description and a warning of the detour to come but a performative act that tries to draw attention to its own performance, to its own possibility. Derrida writes: "Let us take the time for a long detour. Let us consider the manner in which Hegel's speculative dialectic inscribes mythic thought in a teleological perspective. . . . It sublates mythic discourse as such into the philosopheme" (*"K,"* 100).

As Derrida argues in the pages that follow, philosophy becomes serious for Hegel only once it has "abandoned" or rather "sublated its mythic *form.*" For Hegel "philosophical logic comes to its senses when the concept wakes up from its mythological slumber." The mytheme is nothing more than a detour taken by the philosopheme; it *"will have been* only a prephilosopheme offered and promised to a dialectical *Aufhebung"* (*"K,"* 100–101). The serious philosopher would thus avoid such a mythological drift [*dérive*] at all costs, unless he or she were in such perfect possession of philosophical understanding that the mytheme might be ventured for its heuristic value, that is, unless the detour through the mytheme were oriented and mastered from the outset by a philosophical speculation that risks nothing of its philosophical capital. Recourse to mythic detours in a philosopher such as Plato is thus a sign of either his mastery over the subject or "his 'impotence' to 'express himself in the pure modality of thought'" ("*K*," 101). Derrida writes:

> Hegel seems to oscillate between two interpretations. In a philosophical text, the function of myth is at times a sign of philosophical impotence, the incapacity to accede to the concept as such and to keep to it, at other times the index of a dialectic and above all didactic potency, the pedagogic mastery of the serious philosopher in full possession of the philosopheme. Simultaneously or successively, Hegel seems to recognize in Plato both this impotence and this mastery. ("*K*," 102)

As Derrida shows, there is no contradiction in Hegel's oscillation; whether impotent or didactically useful, myth is excluded from the realm of philosophical meaning—that is, from the signified concept. Myth is either the sign of an impotence to which one must resign oneself—and is thus not so much a detour as a dead end—or a dialectic device, a pedagogical tool mastered from the beginning by philosophical understanding. In both cases the pure detour, the detour *as such*, has been bypassed; there has been a detour of the detour, since what Hegel calls the mythic detour is something understood and mastered *by* philosophy. Derrida's point here, I take it, is that for both Hegel and Plato the opposition between mythos and logos is already a distinction of logos, the former always being framed by and subordinated to the latter. My point, in passing through Derrida's detour on Hegel, is that the opposition between a philosophical program and a detour is itself defined by the philosophical program, the detour being always taken and understood in the name and service of that program. This is the philosophical point that Derrida's detour through the texts of Hegel on Plato would have us see. In this sense Derrida's detour through Hegel is indeed speculative insofar as it helps us understand what is at issue in Plato's *Timaeus*. And my detour through "*Khōra*" is speculative insofar as it would help illuminate the structure of the gift in *Given Time*.

If the distinction between mythos and logos is a distinction of philosophy, of logos, what happens in a text like the *Timaeus* when we are confronted with *khōra*—that is, with something that belongs neither to the intelligible nor to the sensible realms, something that exceeds the determinations on which is founded the opposition between logos and mythos, literal speech and metaphor? How would a philosophical program harbor, shelter, or incorporate something that would exceed it, something that would, as Plato himself seems to see, situate the very oppositions of the program in which it is found? How does a text receive such a detour, such a gift? In what time or space? And how does it receive it when *khōra* is the name of that which receives all things into it, when *khōra* would give us the very meaning of reception? Would encountering such a thing as *khōra* within a philosophical text constitute the first *pure detour*—a detour that would signal neither impotence nor dialectical mastery, that would not be simply located within the program but would in some sense situate the program itself, that would not simply take place within the time of the program but would first give the program its time?

One can begin to see the chronological and topographical complexities that such a gift or detour would introduce into the philosophical program. If the detour *through* or *of khōra* would give the time of the philosophical program, it would also give the time for the philosophical detours within that program—and the chance for a detour that would exceed the philosophical program. At this level such a thing as *khōra* could never be simply isolated as a detour within Plato's text, for such a detour would, of necessity, take us out of the Platonic text strictly speaking and lead us— since *khōra* cannot but be received—into other texts, for example, into Heidegger's or Derrida's. We would thus be speaking here of a detour *within* the philosophical program that would open up the possibility of a detour that would exceed that program—indeed, that would, at the limit, show the philosophical program *itself* to have been a long detour that aims to return to the name of an impossibility: *khōra*, the gift, the detour, Van Gogh's shoes—yes, even Van Gogh's shoes, as we will see in a moment. This is why the detour through "*Khōra*" is, if not necessary, at least consonant with a certain reading of *Given Time*.

We are still, I recall, in the opening pages of what Derrida himself calls a detour through the Hegelian understanding of myth as something that is always guided by the philosophical concept. Derrida's detour is necessitated by the question of whether *khōra* can be thought in terms of myth or whether it exceeds this determination and, thus, the opposition between logos and mythos. We are edging ever closer to something in the Platonic text that, as Derrida will argue, does indeed exceed both the Platonic categories of mythos and logos and the Hegelian notions of impotence or didactic mastery. We are approaching something within the Platonic program—a "supplementary reservation," as Derrida calls it—that would "lodge, shelter [*abriter*], and thereby exceed" that program ("*K*," 103). This "reservation" concerning Plato's Platonism would not be a simple modification or refinement of Plato's project or program but something that would actually lodge and shelter it, keeping it from being its own source and origin, keeping it from founding itself. And yet, since such a reservation would not itself be subject to, or be a part of, this program, it would always risk being forgotten in the name of Platonism. We are approaching the *khōra*—or the proper name *Khōra*—in a detour that concerns the Hegelian notion of detour or, at least, of myth in relationship to the philosophical program. Using Hegel's language in part to describe Plato's program, Derrida writes, "First, the programme. The cosmogony of the *Timaeus* runs through the cycle of knowledge on all things. Its encyclopedic end must mark the term, the *telos*, of a *logos* on the subject of everything that is. . . . This encyclopedic *logos* is a general ontology, treating of all the types of being, it includes a theology, a cosmology, a physiology, a psychology, a zoology" ("*K*," 103).

The *Timaeus* would thus seem to be a monolithic discourse of the Hegelian type; it would aim to incorporate or give itself an account of all things. And yet this is not the whole story of the *Timaeus*, probably not the whole story of Hegelian discourse either, certainly not the whole story of Derrida's detour through the Hegelian corpus. After describing this philosophical program of Plato's *Timaeus*, Derrida begins a new paragraph:

And yet [*Et pourtant*], half-way through the cycle, won't the discourse on *khōra* have opened, between the sensible and the intelligible, belonging neither to one nor to the other, hence neither to the cosmos as sensible god nor to the intelligible god, an apparently empty space—even though it is no doubt not *emptiness*? Didn't it name a gaping opening [*ouverture béante*], an abyss or a chasm? ("*K*," 103)

The first two words of this paragraph should cause us to pause and wonder what sort of detour is taking place here. These words—*And yet* (*Et pourtant*)—have a long history in Derrida, and they form, as I suggested at the outset, a sort of eyelet or tear in the textual fabric that lets us see or lets rise up to the surface a whole series of other texts in Derrida's textual corpus—the most obvious being "Restitutions" from *The Truth in Painting*, another text about the nature of the gift. This *And yet* thus *itself* becomes a sort of chasm or abyss, a kind of *khōra*, in which other texts come to be reflected or come to stand, like ghosts, beginning with "Restitutions" but including the texts that Derrida reads in this text—for example, Heidegger's "The Origin of the Work of Art." *"Et pourtant"*—"And yet"—is Derrida's translation of Heidegger's *"Und dennoch,"* a phrase that Derrida characterizes in "Restitutions" in reference to "The Origin of the Work of Art" as "an articulation or rhetorical suspense which is very unusual in Heidegger."[4]

Now, my point here, I recall, is not simply to trace a series of references and self-references within Derrida's work but to rethink the very notion of self-reference, to rethink it as a sort of autodonation that can never be completed, that can take place only in and as the time of a detour.[5] My concern is to rethink Derrida's emphasis in many recent texts on ghosts or phantoms in terms of a textual autodonation or textual detour within the return of the same. Listen once again, then, to Derrida's *own* articulation or rhetorical suspense:

And yet [*Et pourtant*], half-way through the cycle, won't the discourse on *khōra* have opened, between the sensible and the intelligible, belonging neither to one nor to the other, hence neither to the cosmos as sensible god nor to the intelligible god, an apparently empty space—even though it is no doubt not *emptiness*? Didn't it name a gaping opening, an abyss or a chasm?

And now listen to Heidegger, from "The Origin of the Work of Art," as he turns from describing the famous pair of Van Gogh shoes as mere objects separated from their context, from the earth, to equipmental beings situated by the earth:

A pair of peasant shoes and nothing more. And yet [*Und dennoch*]—
    From the dark opening of the worn insides of the shoes the toilsome tread of the worker stares forth. . . . In the shoes vibrates the silent call of the earth, its quiet gift of the ripening grain and its unexplained self-refusal in the fallow desolation of the wintry field. . . . This equipment belongs to the *earth*, and it is protected in the *world* of the peasant woman.[6]

The resonances between these two paragraphs are more than striking and might make us wonder whether Van Gogh's shoes are not themselves coming to inhabit, or be sheltered by, or reflected in, the chasm of the *khōra* or whether the *khōra* is not coming to be figured and reflected in the dark opening of the shoes. Such rhetorical echoes and thematic repetitions make us wonder whether one cannot but begin to project one image or text onto the other, whether one cannot but give or restitute one text to another when we are dealing—in both texts and at precisely this moment—with restitution and the projection of figures into a *khōra* space. It is as if *khōra* and the Van Gogh shoes had become the reversible sides of one another—a glove to be turned inside out: on the one hand, *khōra*, the receptacle of all things, the condition by which all things appear, the "space" on or in which they are projected, and, on the other hand, Van Gogh's shoes, which, as Derrida demonstrates, become things to be restituted in Heidegger's discourse as well as in Meyer Shapiro's, things into which both Heidegger and Shapiro project some figure—be it the figure of a peasant woman or a male city dweller. Such projection, such retrospective interpretation into this "gaping opening," this "abyss" or "chasm," is the moment of what Derrida calls in "Restitutions" Heidegger's "pathetic fall"—his fall into pathos.[7] It is the moment when Heidegger begins to project the figure of a peasant woman inside the shoes, to fill them with some human form. And so having just evoked this gaping opening or chasm of the *Timaeus* in the midst of this detour in "*Khōra,*" Derrida warns against the Heideggerian fall without explicitly mentioning it, as if the ghost of Heidegger were now coming to inhabit the space of "*Khōra*"—that is, the text called "*Khōra.*" Derrida writes:

Let us not be too hasty about bringing this chasm named *khōra* close to that chaos which also opens the yawning gulf of the abyss. Let us avoid [*éviter*] hurling [*précipiter*] into it the anthropomorphic form and the pathos of fright. Not in order to install in its place the security of a foundation, the [and Derrida here cites a book of Marcel Detienne and Jean-Pierre Vernant] "exact counterpart of what Gaia represents for any creature, since her appearance at the origin of the world: a stable foundation, sure for all eternity, opposed to the gaping and bottomless opening of Chaos." ("*K,*" 103)[8]

Derrida thus warns us about this "pathos" of fright, using the very word he had used in the "Restitutions" essay to describe Heidegger's fall, his precipitation in immediately filling the open abyss of the shoes, his refusal to receive the abyss or confront it.[9] The ghosts of Derrida's past readings of Heidegger thus come to inhabit the space of this passage; they are there in the tone, in the *And yet*, in the quotation from Detienne and Vernant that speaks of Gaia—as if to recall Heidegger's reference to earth in "The Origin of the Work of Art"—and in the footnote accompanying this quotation, where Heidegger's own reading of Chaos in the first Nietzsche volume is mentioned. So clear is this evocation that Derrida himself seems compelled to mention Heidegger in the following sentence, in a place and at a time when Heidegger is not explicitly at issue. After citing Vernant and Detienne, Derrida continues: "We shall later encounter a brief allusion of Heidegger's to *khōra*, not to the one in the *Timaeus* but, outside of all quotation and all precise reference, the one which in Plato would designate the place (*Ort*) between the existent and being, the 'difference' or place between the two" ("*K*," 103–4).

Is it a coincidence that in the midst of Derrida's reading of Plato's *Timaeus* a detour should take place whereby the abyss that opens up Plato's text should return to open up Derrida's—as if the only way to receive Plato's discourse on the *khōra* were at once to speak of *khōra and* become consumed or situated by it, opened up to it and other texts—almost, one would want to say, automatically, uncontrollably? Is it a coincidence that this meditation on the logic of the gift, which began with this Derridean detour, would itself come to be consumed by this same *khōric* structure, this same detour, as the only way of receiving it, the only way of receiving *khōra* as gift or detour?

Clearly, such a thought—such a reception of the gift—cannot take place in any present, cannot be received at any identifiable point or time within a philosophical program. After his brief allusion to Heidegger, Derrida continues:

> The ontologico-encyclopedic conclusion of the *Timaeus* seems to cover over the open chasm in the middle of the book. What it thus covers over, closing the gaping mouth [*la bouche bée*] of the quasi-banned discourse on *khōra*, would perhaps not only be the abyss between the sensible and the intelligible, between being and nothingness . . . nor yet between *logos* and *mythos* but between all these couples and another which would not even be *their* other. ("*K*," 104)

The open chasm is closed and the gaping mouth covered over by the projection of a figure onto it: nurse or mother in the case of Plato, a peasant woman in the case of Heidegger. Even Derrida cannot help but cover over this gaping mouth by projecting the figure of a gaping mouth onto it, that is, by interpreting or reading it in some way.[10] And yet, what Derrida's discourse opens up, what it opens itself up to, is a moment of what I have risked calling autodonation, a moment whereby Derrida gives himself, or lets himself be given, an entire tradition of philosophy that has given itself to itself by means of this open mouth but that has then foreclosed and forgotten this opening—foreclosed and forgotten it by projecting a figure within or onto it. *This* is restitution and autodonation: letting oneself be given that which in the tradition can never be made a theme for philosophy and thus can never be given in a present—chaos, *khōra*, Van Gogh's shoes, the gift. Through this autodonation, this textual haunting, one begins to see that each of these names can function as the site—the singular site—of the others, each giving itself to the others both to name and to mark that which is nothing other than the very giving of these names.

Derrida remarks in *"Khōra"* that if there is a *mise en abîme* within the dialogue—namely *khōra*—it is not surprising that the discourse about *khōra*, the very form of Plato's dialogue, should also take on the structure of a *mise en abîme*. Derrida thus painstakingly maps out the various levels of narration in the *Timaeus* to show, in effect, that the *mise en abîme* leads not to an infinite regress but to a series of aporias wherein the contained narrative turns out to contain the conditions for the containing one, and the containing narrative turns out to be a moment or example within the narrative it contains. It should come as little surprise that Derrida's own text would be similarly disrupted. Indeed, this is its chance for autodonation, its chance not simply to give, to give us a new theory of the gift, for example, or to receive, to receive other theories within the tradition, but to question the notions of giving and receiving through a kind of double reading so as itself to become, at the limit, a gift, a gift to itself, but to an "itself" that is now nothing *but* gift—if such a notion could ever be received. Such a self-donation, always absolutely unique, would resemble the giving of a proper name, a proper name that would have nothing proper to it, however, because it would name nothing but this giving.

Derrida in fact speaks throughout *"Khōra"* of *Khōra* as a proper name. Although the name would seem to be that of a woman, it is in fact the proper name of that which is always other than the name, the proper name of that which gives us all our distinctions (between male and female, for example) and our names. Instead, then, of describing *khōra* as the nurse or mother of all beings, instead of projecting the image of some woman onto *khōra*, Derrida gives *khōra* the name *Khōra* so as to mark the singular site where names and, along with them, all our philosophical distinctions, are given. *Khōra* is the proper name of that which has nothing proper to it, a proper name that negotiates between that singular site without properties and the tradition—which begins already in Plato—of projecting figures and properties (the human, the feminine, and so on) onto that site.

Yet there is another proper name to whom or to which Derrida in effect dedicates the entire essay entitled *"Khōra"*: the name (of) Jean-Pierre Vernant.

Vernant was cited without being named in the crucial passage on *khōra* where the ghost of Heidegger came to meet those of Plato and Derrida. That is the only time Vernant's work is cited in the *"Khōra"* text apart from an opening epigraph wherein Vernant speaks of the way Greek myth must be read as the other of the binary logic of logos and philosophy: "myth puts in play a form of logic which could be called—in contrast to the logic of noncontradiction of the philosophers—a logic of the ambiguous, of the equivocal, of polarity" (*"K,"* 88). Although it seems that Derrida implicitly takes issue with Vernant's understanding of myth in the detour through Hegel with which we began, it is also possible to say that what Derrida gets or takes from Vernant is precisely this notion of something that would exceed the binary oppositions of philosophy. That is, what he gets from Vernant is an interest in or attention to things in the tradition like *khōra* or chaos. Considering everything said thus far about the gift, however, considering that Derrida's *"Khōra"* piece is itself a work on donation and the gift, can one simply say that this is what Derrida "gets" or "receives" or "takes" from Vernant when a thought like *khōra* exceeds our understanding of giving, receiving, and taking?

This question leads me to recall the final reason why I wished to begin and, as it turns out, end my reading of the logic of the gift in Derrida's work with a long detour through *"Khōra."* Although one can and, to a certain extent, must read *Given Time* (as well as other texts that treat this subject) as a sort of formal articulation of the logic of the gift, one may also read it as a meditation on the possibility of the text—of writing itself—*as gift*, that is, on the performativity of writing as gift. One way to focus this possibility is to look at those places where Derrida himself gives or makes an offering of his work. Is it a coincidence that "Restitutions" and *"Khōra"*—two texts with rather explicit dedications—have to do with restituting, giving, and offering, that is, with assigning, destining, and dedicating?

As Derrida notes, an earlier version of *"Khōra"* was given in 1987 as part of a Festschrift for Jean-Pierre Vernant and published in a volume entitled *Poikilia: Etudes offertes à Jean-Pierre Vernant*. In the opening pages of *"Khōra"* Derrida recalls this event, thereby situating his work, his offering, and assigning it a place, or so it would seem, as well as a destination. Yet given everything that has been said about gifts, one would be surprised if Derrida simply and unambiguously *presented* or *offered* his work as a gift to Vernant. Indeed one begins to see in *"Khōra"* the philosophical problem involved in the whole idea of a Festschrift. Can one simply offer something to Vernant for his teaching? Can one simply thank him for having helped us think such notions as *khōra*, for having helped us think that which precedes and gives us all our philosophical distinctions? Would not such a giving or thanking reveal that we have in fact understood *nothing* at all of Vernant's teaching, that we have merely reinscribed the traditional notions of giving and receiving, mythos and logos, that Vernant had supposedly helped us rethink? Given this dilemma or double bind, should one then simply *not* give or try to refrain from giving—or would this too be a way of giving, a way of responding by giving in or giving up?

Near the beginning of the *"Khōra"* text, Derrida says that in order to speak of *khōra* it may be necessary to "signal toward [*faire signe vers*] a genre [or gender] beyond genre [or gender]" (*"K,"* 90). In the very next paragraph Derrida repeats the word *signe* and says that "as a token [*signe*] of gratitude and admiration" he is paying "homage in the form of a question to Jean-Pierre Vernant" (*"K,"* 90). Notice, first, that Derrida's homage takes the form not of a receivable gift—like a text—but, as we will see again in Chapter 4 in Derrida's homage to Foucault, of a question. But, more important, the repetition of the word *signe* seems to suggest that a discourse—a giving discourse—in honor of Jean-Pierre Vernant would itself have to signal toward a genre beyond all genres. This would especially be the case if Jean-Pierre Vernant were *himself* a sort of figure or analogue of *khōra*, a parallel that Derrida discreetly but unmistakably draws in the lines that follow, where he praises Vernant as someone who "taught us so much and gave us so much pause for thought about the opposition *mythos/logos*" (*"K,"* 90). In a certain sense Vernant does indeed "resemble" the figure of *khōra*, giving us oppositions yet causing us to rethink them—causing us to go back and begin again. As Derrida later argues, Socrates in the *Timaeus* occupies a place very similar to that of *khōra*, for he is the one who receives all the discourses that Timaeus and Critias are going to produce.[11] The *Timaeus* is precisely a sort of Festschrift for Socrates, who had delivered his own discourse—the *Republic*, it seems, or at least parts thereof—on the previous day. Is it by chance that, in this Festschrift for a noted professor of classical studies, Vernant should himself be figured in place of *khōra*, in the place of what receives all things and discourses? It seems that Derrida's dilemma in giving thanks, in honoring Vernant, has to do not only with how to thank someone for a thought such as *khōra*, that is, for a thought that can never be received, but how to thank the "one" who "gave" him this thought without *projecting* some figure onto him, that is, without some pathetic fall.

There is, therefore, a relationship, a fit, between what is given and what gives, between *khōra* as it appears in the philosophical text called the *Timaeus* and the giving of *khōra*. Must there not be a reciprocal fit between the discourse about *khōra*, or about Jean-Pierre Vernant, and *khōra* itself? Do we not need a third genre of discourse—a *gifted discourse*—in order to speak of this third genre that is the gift? For do we really know any more about Jean-Pierre Vernant than about *khōra*? Do we know any more about how to give than about the giving of *khōra* or Vernant? If not, if we are not certain what the name Jean-Pierre Vernant means, do we not risk not hearing him, not receiving anything he has given or taught us, whenever we simply give back to him what we think we owe? Do we not risk closing the gaping mouth of chaos by projecting some figure onto Vernant so as to give back to him? The problem of thinking that which "gives rise" to the opposition between mythos and logos thus appears inextricably linked to the problem of giving homage to the one who has taught us so much about this "giving rise."[12] Indeed, just a couple of pages later Derrida attributes not only giving but *teaching* to the *khōra*—the very thing for which he is honoring Vernant:

Khōra is . . . anything but a support or a subject that would *give* place by receiving or by conceiving, or indeed by letting itself be conceived. . . . Perhaps we have not yet thought through what is meant by *to receive*, the receiving of the receptacle, what is said by *dekhomai*, *dekhomenon*. Perhaps it is from *khōra* that we are beginning to learn it—to receive it, to receive from it what its name calls up. ("*K*," 95–96)

Perhaps what we learn from Jean-Pierre Vernant first and foremost is not some thesis or other about mythos or logos but what *learning* or *teaching* first means, and perhaps what we receive from *khōra* first and foremost is not some particular philosophical distinction but what *receiving* means. In both cases our learning or receiving must be in some way *adjusted* to that which is learned or received. The discourse on *khōra* clearly cannot be a straightforwardly philosophical discourse that simply talks of or about *khōra*. *Khōra* tells us something about itself—about herself—and our discourse must fit itself to this telling; *khōra* names itself or, indeed, gives itself a name through our discourse, and this is the meaning, I would claim, of the text as gift—that is, of the *dedicated text*.

The question of dedication is, one will recall, directly posed by Derrida himself in *Given Time*. Speaking in the context of Baudelaire's dedication of *Le spleen de Paris*, Derrida writes:

By giving it to be remarked, the dedication situates . . . the *dative* or *donor* movement that displaces the text. There is nothing in a text that is not dedicated, nothing that is not destined, and the destination of this dative is not reducible to the explicit dedication. The name of the dedicatee—or donee—supplies no more proof of the effective dedication than the patronymic name of the signatory (juridically identifiable by civil law) exhausts the effective signature, if there is one. ("*GT*," 87)

The dedication destines a text; in the case of a teacher, of someone you owe, a dedication would be a way of paying back—and, inevitably, of taking more, since by seeking the gratitude or respect of the teacher or master through one's offering one would always be trying to get something in return. Unless, of course, a text were dedicated not to some person but, at the limit, to the name of an impossibility, to the name of that which gives us all our distinctions, to the name of the irrecoverable detour between giving and receiving. Such a dedication, such a giving, can take place only at the limits of an economy, in this case, a textual economy, at the limits of reading and receiving, of Derrida reading and receiving the tradition, of our reading and receiving Derrida, of Derrida reading and receiving himself. The dedication would always be, then, a sort of third kind of discourse to a third kind of entity; it would be neither straightforwardly logical nor mythical but would, rather, "signal toward [*faire signe*]" its object, toward itself as a movement of autodonation that never meets back up with itself. One must thus speak of *khōra*, says Derrida paraphrasing Plato, not always with the same name, but "*in the same manner*" [*de la même façon*] ("*K*," 98).[13] *Khōra* is the name, like *différance*, like *pharmakon*, like the gift, of that which has nothing proper; it is a reference that can have no present referent since it refers to what I am calling—and thus naming—the autodonation of a detour.

This autodonation is both the danger and the chance of the tradition. For this tradition—the one we have received—entails or contains not only a series of themes and objects for philosophical discourse but, more significantly, a way of receiving these themes and objects, a way of reading texts, of taking philosophy. If such a tradition is thus unambiguously received, if it is taken for what it is, for what it itself says it is, then philosophy has in this reception concealed its most becoming gift—the moment of donation. This is what Derrida is trying to draw our attention to, what he is trying to give us in *Given Time*, and in all his other texts on the gift. He is, I would suggest, inviting us to read or take our tradition at the limits of our time and our tradition, that is, to take our tradition in and as the time of a detour.

Derrida asks at the very beginning of "*Khōra*": "And what if, perhaps as in the case of the *khōra*, this appeal to the third genre was only the moment of a detour [*le temps d'un détour*] in order to signal toward a genre beyond genre? Beyond categories, and above all beyond categorial oppositions, which in the first place allow it to be approached or said?" ("*K*," 90). This time, this time of a detour, is the only time, I would suggest, for something like a gift; and it designates the way—which is always the same—of taking a discourse like Plato's *Timaeus* or Derrida's *Given Time*. We must thus take the time for a detour through these texts in order to be given a chance—if only for the time of a detour.

3

Stumping the Sun

THE ODYSSEY OF METAPHOR IN "WHITE MYTHOLOGY"

> Signs are not proof, since anyone can produce false or ambiguous signs. Hence one
> falls back, paradoxically, on the omnipotence of language: since nothing assures
> language, I will regard it as the sole and final assurance: *I shall no longer believe in
> interpretation*. I shall receive every word from my other as a sign of truth; and
> when I speak, I shall not doubt that he, too, receives what I say as the truth.
> Whence the importance of *declarations*; I want to keep wresting from the other
> the formula of his feeling, and I keep telling him, on my side, that I love him:
> nothing is left to suggestion, to divination: for a thing to be known, it must be
> spoken; but also, once it is spoken, even very provisionally, it is true.
> —Roland Barthes, *A Lover's Discourse*

In book 2 of the *Physics* Aristotle helps illustrate the position of those who
"hold that the nature and substantive existence of natural products resides
in their material" with the example of Antiphon, who "took as an indication [*sēmeion*] of this that if a man buried a bedstead [*klinēn*] and the sap
in it took force and threw out a shoot it would be tree and not bedstead
that came up . . . and this is why they say that the natural factor in a bedstead is not its shape but the wood—to wit, because wood and not bedstead
would come up if it germinated."[1]

Antiphon's logic seems quite sound, even natural; indeed, what could
be more natural than a tree sprouting from the earth to illustrate what nature really is? But, curiously, significantly, it is not a simple, naturally sprouting tree that provides Antiphon with this "indication" of nature but a work
of culture, of artifice, which, *by being stripped* of its accidental properties, reveals the natural substance residing beneath or within it. A work of culture,

a bedstead, is used to demonstrate what is natural, and this work of culture, stripped of all human signs, is then itself used as a sign or "indication [*sēmeion*]" in this demonstration. For even if the natural factor of wood in the tree is demonstrated to be in some sense prior to the bedstead, only through demonstration and indication is access gained to what is beyond or before all human artifice and imitation—as if artifice and signs had to come before nature in order to indicate that nature comes before signs; as if signs and indications were necessary to indicate the silence of the naturally sprouting tree prior to all indications and signs.

Such observations suggest not that Antiphon's demonstration or indication is unsound or unnatural but that the nature of indication is perhaps complicitous with the indication of nature. In other words, the question of the relationship between nature and artifice is inseparable from the question of the sign. As we will see, the sign in Aristotle turns out to be itself structured like a bedstead, with a well-wrought covering or husk of artificial language and human indication concealing a sap of natural meaning that would *in fact* never see the light of day without that husk but would *in principle* always be there before and without it. It is thus because the sign is structured like a bedstead that a sign like a bedstead is best able to indicate the nature of the sign.

From all this comes the *inclination* to ask about the bedstead and the sign *together*, to take Antiphon's example at face value and to read right on and not yet behind it all the differences between nature and culture, inside and outside, essential and accidental that seem to structure both its content and its form—as well as the difference between content and form. One way to follow such an inclination would be to turn things around, or upside down—by means of a hypothesis: for instance, what if a bedstead *were* to spring out of the earth when planted, if not only more bedstead but an entire bed, indeed an entire bedroom, home, or cosmos, were to grow out of it? What if the most natural thing in the world were a bedstead? And what if this bedstead grew to the point of detaching itself from the earth, from itself, in order to become a sort of signpost that would always suggest, or point back to, yet another bedstead detaching itself from itself, always another instead of itself, in the stead of a unique nature that it would always figure but to which it could never simply refer? What if Antiphon's distinction between nature and artifice, material and form, were itself the result of a bedstead that will have already been buried, and from the beginning, providing not the prelinguistic force or sap of a natural language but the very possibility of a stead of nature, of a bed in the stead of a tree trunk, a signifier in the stead of a signified, a name in the stead of an identity, a scar in the stead of flesh, a narrative in the stead of a home, a metaphor in the stead of a definition? Would we rest less comfortably, would we rest less assured, knowing that language does not grow on trees but is from the beginning crafted and polished, cut with an ax, turned with an augur, spun round a bedstead that is always being uprooted, that can be a sure sign only insofar as it is always instead of itself?

I will try to show here that the bedstead is always the *focus* of the sign, the axis of its revolutions, the stump at the center of the sun that makes for the seasons at the same time as it seasons all our narratives. The bedstead itself, the crafted stump itself—such will be the focus of this chapter on the relationship, in Derrida, between signifier and signified, the husk of meaning and its kernel. At issue will be the very possibility of a return to an already constituted identity or to a natural language that would precede all cultural institutions.

The aim of the chapter is thus to give a certain figuration of *seasoning* through a rereading of certain signs, sure signs of the seasons, signs anchored in the ground, like a tree trunk, but already crafted, like a bedstead, their legibility assured by their unfathomable truth: sure signs that can be disrupted or uprooted only by the seasoning that they will have assured; sure signs that revolve not around the sun but around the bedstead that eclipses and stumps the sun. For this bedstead grows not beneath and toward the sun but out of it; it is that from which the sun itself rises each morning and into which it sets each evening; it is that about which not even the sun, this greatest of eyes, can keep posted, since it is the bedstead and not the sun that marks youth from old age, present sap from lost bloom, departure from return.

Planted in the ground to help orient our space and mark our time, such a bedstead can be dated and located, even if it is that which accounts for all dates and locations. Armed with the best tools of the archaeological dig, I will locate it on the island of Ithaca in the Mediterranean, some three thousand years ago. Unless, of course, everything the reputedly blind poet says turns out to be there to stump us—a narrative to be plunged into our eye at the moment when we see too well that of which it speaks. For as we will see, the bedstead is what always precedes and orients the journey away from home, away from Ithaca, away from a natural or private language into metaphor and narrative; it is that about which we are condemned always to tell stories since we can never really know what a bedstead means.

*

To show that this bedstead is no mere figure or metaphor but the origin of all metaphor, the axis of "metaphoricity" itself, I will begin by sketching out the opposition between the sun and the earth, the light of presence and the ground of concealment, as it is developed in Derrida's "White Mythology." Underlying both, as we will see, underlying the seeming opposition between the literal and the metaphoric, there will prove to be a notion of presence that is derived from the privileged side of the opposition, namely, from the side of the literal, of the philosopheme, as we saw in the previous chapter. In "White Mythology" Derrida first shows how the philosophical opposition of the literal and the metaphoric invariably assumes a certain understanding of presence and resemblance that itself depends on, or is rooted in, a more original "metaphoricity." Neither simply present nor absent, on the side of neither speech nor writing as they are defined by the tradition, this metaphoricity gives rise to the very difference between the literal and the metaphoric. If I take the risk of giving it some figure here— namely, the figure of a stump or a bedpost—it is to avoid the equally great risk of giving it no figure at all. The stump will be neither a literal expression of metaphoricity nor a metaphorical way of expressing it but a *tracing* or *turning* of it, one that both suggests something about metaphoricity as the place between nature and culture, the literal and the metaphorical, and stumps our understanding of that place.

At the very end of "White Mythology" Derrida explicitly opposes sun and earth, plant and stone, by means of an ambivalent "trope." He speaks there of two "heliotropes," the plant that turns to the sun, the *tournesol* or sunflower, an emblem of the metaphysics of presence, and the reddish purple stone that is called in English the bloodstone. In the final paragraph these two heliotropes are opposed in the forms of anthology, the book or logic of the flower collection, and lithography, the writing in or of stone. Situated between these two heliotropes, however, between a rock and a hot place, is, we will see, a certain stump, a sort of petrified tree or growing stone—just one of the many flowers of Derrida's rhetoric that ornament his essay from beginning to end.

Derrida in fact opens "White Mythology" with the image or figure of a flower "turning away, as if from itself, come round again, such a flower engraves—learning to cultivate, by means of a lapidary's reckoning, patience."[2] This flower, which Derrida presses into the opening page of a text full of metaphors, situates us already between cultivation and engraving, the organic and the inorganic, a flower that turns toward the sun and one that turns away. The virtue of this patience—as opposed to the *impatiens*, the touch-me-not or jewelweed, which bursts open and scatters its seed when ripe—is to teach us that we can never simply "get beyond" or "get over" metaphor, even though we must constantly rethink and criticize our metaphors and their sources, especially the light beneath which they grow, through which they are nourished, and toward which they turn.

Derrida argues in "White Mythology" that the text of philosophy, of metaphysics, is full of metaphors and that philosophy can never escape figurative language. Metaphor itself can thus never be understood completely from within philosophy since metaphors will always have been used to explain metaphor. Because philosophy can never dominate the metaphorology it uses, it always "perceive[s] its metaphorics only around a blind spot or central [*foyer*: hearth] deafness" ("WM," 228). But since metaphor itself is an old philosopheme, no metaphor from outside philosophy can come to dominate an understanding of metaphor in philosophy.

Neither inside nor outside, then, but that is not all, for Derrida tries to mark, inscribe, draw attention to a "metaphoricity" that would precede any particular metaphor, the condition of possibility, so to speak, of all metaphor. "To mark," "inscribe," "draw attention to," these too are, of course, all metaphors, but metaphors of what? At the same time as we are led toward a *mise en abîme* of metaphor, the text "White Mythology" figures or gestures the metaphoricity of metaphor, that which produces metaphor, the trunk from which the flowers of rhetoric and philosophy grow. We are always too late for metaphoricity, for seasoning, and so are already in metaphor, in some season. Yet metaphoricity leaves its trace in the metaphor, a trace that can be described or figured only by more metaphors, themselves the result of metaphoricity. To say either that all metaphorical language is based on some literal meaning that precedes it, or, inversely, that all meaning is based on some primitive, figurative language that has been effaced through usage, is to efface the metaphoricity that first gives metaphor. It is already to know what "likeness" is, what links the vehicle to the tenor of the metaphor, what it means to "share" a quality or to have a characteristic "in common."

In the first scenario, which Derrida labels Hegelian, the "turning" of metaphor is risked only with a view toward reappropriation in the overcoming of metaphor in literal language. In the second scenario, the empirical version of heliocentrism, an original, figurative language gives access to a realm of immediate, sensuous experience that is claimed to be more real, more evident, more powerful and, of course, more natural. According to this latter, abstract or metaphysical language effaces not only the material figures of language but the very fact of this effacement, making its own literal language thus appear transparent. It is this putative transparency of abstract language that prompts Anatole France to say that metaphysicians live a "white mythology."

But Derrida shows that the apparent opposition between what is characterized as the Hegelian overcoming of metaphor and the empiricist retrieval of it rests on the same unquestioned ground. Both sides want to recover an experience or realm of thought that is identical to itself, a realm wherein things are identifiable because they resemble themselves to the point of being taken for themselves. But what about the metaphor of resemblance? Derrida writes, "Metaphor has always been defined as the trope of resemblance; not simply as the resemblance between a signifier and a signified but as the resemblance between two signs, one of which resembles the other" ("WM," 215). The metaphor of resemblance appears to elude the system that is supposed to contain it. As Derrida demonstrates, the foundational metaphor that would claim to be the origin of figurative as well as literal language "cannot dominate itself, cannot be dominated by what it itself has engendered, has made to grow on its own soil, supported on its own base [*socle*]" ("WM," 219).[3]

According to Derrida, then, base or fundamental metaphors can never account for themselves since there is always one more metaphor in this "interminable *dehiscence* of the supplement" ("WM," 220). Such dehiscence multiplies metaphors, breaking them open to a metaphoricity that will have preceded them. Like splitting a piece of wood with an ax—an ax that here splits from within—this dehiscence gives rise to a stump that will have preceded the tree from which it came. Derrida writes: "Already the opposition of meaning (the atemporal or nonspatial signified as meaning, as content) to its metaphorical signifier . . . is sedimented—another metaphor—by the entire history of philosophy. Without taking into account that the separation between sense (the signified) and the senses (sensory signifier) is enun-ciated by means of the same root [*racine*] (*sensus, Sinn*). One might admire, as does Hegel, the generousness of this stock [*souche*]" ("WM," 228). This stock, this stump, will become, for Derrida, the "tropic and prephilosoph-ical resource" ("WM," 229) that can never be a proper origin insofar as it precedes propriety itself.

Metaphysics, therefore, according to Derrida, has conceived of meta-phor in terms of *either* the sun, presence and light, or the ground, in terms of either "dialectical idealism . . . the *relève* (*Aufhebung*) . . . the memory (*Erinnerung*) that produces signs, interiorizes them in elevating, suppress-ing, and conserving the sensory exterior," *or* foundationalism, "the desire for a firm and ultimate ground, a terrain to build on, the earth as the sup-port of an artificial structure" ("WM," 224)—an artificial structure, as we will see, like a bed "anchored" in the earth or a scar "carved" on the surface of the body. *Either* the sun *or* the earth: this is the logic of the sun, the logic of presence as origin, *archē*, foundation, or ground. But to think earth and sun together, earth as that which hides and harbors the sun and sun as that which has the earth in its eye, in its face, another logic is required, one that can never completely dominate or master itself but must always rely on risking a story, on erring in language.

In the section of "White Mythology" entitled "The Ellipsis of the Sun" Derrida concludes that, for Aristotle, metaphor, as an effect of *mimēsis* and *homoiōsis*, is a means of knowledge. It must work in the service of truth, even though, or precisely because, it is inferior to philosophical dis-course. Yet Derrida cites an example from Aristotle's *Rhetoric* that would seem to call this vocation of metaphor into question: "When the poet calls old age a 'withered stalk' he conveys a new idea, a new fact, to us by means of the general notion of 'lost bloom' which is common to both things" ("WM," 238–39). The poet in question here is, of course, Homer, and the man who is compared, who compares himself, to this stalk [*kalamēn*] is Odysseus, who says to the swineherd Eumaeus in book 14 of the *Odyssey*, "Now all [my] strength is gone; yet even so, in seeing the stubble, me-thinks thou mayest judge what the grain was [*all' empēs kalamēn ge s'oiomai eisoroōnta gignōskein*]."[4] Homer's Odysseus seems to say that the old stalk, the stubble, is a sign, or signifier, of what was once contained within it—the grain or sap of youth. Like Antiphon's bedpost, the example chosen by Aristotle to illustrate metaphor doubles the structure of the illustration (it is not merely an example of metaphor but the metaphor of metaphor), the exterior stalk or stubble of the metaphor referring to an interior meaning that allows for the substitution of grain for the sap or strength of youth. Although the line in Greek is literally, "I think that seeing the stubble ye may judge," the liberty taken by the English translation in putting the grain back in seems justified since the metaphor establishes a relationship between the grain and the sap of youth.

Yet Aristotle's interpretation of this line seems implicitly to call all this into question. For unlike the example of the bedpost that would refer to a present sap within or before all artifice, the stubble of old age refers not to some youth still present, not even potentially, nor to some youth once present but now lost, but to "something new," "something fresh," "by means of the general notion of 'lost bloom' which is common to both" ("WM," 238–39). But could one ever grasp such a notion—itself expressed here through metaphor—detached from any particular signifiers? Does not the very notion of "lost bloom" depend on a difference between past and present, what is absent and what is present? Is "lost bloom" ever present *as such*—uncontaminated by the categories of youth or flowers? It seems that what makes metaphor possible here, what makes the above translation possible along with the movement from the particular to the genus, is an impossible notion that two things share—a *literal* "lost bloom." This impossibility compels us to ask whether the Homeric line might not suggest that it is on the basis of the stalk *itself* that one may judge the strength now gone, that the stubble *itself* inscribes the general notion of lost bloom— right on its surface, on its husk—and that one can think the oppositions particular/general, presence/absence, signifier/signified, only on the basis of this husk or stalk, only on the basis of an artificial signifier.

Derrida thus concludes that metaphor in Aristotle "does not just illustrate the general possibilities" of *lexis* but "risks disrupting the semantic plenitude to which it should belong. . . . Marking the moment of the turn or of the detour during which meaning might seem to venture forth alone, unloosed from the very thing it aims at however, from the truth which attunes it to its referent, metaphor also opens the wandering of the semantic" ("WM," 241). Return, Derrida claims, is always disrupted by the turning or trope of the sun, the sun that provides the light of resemblance for all metaphors and, even before metaphor, all identities—including, and first of all, the proper name. "The proper name . . . is the nonmetaphorical prime mover of metaphor, the father of all figures. Everything turns around it, everything turns toward it" ("WM," 243). All metaphorical wandering is done with the retrieval of the proper name in view. "Like *mimēsis*, metaphor *comes back* to *physis*, to its truth and its presence. There, nature always refinds its own, proper analogy, its own resemblance to itself, and takes increase only from itself. Nature gives itself in metaphor" ("WM," 244). But the discourse of presence and propriety is sustained by what Derrida calls "a secret narrative" ("WM," 243). For Derrida, in "White Mythology," this secret narrative is a blind spot around which the sun turns; for me, here, it is a stump at the center of the sun, the stumping of the return of the sun to its origin, to the identity of a proper name. To be a master of metaphors, a polytroper so to speak, is to be able to perceive resemblances in order to substitute one term for another—the *telos* always being the retrieval of univocity through the risking of metaphor and polysemy. This desire for univocity depends, as Derrida shows in Aristotle, on the presence of the sun, on presence itself, on that which illuminates the resemblances or similarities between things.

But the sun is not always present. Just when one might think that it, like metaphor, will return to itself, return from its wandering circuit across the sky to join up with itself in a perfect circle of light and presence, it sets, or even worse, hides beneath the earth. We can thus never know that which makes all things proper—that is, the proper of the sun—because the sun turns and hides. The metaphor of the sun is thus not the proper of metaphor but the metaphor of metaphor, since all metaphor is opened to setting, to hiding, to an endless wandering away from proper language. Derrida concludes: "metaphor means [*veut dire*] heliotrope, both a movement turned toward the sun and the turning movement of the sun" ("WM," 251).

It is at precisely this point in "White Mythology" that Derrida turns around, for what I believe to be the first and only time in the essay, to address what one might assume to be us, the reader. "But let us not hasten to make of this a truth of metaphor. Are you sure that you know what the heliotrope is?" ("WM," 251). Having just said that metaphor *means* heliotrope, Derrida turns, advises caution, and then asks us a question intended, I think, to stump us, his readers. For heliotrope is not, we come to see, a proper name with a univocal meaning; it means *both* the turning of the sun *and* the earth, *both* turning toward the sun *and* the bloodstone, *both* anthology *and* lithography. Hence we can never be sure what heliotrope *means*, for it "is" both anthology and lithography, both sun and stone, not alternatively but at the same time—both at once, since reducing the ambivalence of the heliotrope to a masterable polysemy determined by context would be to turn away from the earth, away from the stump, to the sun alone. In other words, it would be simply to repeat the heliocentric gesture of philosophy that aims to reduce the "both . . . and" to an "either . . . or" in the name of univocity, which is to say, in the name not of the name but of meaning.

Derrida thus turns toward us as if he himself were a heliotropic plant and we were the sun, as if this reserve of turning could itself turn our heliocentric desire to find the truth of metaphor back to earth, back to the lithographic text. With this question, this apostrophe, Derrida turns us away from meaning back toward writing, toward an unmasterable graphic ambivalence. In this apostrophe Derrida is in our face, there to blind us with the stake of writing, there to drill writing into us by crossing out our Cyclopean eye, to turn us toward the blindness at the root of all our vision, all our wanting to know. With this apostrophe Derrida calls into question our very desire for the referent, for meaning, for a unique, unambivalent answer to the question What is a heliotrope? For as Derrida argues, the sun, a unique referent insofar as we on earth have only one, is always already metaphorical, always already nonproper, always already instead of itself. The sun "eclipses itself, always has been other, itself: father, seed, fire, eye, egg" ("WM," 253). As Derrida writes: "All that these tropes maintain and sediment in the entangling of their roots is apparent" ("WM," 253). Yes, root*s*, for neither the stump nor the root is ever singular. And it is this multiplicity, this opening onto narrative, that, paradoxically, makes for the possibility of narrative and, thus, as we will see, the recounting of sure signs:

If there were only one possible metaphor, the dream at the heart of philosophy, if one could reduce their play to the circle of a family or a group of metaphors, that is, to one "central," "fundamental," "principal" metaphor, there would be no more true metaphor, but only, through the one true metaphor, the assured legibility of the proper. Now, it is because the metaphoric is plural from the outset that it does not escape syntax, that it gives rise, in philosophy too, to a *text* which is not exhausted in the history of its meaning. ("WM," 268)

Metaphor thus gives rise to a text that is always at a loss, always stumped, but also, as a result, always open to being repeated, to being read otherwise, to being read *in-stead* of itself.

*

Like metaphor, Odysseus is always trying to return home, always trying to come back to and reappropriate himself. To cite Derrida's description of du Marsais's understanding of metaphor, Odysseus is "a being-outside-one's-own-residence, but still in a dwelling, outside its own residence but still in a residence in which one comes back to oneself, recognizes oneself, re-assembles oneself or resembles oneself, outside oneself in oneself" ("WM," 253). Still in a residence, still with a name, a story, an identity, although always in disguise, never truly home, in his own place, Odysseus longs always for the overcoming of his longing, for an eclipse of nostalgia.

Yet, like metaphor, Odysseus would always risk not returning home. Although he would always have reappropriation in mind—the return to his dear native land, to proximity itself, to hearth and home, to the natural stump at the center of the *cosmos*—he would always risk not only delay but nonreturn, perpetual wandering or erring in language. This is not simply a question of some contingency that would cause him to get lost along the way home. For, as we will see, when Odysseus—like metaphor—finally returns to his proper abode, to Ithaca, what he finds or reappropriates is not himself but himself as other, himself as he has never been, himself no longer as the hero of narrative but as the very opening onto it. When this man of many resources returns to Ithaca after some nineteen years of ab-sence, what he discovers, or rather invents, through his *mētis* or ruse, is not some meaning, some significance, he once left behind but the signs he will have once inscribed, the *sure signs* of a stump. Odysseus does not simply discover the thought, the *dianoia*, behind the language or *lexis* of Penelope, who is trying to stump him with the question of the bed; he does not sim-ply unveil some thought buried deep in the mind, waiting, as Derrida writes, to be "brought to the light of language" ("WM," 233). No, he in-vents in narrative the resource or source of both thought and language, a source that breaks out of the earth yet, if it is to be sure, must remain rooted within it. And what will turn out to link the past stump to the pre-sent will be not an assumed, theoretical apprehension of resemblance, of *homoiōsis*, but the stump itself, the center or prephilosophical *foyer* called the "sure sign."

Let us turn, then, to this man of many turns, to this sort of "wandering signifier" who provides Aristotle with one of his most pertinent examples of metaphor. Let us turn to him at the very moment in the *Odyssey* when, after having returned to Ithaca and killed the suitors, he is ready to reveal himself to Penelope. In this scene from book 23 the master of ruses and disguises appears to face his ultimate uncovering and discovery, the moment when he can peel off the final layer of artifice, the last thread of false identity, in order to be home, truly home, with his wife. As Jean Starobinski notes, Odysseus's "mastery derives from his ability to appraise, while moving through an almost ubiquitously hostile world, the exact portion of himself that can be externalized."[5] Now that he is home, he can, it seems, portion himself out without remainder, externalize everything, hold nothing back.

But this is not what happens. Bathed and well clothed after the slaughter, Odysseus sits opposite Penelope in the palace, holding himself back from embracing her, from pouring himself out completely in front of her. And Penelope too, as if she were a mirror in front of Odysseus (unless Odysseus is the mirror image of Penelope), remains implacable, not yet satisfied with the signs the stranger has given her to assure his identity as Odysseus. Hence the final encounter, the final mediation, the moment when Odysseus is recognized as himself, as being truly home, does not occur spontaneously (as it perhaps did with Argos, Odysseus's dog) but requires a sign—and not just any sign but the sign that gives meaning to all other signs. What Penelope wants, in the end, is a *sure sign*, one that cannot be repeated, imitated, or reproduced, one that only Odysseus could give. What she wants is the revelation of a private sign: "we have signs," she says, "which we two alone know, signs hidden from others" (*Od.*, 23.109–10). What she wants is a final sign, a final proof, beyond all signs and proofs. Penelope thus orders the nurse to remove her and Odysseus's bed from the bridal chamber and prepare it in the hallway for the stranger to sleep on. Seeming to be taken in by this ruse, Odysseus, this most suspicious and ruseful of men, recounts in indignation the story of the bedpost he had once built, the bedstead that had been at the center of his universe, the magnetic pole that had oriented his nineteen years of wandering:

"Woman, truly this is a bitter word that thou hast spoken. Who has set my bed elsewhere? Hard would it be for one, though never so skilled, unless a god himself should come and easily by his will set it in another place. But of men there is no mortal that lives . . . who could easily pry it from its place, for a great token [*mega sēma*] is wrought in the fashioned bed, and it was I that built it and none other. A bush of long-leafed olive was growing within the court, strong and vigorous, and in girth it was like a pillar. Round about this I built my chamber. . . . I cut away the leafy branches of the long-leafed olive, and, trimming the trunk from the root, I smoothed it around with the adze well and cunningly, and made it straight to the line, thus fashioning the bed-post; and I bored it all with the auger. Beginning with this I hewed out my bed. . . . Thus do I declare to thee this token; but I know not, woman, whether my bedstead is still fast [*empedon*] in its place, or whether by now some man has cut from beneath the olive stump, and set the bedstead elsewhere."

So he spoke, and her knees were loosed where she sat, and her heart melted, as she knew the sure tokens [*sēmat'... empeda*]. Then with a burst of tears she ran straight toward him, and flung her arms about the neck of Odysseus. . . . "Since thou hast told the clear tokens [*sēmat' ariphradea*] of our bed . . . thou dost convince [*peitheis*] my heart, unbending as it is." (*Od.*, 23.183–208, 225–26, 230)

Penelope accepts the man before her as Odysseus only when she hears the sure signs. Only Odysseus could have known about the bedpost and thus have told the story about it. But there seems to be some confusion here—a confusion that is *perfectly telling*—about what is the sign of what. Odysseus says that a "great token [*sēma*] is wrought in the fashioned bed," while Penelope is said to have melted when she knew, or had revealed to her, the sure signs [*sēmata*], those that Odysseus, it seems, had just recounted. Is the anchored bedstead the sign, or is the story about the bedstead the sign, or the signs? If the latter, what would ever make these signs sure if they were simply the signs of narrative—signs that could be mimed, imitated, stolen, inspired by the gods, made into instruments of deception? In other words, what would anchor the sure sign, give it its sureness, its reliability? What would ensure that the sign could not be uprooted and placed outside its proper context, outside its private chamber? Just as the sign seems to apply to both the bedstead and the story of the bedstead, so the notion of sureness or steadiness seems to apply to both the sign and the bedstead. Odysseus asks whether his bedstead is still fast [*empedon*], still bound or anchored where it was, or whether some man has cut it at the root, stolen or usurped it: his bed, his wife, his rule. But the signs are also said to be *empeda*, steady, as Penelope recognizes in Odysseus's words "tokens" that are reliable, "sure [*empeda*]."

Odysseus thus makes manifest the sureness of signs, the private language that he shares with Penelope alone, the idiomatic language of their bedroom, which has not been uprooted by some other man and put into the general economy of language and the state. Yet to assure his identity, Odysseus must make this private language manifest, public, make the idiomatic tale a story for an outside ear—or voyeuristic third party, a narrator, perhaps, who might now watch over himself, being both hero and narrator, able at once to seal and unseal his own private language, to affirm his own unique identity only by repeating it in narrative. Starobinski writes that "it is through the outside, through the mediation of exteriority, that the hidden part, the dissimulated identity, can become manifest. . . . The narration of external activity stands in place of (in the fullest sense of that term: it develops in space, it establishes itself in space) the expression of internal identity" ("IO," 348, 350).

In the final book of the *Odyssey* the recounting of sure signs once again persuades someone close to Odysseus, and once again these sure signs are rooted in narrative and attached to trees. Old Laertes says to his son, "If it is indeed as Odysseus, my son, that thou art come hither, tell me now some clear sign [*sēma . . . ariphrades*], that I may be sure" (*Od.*, 24.328–29). So Odysseus shows his father his scar, tells him the story of it, and names the various trees his father had once given him; at this, Laertes' "knees were loosed where he stood, and his heart melted, as he knew the sure tokens [*sēmat' . . . empeda*]" (*Od.*, 24.345–46).

What is the effect of this conjunction of the sign and sureness, *sēma* and *empedos*, in these final scenes of the *Odyssey*? And what does such a conjunction tell us about a bedstead that would be able to indicate, for Antiphon, the true nature of wood, or, for Odysseus, the true nature of his identity? In Homer a *sēma* is a distinguishing trait or sign of some sort, a mark that allows someone to identify or to be himself identified.[6] It can thus be the personal mark one puts on a stone when casting lots or else a mark on the body that allows one to be identified—such as the scar of Odysseus, a "manifest sign [*sēma ariphrades*]" that can either prove one's identity or give one away (*Od.*, 21.217; cf. 23.73). Yet because every sign is precisely a "sign," that is, only a sign of the thing and not the thing itself, the manifest sign needs to be secured, anchored, buried.[7]

In the *Odyssey* the sure sign and the manifest sign meet in the bedpost and the scar. But there is yet one more manifest sign that points us outside or beyond the narrative proper. This sign is recounted in Hades by Tiresias, the half-male, half-female, blind seer. Tiresias tells Odysseus that to appease the wrath of Poseidon, god of the sea, angry because Odysseus had blinded his son the Cyclops with a well-turned stick, he must leave Ithaca once he has returned, travel back to the mainland, and journey inland bearing an oar on his shoulder: "And I will tell thee a sign right manifest [*sēma ariphrades*], which will not escape thee. When another wayfarer, on meeting thee, shall say that thou hast a winnowing-fan on thy stout shoulder, then do thou fix [*pēxas*] in the earth thy shapely oar and make goodly offering to lord Poseidon" (*Od.*, 11.126–30; 23.273).[8] So Odysseus must once again

leave Ithaca, and when he has been given a manifest sign—someone mis-
taking his instrument of seafaring for one of agriculture—he must plant or
anchor his oar and make offerings to Poseidon. (And I remark in passing
that if this oar were to throw out a shoot, a nonseafaring people would interpret it as more wood, perhaps as more winnowing fan, but never as
more oar.) At that point, with that point, that sign, Odysseus's journey will
end, says Tiresias, and he will return to Ithaca to die a comfortable death in
old age.

But Odysseus's bed—the bed on which Odysseus will probably die if
he fixes his oar in the ground for Poseidon—is not only a manifest but a
"sure" sign, a sign that is *empedos*. As an adjective *empedos* denotes in Homer
firmness, steadiness, safeness, or protection against decay; it is used to describe things or men who are vigorous, unimpaired, well balanced, secure,
assured, unfailing. Thus chains, men in battle, and even the human heart
can all be steady, firm, secure, *empedos*. As an adverb *empedon* or *empedōs*
means unceasingly, steadily, without hesitation or break. Hence snow can
fall continually, or sticks and stones can rain down steadily from a city wall
during a battle. *Empedos* thus indicates both steadiness at a particular moment in time, steadfastness of or in space, and continuity across time—
like a seasoned stump that reaches down to another time, an inscription of
time in the earth, or a scar provoking narrative, an emblem of narrative,
that is, not just another sign but the place from which the sign—and the
likeness of the sign—is given.

Indeed what could be a surer sign of one's identity than a cicatrix or
scar? Recall that it is precisely at the moment when the scar is discovered
by the aged nurse during the bathing scene of book 19 that the poet breaks
into the narrative, interrupting Odysseus's reaction to the discovery, cutting in like a scar across the narrative, to tell the story of Odysseus's birth
and name. Odysseus's name, "child of wrath," itself thus cuts into the narrative like the boar's tusks once cut into his flesh. To stump the host is, it
seems, to cut into his flesh and give him a name. For this scar is the cut of
the name and of language, the unique cut that provides certainty and yet
must be manifest, that is hidden in the flesh and yet must be deciphered
or read on its surface. It is the point where the body is opened to and inscribed in narrative: my name, my body, my bed, my wife, my house, my
kingdom . . . but then, my story, my narrative, the story of my name, of
my body, of my bed, of my kingdom. To be given a name is to be inscribed
into the flesh of narrative.

So the tree stump, the bedstead, the sure sign, seems to refer back to itself in the past, back to the experience of making the bed. This duration, this relation between past and present, is what would give the sign its sureness and stability. Yet this past is not given in a *nonlinguistic* moment that would precede all signs; it is open to experience only in the experience of narrative, whereas narrative is itself opened up only by means of the sure sign that gives to all signs their light and legibility, their stability and identity with themselves. What assures the stability of the bed, then, is not the presence of an experience, not the making of the bed under the light of day, but the fact that the bed is half buried, its roots reaching down into the stable earth. Such a sign can thus become manifest, and so truly be a sign, only by uprooting itself, by detaching itself from itself.

On the one hand, then, signs in the present link up with signs or things of the past to produce sure signs. On the other hand, a sign in the present supplements, but does not reveal, the sure sign, for it produces that which precedes it and thus gets its sureness not from a past once present but from its own autoaffective movement, the sure sign being not the tree once and still present but the narrative about the tree. The narrative thus substitutes for itself, substitutes its own signs beneath the light of day, signs that can be learned, mimed, imitated, and repeated, for the sure signs that offer no proof or possibility for reference, for roots that plunge down into the earth. To make these roots present, to make them manifest, would be to destroy the hidden, private signs they ensure. Yet how else to offer proof? The sure sign must become manifest. It must become itself by becoming other—so that its sureness is never sure, never absolute, never inimitable, always repeatable. The sure sign is not, then, simply the limit of experience; it is not some idea or intuition that would precede experience and narrative; it is that which gives rise to the difference between experience and narrative, experience of the present and tales of the past; it is that which first gives the sign and so is at once the *first* sign and the *impossible* sign.

The sure sign is the trace of its own unfathomable depth: both narrative and root, both artificial and natural, both the object of human artifice and the nature that precedes artifice. The stump of the bed is the first sign and the first metaphor, which is to say that it is already multiple, the divided center of a private language. This language recognizes itself, indeed becomes itself, only in being brought back to itself after a circuit (of, say, some nineteen years) around the stump at the center of the sun, around a certain *seasoning* of time and space.

The stump is indeed an *axis mundi*, not just the center of the world but a worldly axis, the very difference or ax cut between nature and culture. It grows beneath the sun toward itself, toward the stump at the center of the sun. The sun thus turns on itself around the stump that precedes it. As the sun goes down beneath the earth, the stump grows at the center of the sun, a line at the center of the circle. The stump of the sun is thus no mere metaphor but the inclination of metaphoricity itself. Whereas the circle of the heliotrope is the dominant metaphor of metaphysics, the ambivalent heliotrope, the very stumping or posting of the heliotrope, would be the metaphor of metaphor, the very figure of postmetaphysics or *post-metaphorics*.

*

At the end of "White Mythology," just before introducing the other heliotrope that is a rock, Derrida summarizes two autodestructions of metaphor, the first, that of the Hegelian *Aufhebung*, and the second, it seems, that of deconstruction. Of this latter he writes: "The *other* self-destruction of metaphor thus *resembles* the philosophical one to the point of being taken for it" ("WM," 270). *Other* and *resemble* are in italics, indeed must be in italics, for the similarity between these two self-destructions can no longer be a simple resemblance. The other self-destruction of metaphor is taken for philosophy because it resembles it—resembles it both without and with italics—that is, both resembles it and *resembles* this resembling. What Penelope welcomes home at the end of the *Odyssey*, what she tries to stump even after the beggar has doffed his disguise and donned the appearance, voice, and memory of Odysseus, is an Odysseus both with and without italics, an immovable center that nonetheless inclines, slants away from itself, and, in this inclination, first becomes itself.

The poet Richard Wilbur once wrote, "Odd that a thing is most itself when likened."[9] Yes, odd that Odysseus is most himself when likened to himself, when he is both disguised and revealed, both hero and poet, both with and without quotation marks, both the object and subject of narrative. Odd that Odysseus is most himself when he has returned to himself, or, rather, to his proper name, when he must at last recall and cite himself, tell his own story, put himself in italics, resemble himself to the point of being taken for himself, to the point of stumping not only us but himself, since he must now put even himself on, and, like Penelope, weave an identity by day that is unwoven at night, the sun no longer there to assure the transparency and property of his name, the bed now uprooted and put into narrative.

PART TWO

FRENCH RECEPTIONS

4

Derrida's Watch/Foucault's Pendulum

A FINAL IMPETUS TO THE COGITO DEBATE

> Derrida's weaving of irony and openness in his claims for discipleship bears further
> thought. Since I find our voices passing and repassing in the experiments I have
> made with certain of the passages of an early essay of his, and of certain others,
> I am led to take his reflections on discipleship as, more generally, or more specifi-
> cally, reflections on reading at its most faithful—as if at its most faithful reading
> consists of this competition or mutual inhabitation or mutual subjection of voices.
> Then one had better be careful of what it is one is drawn to read faithfully.
> —Stanley Cavell, "Naughty Orators"

Derrida/Foucault: two master names brought together in a single title, two
masters separated by a single, silent virgule, by a discreet suspension of the
breath, by the almost imperceptible yet thoroughly dramatic moment when
the pendulum has reached its apex and is about to descend. Derrida/Foucault:
separately, these names suggest many things, too many even to begin to
enumerate here, but when combined, when joined together like the two
terms of a pendulum movement, or like the two rivals in a debate, these
names recall in their alternation and rhythm a single but significant episode
or chapter in French intellectual history—a single episode or chapter that is
nonetheless divided and scanned within, that will have lasted for more
than thirty years, from even before Derrida's full appearance on the scene
to even after Foucault's disappearance from it, that is, from even before the
publication of Derrida's 1967 essay "Cogito and the History of Madness"
in *Writing and Difference* to even after his more recent 1991 essay on Foucault, "'To Do Justice to Freud': The History of Madness in the Age of Psychoanalysis." Even before/even after: even before 1967, while Derrida was

still, as he himself says, an admiring student of Foucault, delivering a version of the "Cogito" essay in March of 1963 before the master; and even after, at the end of the 1991 essay "'To Do Justice to Freud,'" where Derrida poses a final question to the master, long after his disappearance, and, in place of the master, attempts not to answer for him but at least to formulate the principle of a response.

Derrida/Foucault: to join these names yet again in this way, to wish to return to this *fort/da* scene, to revisit and give this debate a new impetus, might appear, if not simply passé, meddlesome and inappropriate. For the debate over Descartes, over the exclusion of madness in narrative, was, after all, between them, and even if others got into the act and contributed to it, becoming more involved, perhaps, than either Derrida or Foucault, it had only so much energy, held only so much interest, so that good taste should dictate not returning to breathe new life into something that Derrida himself seems to have punctuated one last time and laid to rest— leaving the last word, which will remain unspoken, to Foucault.

Good taste and respect should lead us to be silent here, to let those touched by the debate speak for themselves, speak of and to themselves. Yet to reread this debate, one cannot but be touched to some degree by it, touched not necessarily by the issues involved but by their rhythm, not so much by the actors in the debate but by the pendulum-like motion that scans their relation to each other, to themselves, and, ultimately, to us. For if there is anything that is not and cannot be properly theirs, if there is anything "in" this debate that cannot but touch others, it is this suspension of the breath, this pause between breaths, between Derrida's and Foucault's, this pause that inscribes death into the heart of every rhythm, that marks every breath by a last breath and every word by silence.

Let me begin, then, by simply recalling a few dates: Foucault's *Folie et déraison: Histoire de la folie à l'âge classique* (which I will refer to throughout as *The History of Madness*) was originally published in 1961. In 1964 a much abridged French version was published and then translated into English the following year by Richard Howard under the title *Madness and Civilization: A History of Insanity in the Age of Reason*. The original was then reprinted with a different pagination by Gallimard in 1972 and included as an appendix "My Body, This Paper, This Fire," Foucault's response to Derrida's essay "Cogito and the History of Madness."[1] This essay of Derrida's was first presented as a lecture in 1963 at the Collège philosophique and was published the following year in the *Revue de Métaphysique et de Morale* before being republished in 1967 in *Writing and Difference.* Foucault's 1972 response goes pretty much unanswered, or answered only by a silence that will last, as Derrida himself says, for some ten years, until January of 1982. Finally, if it is possible ever to say "finally," Derrida delivered in 1991 and published in 1992 the essay "'To Do Justice to Freud': The History of Madness in the Age of Psychoanalysis," an essay written for the thirtieth anniversary of the publication of *The History of Madness.*

Now, I recall these dates not simply to archive this debate or dialogue, to recount its history, but to evoke its periodicity, which, more than thirty years later, has the appearance of falling into roughly three distinct ten-year periods: the first, marked by the publication of Foucault's book, Derrida's response to it, and Foucault's silence concerning this response; the second, beginning with Foucault's response to Derrida and Derrida's silence; and the third, beginning with the end of a decade of silence in 1982 and continuing, through Foucault's death in 1984, up to Derrida's essay of 1991 and the silence of Foucault that has inevitably followed.[2] My intention here is thus not simply to revisit and reanimate a debate or dialogue that does not and should not really concern me but to shift emphasis to the debate *as* a debate, that is, to Derrida's relationship to Foucault in 1963 and after and to both of their relationships to the movement of the pendulum between them. I wish to ask, therefore, not simply about two moments or positions or even two names, like Derrida and Foucault, that can be identified and thereby mastered but about two notions of time and exclusion, not simply about the watch or the pendulum but about the constant scansion, the constant vigilance of the watch by the pendulum, not simply about the relationship between master and disciple but about the impetus given to an unmasterable dialectic between inclusion and exclusion, mastery and discipleship, an impetus that, as we will see, always comes back to haunt the one who sets it in motion.

In what follows I will look at how this dialogue is itself marked by the very things at issue in the dialogue, that is, by exclusion and inclusion, mastery, control, communication with the other, and silence. In other words, I will be concerned with how the terms of the debate over the mastery of madness in Descartes, and, later, over the role that Freud plays in Foucault's corpus, come to haunt the debate *as* a debate, come to scan it with moments of inclusion and exclusion, silence and communication, that can now be read as either a series of ages of the debate, a series of chapters in an ongoing history, or as a debate whose history must remain at issue insofar as temporality and historicity are exactly what are at stake there. This back and forth, pendulum-like movement of the debate can thus be read, I will argue, either as one extremely significant chapter within French intellectual history or as a movement that first scans and situates that history, a movement that promises not just the return of one side in response to the other but the return of a certain impetus or periodicity—a return of the silence between two breaths, of the little death between one response and another. In the end the debate might be read not only as a dialectic or competition between master and disciple, teacher and student, Foucault and Derrida, but as a process of mourning, an unmasterable dialectic of mourning that will have begun already in 1963, more than twenty years before Foucault's death, and that would go on even today—providing the impetus for all this talk about Foucault, about Derrida, and about the debate between them.

It would be impossible to do justice here to the rich and complex dialogue between Derrida and Foucault that began just about thirty years ago when Derrida challenged the reading Foucault devotes to a couple of paragraphs of Descartes's first meditation in a three-page introduction to the second chapter of *The History of Madness*. To oversimplify to the extreme, Derrida takes Foucault to task for claiming that in the first meditation Descartes summarily excludes madness from the cogito by distinguishing sharply between, on the one hand, the deceptions of dreams and illusions, which are overcome because of a residue of truth in the things themselves, and, on the other hand, madness, which is outright rejected by the cogito so that the Cartesian project of rationality might be pursued and protected. Foucault writes, "In the economy of doubt, there is a fundamental disequilibrium between madness, on the one hand, dreams and error, on the other. They are differently situated with relation to the truth and to the one seeking it; dreams or illusions are overcome in the very structure of truth; but madness is excluded by the subject who doubts."[3] Whereas Montaigne, in the sixteenth century, was forever haunted by the possibility of being mad, Descartes, in the seventeenth, Foucault claims, banished this threat, reducing madness "to silence by a strange act of force [*étrange coup de force*]."

In "Cogito and the History of Madness" Derrida argues that madness is not excluded at this point in the *Meditations*, confined to the outside of the cogito, but actually incorporated into it. Descartes moves in the *Meditations* from doubts concerning madness to doubts arising from dreams because of a rhetorical and pedagogical need to convince the nonphilosopher who would never believe himself mad. Whereas the nonphilosopher, who is, Derrida claims, Descartes's implicit interlocutor in this part of the first meditation, would simply dismiss the possibility of being mad, the experience of being deceived in dreams is something that the nonphilosopher not only has experienced but experiences every night. Hence madness is not simply excluded but, in a sense, radicalized in the form of dreams, which, for the nonphilosopher, would prove more convincing than madness and, in a sense, more mad than madness itself. When, just after, the moment of hyperbolic doubt is achieved through the fiction of the evil genius, the cogito is not protected from a madness that it has already excluded but opened up to a madness that encompasses the entirety of the factual world without, however, affecting the sole fact of the cogito's existence. Derrida writes:

The certainty [of the cogito] thus attained need not be sheltered from an emprisoned [*sic*] madness, for it is attained and ascertained within madness itself. It is valid *even if I am mad*—a supreme self-confidence that seems to require neither the exclusion nor the circumventing of madness. Descartes never interns madness, neither at the stage of natural doubt nor at the stage of metaphysical doubt. *He only makes as if he is excluding it [il fait seulement semblant de l'exclure] during the first phase of the first phase, during the nonhyperbolic moment of natural doubt.*[4]

According to Derrida the artifice of hyperbolic doubt enables Descartes to open up the *Meditations* to the very point at which the philosophical project is exceeded by a silence that precedes all philosophical reasoning, to what Derrida calls a "historicity" in general that precedes all narrativization and etiological argumentation. Once this point is reached, however, Descartes immediately begins covering over this silence, grounding the cogito in the existence of a God who could not be a deceiver, establishing criteria for truth, and so forth. At the moment of hyperbolic doubt, however, the *Meditations* are opened to the silence that would accompany a historicity in general, the historicity that would be at the origin of a history such as a "History of Madness in the Classical Age."

Now, Derrida uses this rereading of Descartes to question Foucault's entire project. If within this project or this history of madness a point is revealed that opens this history onto the origin of history itself, then a whole series of questions concerning the periodization and historicity of this history needs to be addressed. Although Derrida finds signs of such questions in various places in *The History of Madness*, he ultimately argues that they are not raised explicitly enough or in a determined enough fashion.

All this, I recall, takes place in 1963 and is published in the French edition of *Writing and Difference* in 1967. And Foucault does not respond until 1972, in an appendix to a new edition of *The History of Madness*. In his response Foucault defends his reading of the *Meditations* some eleven years earlier and, although giving credit to Derrida for having raised several important points in his reading, insists that Derrida has elided the important differences between dreaming and madness just as the traditional interpreters of Descartes have done. Foucault writes near the end of "My Body, This Paper, This Fire":

It is not as an effect of their lack of attention that before Derrida and in like manner the classical interpreters erased this passage from Descartes. It is by system. A system of which Derrida is the most decisive modern representative, in its final glory; the reduction of discursive practices to textual traces . . . the invention of voices behind texts to avoid having to analyze the modes of implication of the subject in discourses.[5]

Foucault depicts Derrida as the inheritor of an old tradition, the last in a long line of masters who genuflect before the sovereign text in order to claim, as the master, sovereignty over the text and its disciples. Here is the penultimate paragraph of Foucault's response, which I cite not for the dramatic effect of its stinging remarks but to bring us back to the terms of the debate *as* a debate—that is, to exclusion and inclusion, silence, mastery and discipleship, and to Derrida's and Foucault's relationship to the tradition and history of philosophy:

I will not say that it is a metaphysics, metaphysics itself or its closure which is hiding in this "textualisation" of discursive practices. I'll go much further than that: I shall say that what can be seen here so visibly is a historically well-determined little pedagogy. A pedagogy which teaches the pupil that there is nothing outside the text, but that in it, in its gaps, its blanks and its silences, there reigns the reserve of the origin; that it is therefore unnecessary to search elsewhere, but that here, not in the words, certainly, but in the words under erasure, in their *grid*, the "sense of being" is said. A pedagogy which gives conversely to the master's voice the limitless sovereignty which allows it to restate the text indefinitely. ("MBTP," 27)

Again, much more can and should be said about Foucault's pointed and thoughtful response to Derrida. But I recall that my intention here is simply to lay out the terms of the debate to show how these very terms come to characterize the debate *as a debate*. So without doing justice to any of these texts I now move on to the final written installment of this debate, Derrida's 1991 essay, "'To Do Justice to Freud': The History of Madness in the Age of Psychoanalysis." Derrida returns in this essay to questions concerning historicity in general and the very possibility of writing a history of madness by focusing not on the exclusion of madness in Descartes but on the role Freud plays in Foucault's corpus from *The History of Madness* right up through *The History of Sexuality*. Derrida demonstrates Foucault's fundamental ambivalence with regard to Freud, who is sometimes praised and sometimes condemned, sometimes included among those who liberated us from the strategies of power and knowledge and sometimes put on the side of those who subjected us even further to them. Derrida follows the various shifts in emphasis and value attached to the name of Freud throughout Foucault's corpus and ends up characterizing this back-and-forth movement as a sort of pendulum or *fort/da* relation that runs from Foucault's very earliest texts right up to his last.

Derrida suggests that this ambivalence with regard to Freud be understood not as some error on Foucault's part but as an inevitable reflection of an ambivalence in the things themselves—that is, an ambivalence inherent to Freud and to the very objects of psychoanalysis. If Foucault is to be criticized for anything, it would be for not recognizing and clarifying in a theoretical fashion this fundamental ambivalence within Freud. Derrida thus ends the essay by referring to a fundamental duality within Freud that is sometimes reflected but rarely recognized in Foucault's work. Citing Foucault's reference in *The History of Sexuality* to a "double impetus: pleasure and power,"[6] Derrida suggests that were Foucault to have followed up on this double impetus with a close reading of *Beyond the Pleasure Principle*, he would have found "already in Freud, to say nothing of those who followed, discussed, transformed, and displaced him, the very resources for the objection leveled against the 'good genius,' the so very bad 'good genius,' of the father of psychoanalysis" (*RP*, 114)—this word *genius* resonating some thirty years later with the debate over Descartes and the status of the evil genius in the *Meditations*. Derrida writes a couple of pages later:

The question would thus once again be given a new impetus: is not the duality in question, this spiraled duality, precisely what Freud tried to oppose to all monisms by speaking of a dual drive and of a death drive, of a death drive that was no doubt not alien to the drive for mastery? And, thus, to what is most alive in life, to its very living on [*survivance*]? (*RP*, 118)

It is precisely here that I would like to turn the entire discussion from the terms *in* the debate to the terms *of* the debate. I do so, as I said, not to reanimate the debate or breathe new life into it but to approach this drive for mastery that is no doubt not foreign to a certain death drive. For in one sense the debate between Derrida and Foucault over Descartes or Freud was from the beginning a debate about mastery and exclusion, mastery and discipleship, and the ambivalence of a relation that can never be controlled. From the opening lines of Derrida's 1991 essay we can hear how the debate that Derrida says he does not wish to reopen cannot but be reopened insofar as the terms of the debate are the very ones that frame Derrida's desire not to reopen it. Thirty years after the original publication of *The History of Madness*, nearly twenty years after Foucault's response to Derrida, Derrida responds to the expectations of his audience to say something about this historic debate in French intellectual history:

There was in all of this a sort of dramatic chain of events, a compulsive and repeated precipitation that I do not wish to describe here because I do not wish to be alone, to be the only one to speak of this after the death of Michel Foucault—except to say that this shadow that made us invisible to one another, that made us not associate with one another for close to ten years (until January 1, 1982, when I returned from a Czech prison), is still part of a story that I love like life itself. . . . Second, because this whole thing is more than just overdetermined . . . it has become too distant from me, and perhaps because of the drama just alluded to I no longer wished to reopen it. In the end, the debate is archived and those who might be interested in it can analyze as much as they want and decide for themselves. By rereading all the texts of this discussion, right up to the last word, and especially the last word, one will be better able to understand, I imagine, why I prefer not to give it a new impetus today. (*RP*, 71)

Nothing would seem to be clearer. Tact, reserve, and the distance of time dictate not returning to an old debate. But as we read on, we cannot but become attentive to the very terms of this reserve. I will focus on just three—the terms or values of reopening, associating, and giving a new impetus. First, reopening, the reopening of the drama with Foucault, for it just so happens that reopening was already the operative term in *The History of Madness*, where Foucault claims, for example, that Freud and Nietzsche "reopen" a dialogue with madness that had been twice interrupted since the Renaissance. In "Cogito and the History of Madness" Derrida asked about the presuppositions behind Foucault's archaeology of the silence surrounding madness and the intermittent attempts to reestablish or reopen a dialogue with it. Derrida remarks on this value or theme of reopening at several points in his 1991 essay. He says, for example, that "it is through a return to unreason, this time without exclusion, that Nietzsche and Freud reopen the dialogue with madness *itself* (assuming, along with Foucault, that one can here say 'itself')" (*RP*, 83). And later, "what inscribes both Freud *and* Nietzsche, like two accomplices of the same age, is the reopening of the dialogue with unreason, the lifting of the interdiction against *language*, the *return* to a proximity with madness" (*RP*, 97–98).

In claiming that he does not wish to reopen a debate with Foucault, Derrida gives, it seems, a new impetus to the entire debate concerning the very value of reopening; can one really refrain from reopening a debate simply by remaining silent? The word *reopens* seems in Derrida's essay to describe both the dialogue with unreason and Derrida's dialogue with Foucault. This helps us understand, I think, the fact that Derrida does, in a couple of important paragraphs, return to the "debate itself," before reiterating his wish not to do so. Here is one example that might be read, to use Derrida's words, as the sign of a "compulsive and repeated precipitation": "I had stressed that this methodical mastery of the voluntary subject is 'almost always' at work and that Foucault, therefore, like Descartes, is 'almost always right [*a . . . raison*],' and almost always wins out over [*a raison de*] the Evil Genius. But that is not what is at issue here, and I said that I would not reopen the debate" (*RP*, 85). A couple of lines later Derrida, still responding to Foucault's response of 1972, interrupts himself once again to say, "But let us move on. As I said earlier, I am not invoking this difficulty in order to return to an old discussion" (*RP*, 85).

The second point to be noted in Derrida's opening gesture in "'To Do Justice to Freud'" is the value of association: Derrida speaks of this "shadow that made us invisible to one another, that made us not associate with one another for close to ten years (until January 1, 1982, when I returned from a Czech prison)." Again this would all seem rather straightforward were it not for the fact that Derrida's description of his relation with Foucault is echoed just a bit later by his description of Freud's relation to Nietzsche. At one point in the Foucauldian corpus Freud is, says Derrida, "immediately associated with Nietzsche, the only one to be associated with him, on the 'good' side, so to speak, on the side where 'we' contemporaries reopen the dialogue with unreason that was twice interrupted" (*RP*, 86). But at another point, a certain relationship to language "separates Freud from Nietzsche," making them "unable to associate or to be associated with one another from the two sides of a wall that is all the more unsurmountable insofar as it consists of an asylum's partition, an invisible, interior, but eloquent partition, that of truth itself as the truth of man and his alienation" (*RP*, 98). Hence, "the name of the one who was not crazy, not crazy enough in any case, the name of Freud, is dissociated from that of Nietzsche" (*RP*, 90).

Considering that Derrida's "'To Do Justice to Freud'" could be read as a sort of defense of Freud against Foucault's sometimes unequivocal claims against him, one has to wonder whether Derrida is figuring himself in the place of Freud here. Such a hypothesis appears more plausible when one considers that this entire debate, from 1963 on, seems always to have revolved around a *fort/da* between two figures or terms: already in *The History of Madness* Montaigne was played off Descartes, Nietzsche off Freud, so that, later in the debate, when Derrida comes to defend, in some sense, Descartes or Freud, these names seem to mask or serve as foils for the proper names of the debate itself, right up to an almost compulsive repetition of letters: *fort/da*, *folie/déraison*, Freud/Descartes, Foucault/Derrida.

But returning again to the opening of "'To Do Justice to Freud,'" Derrida writes that he would prefer not to give the debate with Foucault "a new impetus today." This too would be straightforward enough were the word *impetus* not taken right from the analysis of Freud we are about to read. In *The History of Sexuality*, for example, Foucault spoke of "how wonderfully effective [Freud] was—worthy of the greatest spiritual fathers and directors of the classical period—in giving a new impetus to the secular injunction to study sex and transform it into discourse" (*HS*, 159). For Foucault this impetus would appear to be something *within* a history of sexuality, a new impetus to already existing "strategies of knowledge and power" to control sexuality. But elsewhere in "'To Do Justice to Freud'" Derrida applies the notion of a "new impetus" not to a particular movement within a history of sexuality or psychoanalysis but to the very movement that scans and opens up such histories to the historicity that precedes them: "If one is still willing to follow this figure of the pendulum [*balancier*] making a scene in front of psychoanalysis, then one will observe that the *fort/da* here gives a new impetus to the movement, a movement with the same rhythm but with a greater amplitude and range than ever before" (*RP*, 111). The movement Derrida is referring to—Foucault's inclusion/exclusion of Freud within the list of mad geniuses—is thus given a new impetus *as the movement* of historicity itself and not as a determined moment within some history. Derrida's claimed desire not to give a new impetus to the debate between himself and Foucault could be read, then, without contradiction, as a desire not to return to the themes of exclusion and madness in Descartes, that is, to a particular historical debate, but to give a new impetus, in the absence of the other and perhaps from the absence of the other, to the question of what an impetus is, to give a new impetus, then, not to the debate as such but to the impetus of the debate.[7]

This movement from the particular terms of the debate to their movement or alternation, that is, from their discrete appearance in a text to their repetition, comes to touch and transform just about every other major term in the debate. Consider, for example, silence.[8] In *The History of Madness* Foucault performs, Derrida argues, a sort of archaeology of the silence of madness—of the silence with regard to madness when one does not speak with it, of the silence to which madness is condemned when one does speak to it, and of the speechlessness and silence of psychology when faced with the silence of madness. In "'To Do Justice to Freud'" Derrida himself performs a sort of archaeology of Foucault's own silence with regard to Freud. He writes, for example, "[The name of Freud] is regularly passed over in silence when, according to another filiation, Hölderlin, Nerval, Nietzsche, Van Gogh, Roussel, and Artaud are at several reprieves named and renamed—renowned—within the same 'family'" (*RP*, 90). Or, "Freud is once again passed over in silence, cut out of both the lineage and the work of mad geniuses. He is given over to a forgetfulness where one can then accuse him of silence and forgetting" (*RP*, 103). But as we will see in a moment, Derrida's 1991 essay ends by turning us toward yet another silence—not the silence of psychology or philosophy when confronted with madness, not the determined silence of madness at a particular historical moment, but the silence that is, as Foucault would say, the "absence of the work," the silence that must be broken in order not only to speak but to remain silent in a determined way. It is the silence, I will argue, between two breaths, between the living and the dead.

This brings us to the question of *mastery*—the master term of the entire debate. Whereas the debate about the *Meditations* revolved around the mastery and exclusion of madness, the issue in "'To Do Justice to Freud'" appears to be, in a first moment, Foucault's mastery and exclusion of Freud. Here is just one example of the relationship between mastery and ambivalence within the Foucauldian text, an interminable ambivalence that is, as

Derrida says, a reflection of the ambivalence of the things themselves, an "interminable and inexhaustible *fort/da*" (*RP*, 103) that Derrida shows can be traced throughout the entire Foucauldian corpus: "Taken at this level of generality, things will never change for Foucault. There will always be this interminable, alternating movement that successively opens and closes, draws near and distances, rejects and accepts, excludes and includes, disqualifies and legitimates, masters and liberates" (*RP*, 78). Yet, as Derrida knows, this theme of mastery cannot be simply isolated within the Foucauldian text. As a theme, it cannot be isolated without betraying the mastery involved in such isolation, such thematization, and even when this mastery too is recognized or taken into account, there still remains the mastery of recognition. There is thus an inevitable slippage from Foucault's analysis of Descartes's or Freud's mastery of madness to Derrida's analysis of Foucault's mastery of the ambivalence within his text with regard to Descartes or Freud, to, finally, the relationship of mastery between Derrida and Foucault. There is a movement from the analysis of some determined mastery to the analysis of the very concept of mastery to the question of recognizing the aporias of this concept and, thus, the aporias of one's own attempt to master this concept. In the following passage, which I cited in an abridged form just a moment ago, one can begin to see a slide from mastery in Foucault to the mastery of Foucault, from Foucault doing justice to Freud to Foucault doing justice to Derrida. Derrida writes, reopening the debate he said he wished not to reopen:

He accuses me of erasing "everything that shows that the episode of the evil genius is an exercise that is voluntary, controlled, mastered, and carried out from start to finish by a meditating subject who never lets himself be surprised" ("MBTP," 26). (Such a reproach was indeed unfair, unjust, since I had stressed that this methodical mastery of the voluntary subject is "almost always" at work and that Foucault, therefore, like Descartes, is "almost always right [*a . . . raison*]," and almost always wins out over [*a raison de*] the Evil Genius. But that is not what is at issue here, and I said that I would not reopen the debate.)[9]

The first thing to note here besides Derrida's return to the debate of "Cogito and the History of Madness" is his parenthetical complaint that "such a reproach was indeed unfair, unjust." What does it mean for Derrida in an essay entitled "'To Do Justice to Freud'" to claim that he has been treated unjustly? By using Foucault's own phrase for his title, is Derrida—who takes the side of Freud, in some sense, throughout the essay—also claiming that justice needs to be done to him? Derrida says of the phrase that forms his title:

When one says, "one must do justice," "one has to be fair" [*il faut être juste*], it is often with the intention of correcting an impulse or reversing the direction of a tendency: one is also recommending resisting a temptation. Foucault must have felt this temptation, the temptation to do an injustice to Freud, to be unfair to him—that is, in this case, to write him into the age of the psychopathological institution. . . . He must have felt it outside or within himself. Indeed, such a temptation must still be threatening and liable to reemerge, since it is still necessary to call for vigilance and greater justice. (*RP*, 81)

By titling his essay with Foucault's words, Derrida seems to wish to get Foucault to keep his word, that is, to do justice to Freud, to get him to be consistent in his treatment of him, rather than, as Derrida shows, giving credit and then taking it away, including him and then excluding him from the list of mad geniuses who begin again to lend an ear to unreason without mastering it. "'To Do Justice to Freud'" would thus betray a desire on Derrida's part that Foucault rectify an ambivalence that runs throughout his corpus with regard to Freud, with regard to Freud's own notions about ambivalence, to set the record straight concerning him. But is Derrida himself also claiming justice from Foucault? And what would this mean when the one from whom justice is being claimed is no longer living? Might such a claim have something to teach us about the work of mourning?

We are perhaps here approaching a limit where doing justice would entail not simply rectifying some situation by paying homage to someone for past services rendered or compensating them for past wrongs committed but remaining faithful to an ambivalence within thought insofar as it reflects the ambivalence of the things themselves. In this case doing justice would consist in taking account of the ambivalence rather than in trying to overcome, rectify, or master it. It would consist in demonstrating that such ambivalence is not some fault on the part of a thinker but a reflection—as long as it is a just reflection—of a fundamental ambivalence in the things themselves. Derrida would thus be just to Foucault insofar as he takes into account the ambivalence that Foucault must have sensed in Freud and so reproduced in his own corpus. Doing justice would consist, then, not in rectification, or not only in rectification, but in remaining attentive to the justice that precedes rectification, a justice related to the movement of the scales of justice rather than any particular determination or verdict based on that movement.

Giving a new impetus to the debate would thus be a way of continuing to do justice to it, to do justice to the ambivalence of exclusion and inclusion within it (that is, within Descartes or Freud, or within Foucault's reading of Descartes or Freud), but also to the ambivalence of the dialogue or debate *as* a debate, as an unmasterable debate between master and disciple, the dead and the living. This would be, perhaps, yet another way of doing justice to the other, to the disappearance of the other, another way of mourning, of paying one's respects with the hope that, at the limits of respect, such payment will not be returned. To do justice to Freud, or to Foucault's doing justice to Freud, or to Derrida's doing justice to Foucault, would thus be not simply to give to each side its due, to reckon accounts and do justice to each individually, but to pay respect to the pendulum-like, *fort/da* movement between them, *between* Foucault and Derrida, as well as within each one of them, each one of them bearing the traces of the other.

Yet can one do justice to the pendulum without identifying its terms or termini? Is not every attempt at exclusion, at mastering the situation—including Derrida's own repeated attempts to exclude his past debate with Foucault from this most recent reading—destined to involve a reappropriation and interiorization of what Derrida calls in the 1963 "Cogito" essay the "voice of the master"? Can one really exclude a past debate or question from a present analysis? Can one isolate the impetus of a pendulum from its two poles without having the "silhouette" of these poles, of some past debate or question, haunt one's discourse? Derrida himself admits at the beginning of "'To Do Justice to Freud'" that it would be impossible completely to exclude or summarily dismiss the debate of thirty years ago surrounding the Cartesian cogito:

Though I have decided not to return to what was debated close to thirty years ago, it would nevertheless be absurd, obsessional to the point of pathological, to say nothing of impossible, to give in to a sort of fetishistic denial and to think that I can protect myself from any contact with the place or meaning of this discussion. Although I intend to speak today of something else altogether . . . I am not surprised, and you will probably not be either, to see the silhouette of certain questions reemerge: not their content, of course, to which I will in no way return, but their abstract type, the schema or specter of an analogous problematic. (*RP*, 71–72)

Derrida clearly recognizes that recognizing and asserting the difference between one discussion and another is not enough; in spite of one's intentions, no matter the rigor of one's discourse and thought, the ruses of reason and mastery come to haunt all assertions and distinctions. In the following passage Derrida speaks of the difficulty, the impossibility even, of mastering the problematic of reason, since it is no doubt coextensive with mastering the concept of mastery itself: "One would be able to master this entire problematic, assuming this were possible, only after having satisfactorily answered a few questions, questions as innocent—or as hardly innocent—as, What is reason? for example, or more narrowly, What is the principle of reason? . . . You will forgive me here, I hope, for leaving these enigmas as they are" (*RP*, 100).

We thus move from the mastery of madness to the mastery of the problematic of reason, a mastery that would, clearly, always require aid from that which it is to master, a mastery, therefore, that would always be undone—or exceeded—in its very execution. Derrida himself makes this connection when he speaks of Foucault's claim that psychology must remain "speechless before the language of madness," that it "can never master madness" because it "became possible in our world only when madness had already been mastered and excluded from the drama." The "consequences—the ruinous consequences"—of this logic are, writes Derrida, that "what has already been mastered can no longer be mastered, and that too much mastery (in the form of exclusion but also of objectification) deprives one of mastery (in the form of access, knowledge, competence). The concept of mastery is an impossible concept to manipulate, as we know: the more there is, the less there is, and vice versa" (*RP*, 103).

Although Derrida claims that "'To Do Justice to Freud'" is about something else altogether than the "Cogito" essay was some thirty years earlier, since what is at issue is now Foucault's relationship to Freud and not Descartes, all this assumes that he—that anyone—can unambiguously identify what either essay is about. Despite the appearances I would argue that both essays are in fact about the "same" thing, the question of mastery in general, the unmasterable concept of mastery, and Derrida's relation to Foucault as a master in particular. Derrida in fact began his 1963 essay "Cogito and the History of Madness" with an explicit and self-conscious invocation of the master/disciple relationship in the context of his own relationship to Michel Foucault. Referring to Foucault's *The History of Madness*, Derrida wrote:

This book, admirable in so many respects, powerful in its breadth [*souffle*] and style, is even more intimidating for me in that, having formerly had the good fortune to study under Michel Foucault, I retain the consciousness of an admiring and grateful disciple. Now, the disciple's consciousness, when he starts, I would not say to dispute, but to engage in dialogue with the master or, better, to articulate the interminable and silent dialogue that made him into a disciple—this disciple's consciousness is an unhappy consciousness. . . . And when, as is the case here, the dialogue is in danger of being taken—incorrectly—as a challenge, the disciple knows that he alone finds himself already challenged by the master's voice within him that precedes his own. He feels himself indefinitely challenged, or rejected, or accused; as a disciple, he is challenged by the master who speaks within him and before him, to reproach him for making this challenge and to reject it in advance, having elaborated it before him; and having interiorized the master, he is also challenged by the disciple that he himself is. This interminable unhappiness of the disciple perhaps stems from the fact that he does not yet know—or is still concealing from himself—that the master, like real life, may always be absent. The disciple must break the glass, or better the mirror, the reflection, his infinite speculation on the master. And start to speak. ("C," 31–32)

I recall here that the great drama surrounding "Cogito and the History of Madness" stemmed from the fact that when it was first given in March of 1963, the master was not—or so it would seem—absent, for Foucault himself was in attendance and apparently expressed his appreciation for Derrida's work and did not publicly reveal his apprehensions about it until some nine years later, in an appendix to *The History of Madness*. There is obviously much more that could be said about this scene of the admiring student paying homage to the work of the master, much more about Derrida's choice of the phrase "to engage in dialogue with the master" considering the fact that "Cogito and the History of Madness" revolves around the question of whether or not Descartes breaks off a dialogue with madness, and that, thirty years later in "'To Do Justice to Freud,'" the question is whether or in what way Freud reestablishes a dialogue with madness.[10]

But notice that Derrida says in the beginning of this essay that the interminable unhappiness of the disciple "perhaps stems from the fact that he does not yet know—or is still concealing from himself—that the master, like real life, may always be absent." Derrida seems to be suggesting not that the master is lacking, that there never is a master, but that the master is—*as a master*—perhaps always absent. This is, I think, what "'To Do Justice to Freud'"—a text written almost thirty years later—also reveals. It reveals that what a text teaches, what it gives us, is never simply an argument or a theme but—most especially—a question, a question that always proceeds from the master *as* absent. Perhaps today, thirty years after "Cogito and the History of Madness," today after the death of Foucault, we can listen once again to Derrida's statement of 1963 in order to receive something that perhaps only death could have brought us. For it is not only the master, Derrida says, who is perhaps always absent but, like the master, "real life." Today, after "'To Do Justice to Freud,'" this allusive reference to Rimbaud, this cultural *clin d'oeil* between Derrida and his audience, can perhaps be heard as suggesting even more than it did in 1963. It can be heard as suggesting not that real life is presently elsewhere or lacking, that it once was at some time and is no longer or else is waiting for us in the future, but that it, like the master, and thus like the master's life, is *always absent*. This life, this absent life, which would have to be opposed to the life of the author, to the *souffle*, style, and energy of the master or the master's voice and work, is what is most living in life, what is most living in a work—for it is, it seems, the very respiration or impetus, the very surviving, the very receiving or self-receiving, of a work or text. At the conclusion of "'To Do Justice to Freud,'" Derrida says, in effect, that if we are to pay tribute to Foucault, it must be not for this or that work or theory but for a question that his work harbors within itself, the question, I would say, of *mastery* "itself." Derrida writes:

When confronted with a historical problematization of such scope and thematic richness, one should not be satisfied either with a mere survey or with asking in just a few minutes an overarching question so as to insure some sort of synoptic mastery. What we can and must try to do in such a situation is to pay tribute to a work that is this great and this uncertain by means of a question that it itself raises, by means of a question that it carries within itself, that it keeps in reserve in its unlimited potential, one of the questions that can thus be deciphered within it, a question that keeps it in suspense, holding its breath [*tient . . . en haleine*]—and, thus, keeps it alive. (*RP*, 115)

Here, in the final pages of "'To Do Justice to Freud,'" Derrida tries, I think, to do justice to Foucault. Such justice would consist neither in acquiescing to the voice of the master nor in paying tribute to it with the discourse of an admiring disciple. Both strategies, as we know, fall quickly into an inescapable and interminable dialectic. Derrida thus seems to suggest that the only way to pay tribute is to locate a moment, a questioning moment, within a text that keeps us holding our breath—and thus keeps us alive. Hence the breath returns, but instead of referring to a breath that animates the text, to the *souffle* or spirit behind the text, it now refers to a question that keeps the text in suspense, that punctuates or scans it like a pendulum, that keeps it alive and open to a future.

The question with which Derrida wishes to pay tribute concerns, once again, the ambivalence of the drive for mastery—as if the only way to inflect differently the dialectic between disciple and master were to recognize that which first opens up the difference between generations, between masters and disciples. Grafting a difficult and enigmatic passage on an "original drive for power or drive for mastery" from *Beyond the Pleasure Principle* onto the Foucauldian corpus, placing this passage now within Foucault's purview after his death, Derrida asks: "How would Foucault have situated this drive for mastery in his discourse on power or on irreducibly plural powers?" (*RP*, 117). Derrida thus ends "'To Do Justice to Freud'" with the very same theme he had used some thirty years earlier to open the "Cogito" essay, opening and closing three decades of debate, therefore, with the theme and question of mastery. Posing a question to the absent master in order to interrogate the master as absent, refusing to speak for the master although taking the risk of imagining the principle of a response, Derrida concludes "'To Do Justice to Freud'":

In this place where no one now can answer for him, in the absolute silence where we remain nonetheless turned toward him, I would venture to wager that, in a sentence that I will not construct for him, he would have associated and yet also dissociated, he would have placed back to back, mastery and death, that is, the same—death *and* the master, death *as* the master. (*RP*, 118)

I have suggested that the entire debate or dialogue between Derrida and Foucault might be read not only or not simply as some overcathected chapter in a history of the anxiety of influence in French intellectual life but, perhaps, as a work of mourning—a mourning for the master, for oneself as the disciple of the master, and for that which relates the disciple to the master, a mourning, then, for an unmasterable ambivalence and an impossible incorporation. For mourning a master or teacher perhaps always involves not only pain over losing the master, pain mixed with a troubling jubilation over having survived, over being able to have the last word and so be the master of the master, but a profound sadness over no longer being able to receive the approbation of the master, perhaps even the recognition by the master that he was not really the master but the disciple, the disciple of his disciple. This desire for recognition from the master would, however, always be the desire for an impossible recognition, and the death of the master would only confirm the fatality that would have structured the master/disciple relationship from the beginning. It would be the desire to be acknowledged by a master who, in speaking from his position as a master, would simultaneously—in a single moment that is already divided—relinquish that position, the desire to be recognized, then, by a master who both is and is not himself, who thus cannot be recognized as such, and so who, precisely as the master, is always absent.[11]

Derrida ends "'To Do Justice to Freud'" in 1991 by giving the last word to Foucault, or, rather, by leaving open a space where Foucault might respond—even if he will now never do so, or will do so now only in us. But if the master is always absent, then perhaps he never could have responded as the master, since to respond is always to put oneself on the scene not as the master "as such" but as the master of the disciple, of a disciple who desires to be, or who will show himself already to have been, the master of his master.

I too will end by giving the final word to Foucault. I do so because of its uncanny proximity to Derrida's final word and because Foucault here too gives the last word to another, to one of his own masters, the one who taught him so much about mastery and about the grand master of mastery itself, that is, of course, about Hegel. Foucault says at the very end of "The Discourse on Language," the lecture he delivered in 1970 on his appointment to the Collège de France:

Because I owe him so much, I well understand that your choice, in inviting me to teach here is, in good part, a homage to Jean Hyppolite. . . . I now understand better why I experienced so much difficulty when I began speaking, earlier on. I now know which voice it was I would have wished for, preceding me, supporting me, inviting me to speak and lodging within my own speech. I know now just what was so awesome about beginning; for it was here, where I speak now, that I listened to that voice, and where its possessor is no longer, to hear me speak.[12]

5

Lacunae

DIVINING DERRIDA'S SOURCES THROUGH "TELEPATHY"

> Thales . . . says that [the original source of all existing things] is water (and therefore declared that the earth is on water).
>
> Thales declared that water, of the four elements, was the most active, as it were, as a cause.
>
> Thales, too, seems, from what they relate, to have supposed that the soul was something kinetic, if he said that the (Magnesian) stone possesses soul because it moves iron.
> —G. S. Kirk and J. E. Raven, *The Presocratic Philosophers*

This time it was not easy to find the words. So long and hard did I search that these words on the work of Jacques Derrida represent less the results of my search than simply a few reflections on the path my search took. For what I discovered in the end was not some new theme, concept, or principle in the work of Derrida but, simply, a way of conducting the search, a means of feeling my way, of taking the lay of the land, of marking out the boundaries of the terrain of thought by following not the differences already present on the terrain or hidden beneath it but the movement of these differences along its surface.

No, this time it was not easy to find the words—especially here at Cerisy, where, some twelve years ago, so many found such right and fitting words to address the work of Jacques Derrida. But too much time has passed, too many texts have been published, too many things have *happened* to the work of Jacques Derrida since 1980 to write today as one would have then. What will concern me here, then, will be less the themes, concepts, or principles (if we can call them that) of deconstruction than deconstruction's relation to itself, deconstruction's way of constantly searching for the very meaning, the very origin or *source*, of deconstruction. To say it all too crudely, there is a way in which a text *by* or even *on* Derrida cannot but be self-reflective today, even autobiographical; it cannot but speak of itself and its relation to the text or texts being read, of the relation between the figure of the critical text and the figure of the text undergoing critique, that is, between the reception and the source. Today more than ever, therefore, we must ask what happens when we read a text by Derrida or write on him, what kind of specularity transpires between his text and ours, between his text, ours, and the text he is reading. We must ask how one text comes to "affect" another, to make it move—as if of itself—in an at once foreseeable and unexpected fashion, what sort of causality is operating between texts, what is transmitted between them, and, thus, where the boundaries between texts might lie.

But, as I said, it was not easy for me to find the words, for I had begun otherwise—that is, with a theme—thinking I knew that it was a theme I should be looking for: in this case the theme of Derrida's *sources*. Not the sources *of* Derrida's work, whether relatively obvious ones, like Nietzsche or Freud, Husserl or Heidegger, or more concealed ones, like—according to some—Merleau-Ponty or Lacan. Derrida himself criticizes just such an understanding of sources as origins in many places, "Qual Quelle: Valéry's Sources" being only the most transparent example.[1] No, this time I decided to follow the sources *in* Derrida, the way Derrida reinterprets the source, opposing all self-reflecting and narcissistic sources to the source points or blind spots that always—or at least this was my hypothesis—interrupt such reflection.

I thus turned myself into a sort of water diviner or water dowser in order to locate the sources of a thinking of sources in the work of Derrida. Divining rod in hand, in my two hands, I let myself go, following the magnetic attraction of water into so many unexpected and often idyllic places. I was initially attracted, of course, by the river Illisus in "Plato's Pharmacy," by the "diaphanous purity of these waters" ("P.P.," 69).[2] Resisting, however, my attraction for water on the other side of the border, that is, in the works of Derrida before 1980, I let myself be pulled instead by all the sources in "Ulysses Gramophone," by all its seas and lakes, by the figure of the Mediterranean in *The Other Heading*, by the tears of "Circumfession" and

Memoirs of the Blind, and so on. But after just a few days I was in over my head, drawn into a veritable flood that overflowed my capacities and threatened to capsize my project. The divining rod turned in so many directions at once that I knew not where to begin or what to read.

Unable—to borrow a phrase from "Circumfession"—to "find the vein,"[3] a particular vein, I eventually turned or let turn the divining rod toward itself, so as to ask myself, with a comparison that no doubt risked obscurantism, if this "occult knowledge" of the divinatory art I was practicing did not already have something in common with deconstruction. But, once again, I knew not where to begin or what to read, not even how to *divine* doing so. Yet begin one must. Like those who practice the divining art, the art of the divining rod, one must begin to cover the terrain, knowing that failure is always possible. I thus walked all around the work [*autour du travail*] of Jacques Derrida, as the subtitle of this Cerisy colloquium suggests. As usual, there were witnesses, and both my anxiety and embarrassment grew as little happened. But then at a certain moment—one already divided between the reception and the source—I felt a vibration. Since the divining rod typically turns not toward the source, as we might think, but in the opposite direction, pivoting round and round in proximity to the source, I did not know if the vibration indicated some source hidden beneath the earth, in consciousness or the unconscious, or only itself in a movement of self-reference or autoaffection. I thus briefly thought of making the divining rod *itself* a theme, to seek out and gather all the sticks, wands, rods, and canes in the work of Derrida, all these supplements, prostheses, arms, or instruments of writing that one holds in the hand, or else in *two hands*, from the chapter "That Movement of the Wand . . ." in *Of Grammatology* to the blind man's staff or Butades' stick in *Memoirs of the Blind*.[4] Yet I also knew that it would be nearly impossible to avoid the wand of Thoth, god of writing, magic, and the "occult sciences," Thoth, or Theuth, archetype of Hermes, who uses his staff or magic wand to measure and mark off parcels of land,[5] leading some to speculate that if our borders are sometimes so irregular, it is because they follow not natural lines of demarcation visible on the surface but subterranean sources revealed only by a divinatory art.[6]

I was thus back to the beginning, back to my sources. But to return to my testimony, it was not long before the attraction became so intense that I eventually had the impression of having found the vein or struck gold. It happened in a little text entitled, precisely, "Telepathy."[7] In principle I should not have been able to speak here of this text, since it was written before 1980, but I allowed myself to do so because it is a text that will have transgressed borders from the very beginning. It should have been published in 1980 in *The Post Card* but was omitted, says Derrida, "by a semblance of accident" at the moment *The Post Card* was going to print. It was later found, Derrida recalls, "very close by me, but too late" ("T," 39), so it was not published until 1981 (in the journal *Furor*, and then again in 1983 in *Confrontation*, before being included in 1987 in *Psyché*). As we will see, the story or history of this little text will not be unrelated to its content and strange movement. Indeed, this little lacuna of *The Post Card*, this short text that should have found its place in the "Envois" between the ninth and fifteenth of July 1979, this foreign body that seems to have undergone a very fortuitous sort of *décalage horaire*, a very singular text lag, poses the question of sources in a truly exemplary and, as we will see, fateful way.

The thirty-five pages entitled "Telepathy" take as their pretext, their source, the status or importance that Freud had attributed to telepathy during the 1920s. Everything turns around a 1926 letter in which Freud speaks of his supposed "conversion to telepathy." Everything is played out, for Freud, around the question of the source of telepathy, namely, whether it originates from within, in the inner recesses of consciousness or the unconscious, or whether it comes from without, finding a place within only as a sort of foreign body. Everything hinges on whether what is called telepathy can be assimilated to psychoanalysis, reduced, like the dream, to an internal affair of the psyche, or whether telepathy really is the correspondence between a psychic phenomenon, such as a telepathic dream, and the realization of an external event, an event that "comes true" in accordance with the dream. At issue is the very status of truth and causality in psychoanalysis and, thus, the very cause of psychoanalysis.

This entire piece of Derrida's on Freud unfolds, therefore, in an atmosphere of telepathy, around the turning axis of a kind of divination. To give just a single indication before placing this little text within the context of *The Post Card*, I cite a few lines from the envoi of July 10. A few pages after a reference to the so-called conversion of Freud to telepathy, the author of the envoi himself, as if through a telepathy of conversion, announces, also in a letter, his own conversion:

When you asked me the other day: what changes in your life? Well you have noticed it a hundred times recently, it is the opposite of what I was anticipating [*prévoyais*], as one might have expected: a surface more and more open to all the phenomena formerly rejected (in the name of a certain discourse of science), the phenomena of "magic," of "clairvoyance," of "fate," of communications at a distance, of the things said to be occult. ("T," 13)

Before continuing with this story of Freud's—or Derrida's—conversion to telepathy in "Telepathy," let me jump to the end of the story, told in *The Post Card*, some nine days later, just enough time (as we learn, for example, in Joyce's *Ulysses*) for a foreign body to resurface in a lake. For it was on July 19, 1979, *exactly thirteen years ago today*, that the very source of *The Post Card* was discovered. It was on this day, in the Bodleian Library at Oxford, that the author of the envois—whom I call for convenience Jacques Derrida— saw for the first time the famous *Fortune-Telling Book*, this book of "occult knowledge" containing the infamous postcard representing "Socrates" and "plato." It was on this day that he laid eyes on the source of a discourse that had been, we could say, already influencing or "moving" him for years.

When the librarian at the Bodleian finally brings him the book, he does not know where to begin; the field is open before him, but he does not know where to look. Like a master diviner, he is not totally unaware of what he seeks, but that does not make his reading any less of a quest or a drama: "And all of a sudden, I am abridging, the small volume was there, on the table, I didn't dare touch it. I think that this lasted a rather long time. . . . I didn't know where to start reading, looking, opening."[8] But this doesn't prevent him from opening, looking, and reading. Leafing quickly through the pages, surveying the whole landscape, he suddenly sees Socrates and Plato appear and disappear: "I hadn't dreamed! I set myself back to digging around patiently, but truly, I exaggerate nothing, as if in a forest, as if they were thieves, squirrels, or mushrooms" (*PC*, 209). Derrida thus searches the pages of the *Fortune-Telling Book*, just like a diviner, and I note in passing that the divining rod was frequently used in past centuries, and particularly in France, to track animals and search for criminals. After digging around for a while, he finally catches up with them, captures them, takes them in hand—and then takes them in confidence.[9] "Finally I've got them, everything stands still, I hold the book open with *both hands*. If you only knew my love how beautiful they are. Very small, smaller than in the reproduction. . . . What a couple! They could see me cry, I told them everything" (*PC*, 209; my emphasis).

Holding the *Fortune-Telling Book* in his own two hands, this book that explains "how to question it in order to decipher one's *fate*" (*PC*, 211)—

the questioner outside the book thus corresponding with what is inside the book so as to determine what is foretold outside the book—Derrida sees what is destined or had long been destined to become *the* exemplary post-card. He thus sees a certain destiny, even though in this very seeing he is himself seen and implicated. There would be much to say about the fact that the author sees and is seen by this couple, Socrates and Plato, about the fact that they reflect his gaze—like the calm waters of a lake, or like a tear. For what Derrida sees in the end, as if the outside already both acted on the inside and reflected it, are (his) two hands—a Socrates "writing with both hands" (*PC*, 211), a Socrates who writes or perhaps types like Derrida, who perhaps has the same *daimon*, hears the same voice(s)—as if by telepa-thy. And what we see, what Socrates and Plato see, is the seer crying.[10] And I remark again in passing that tears also play a significant part in the rhetoric of the divinatory art, the art of the water dowser. In a collection of tales about divining taken from England at the end of the nineteenth cen-tury—the place and period in which we will be interested when we return to Freud—people are often seen crying just after having discovered a source, as if the external source made the water flow within, as if the diviner were not only influenced by a source but were himself transformed into one. Water attracts water, makes it well up; the tears begin to flow, and then, all of a sudden—as if the "revelation" of the divining rod were the figure of a metaphoricity that permitted movement among different rhetorical regis-ters, from the political to the scientific to the theological—a turning point, the moment of revolution, transformation, or conversion.[11]

But let us return to the great turning of "Telepathy," on the other side of the Channel, five days before the revelation of the postcard. It is July 14, the day of another Revolution, and Derrida already has forebod-ings of the Bodleian incident: "Socrates and Plato in person, they are wait-ing for me over there, at the turn, just after the anniversary" ("T," 31). And then, the following day, the anniversary, four days before the revelation at Oxford, right at the end of "Telepathy":

the big Turn [*le grand Tournant*], it's going to go very quickly now. I am going to re-read everything trying out the keys [*clés*] one after the other, but I am afraid of not finding (or of finding) all alone, of no longer having the time. Will you give me your hand?

no more time to lose,
ho gar kairos engus, Telepathy comes upon us, *tempus enim prope est.* ("T," 38)

And finally, near the beginning of that day's envoi: "I pass on to the second and last great epoch today, the turn [*le tournant*] has begun, I was starting to get wedged [*à être calé*], I am going to tip over, I am tipped over already" ("T," 36).

July 15, 1979: it is Derrida's forty-ninth birthday, a moment of Turning, of celebration, a day apart, between two times or epochs, an inter*cal*ary day, so to speak. But how do we get from this "Turning" to "Telepathy," from the time between two epochs to "the time is near," from this one day on the *cal*endar to the Apo*cal*ypse? Even if all fifty-two missing letters were restored before the phrases "the big Turn" and "no more time to lose," it would require a rather good analyst, someone talented and adept—indeed *bien calé*—to decipher the fate of this Turning. But what exactly does the French word *caler* mean here—to be *calé*? Might it turn out to be one of the keys [*clés*] Derrida says he must try, a "password" ("T," 28) or a shibboleth to this entire text? Once again, curiously, we are led back to water, for the French *caler*, from the Greek *khalaō*, meaning to slacken, loosen, or release, is a navigating term that means to drop or bring in a mast. The verb can also be used to describe the sinking of a ship or the sudden stalling of an engine. Figuratively, then, it means to give up, to soften or yield, to back off. The noun *cale* designates the hold of a ship or a piece of lead used as a sinker in fishing, or, most commonly, a piece of wood put beneath a table or chair to stabilize or prop it up—a shim, block, or wedge. To be "at the bottom of the *cale*" means to be broke, while being *calé* means, on the contrary, to be in a comfortable position, to be talented at or knowledgeable about something.

On the basis of these various meanings of *caler* I offer a first gloss or telepathic rendering of what Derrida might be suggesting here with *calé*: Having come to the Turning, he's all set up, *bien calé*, safe and secure, living a moment of equilibrium, of mastery even, yet all of a sudden he's beginning to stall, to give up, to *caler*, to tip or tip over, to sink, to lose his balance or his grip, to go down; it is the beginning of the end—the apo*cal*ypse is upon him.[12]

Here at the Turning, the word *caler* appears to turn inside out, or upside down; it flips over or flips out, from mastery in life to being mastered in death. Located at the great Turning, it overturns itself and leads us right back to the beginning of this drama, where it is this same word, or rather syllable—these letters—that seek themselves out. I recall that this little text, "Telepathy," treats Freud's interpretation of and belief in the phenomenon of telepathy in texts such as "Dreams and Telepathy" and "Dreams and

Occultism." We should thus not be surprised if, in this oneiric atmosphere, sounds and syllables inundate the text and echo throughout it like incantations—which also play a large part, I should note, in the practice of the divinatory art.[13]

Let us look, then, at the beginning of this drama, at the beginning of these fateful ten days—the beginning of another *décade*. It is July 9, and Derrida writes in an envoi concerning several cards and letters of Freud:

I felt, from a distance and confusedly, that I was searching for a word, perhaps a proper name (for example Claude, but I do not know why I choose this example right now, I do not remember his presence in my dream).[14] Rather it was the term [*vocable*; syllable] which was searching for me. . . . You ask me, I ask myself: where is this leading us, towards what *place*? We are absolutely unable to know, forecast [*prévoir*], foresee, foretell, fortune-tell. ("T," 3)

Once again, the poles of attraction get reversed: it is not Derrida who seeks the syllable but the syllable that seeks him, that calls him. At the beginning of the letter he evokes "a piece of worm that would be a piece of word, and that would seek to reconstitute itself, slithering, something tainted which poisons life" ("T," 3). Might not this piece of word, this syllable, indeed this abbreviation of a place name destined to play such an important part in Derrida's life, be *cal*? Might not this syllable be the wedge, the *cale*, that keeps the whole thing balanced, the whole thing afloat—or not? One finds *cal*s wedged in just about everywhere in the following pages, in the French *décale*, *calendrier*, *caléidoscopée*, *calcul*, *calée*, *calmement* (three times in a single paragraph), *calque*, in the Professor Kahl, and "Kahlenberg, so well named," and of course in "apo*cal*ypse," but then also, inverting the letters like Derrida himself does for all this, for *tout cela*, in *cela*, *place*, *déplace*, *classer*, *classes*, *classifies*, *nomenclaturée*, *clair*, *clairement*, *clairvoyance*, *claire-ouïe*, *spectacle*, *clan*, *Claude*, and so on. Derrida himself realizes that something is surfacing here when he says, for example, "Notice that this word 'calculation' [*calcul*] is interesting in itself, listen to it carefully" ("T," 12), or when he evokes Flaubert's phrases (emphasizing their addressee, "*C'est à Louise*"), "to have callus [*du cal*] in one's heart," "lake of my heart [*lac de mon coeur*]" ("T," 12). And again, "I can no longer see very clearly [*claire*], I am stalling [*cale*] a bit" ("T," 5); "I give up [*je cale*]. . . . I will have to make enquiries and clear things up [*tire cela au clair*]" ("T," 7). And finally, "From *cal* to *lac* is enough to make one believe that that fellow also had a limp [*sa claudication*]" ("T," 12).

His *claudication*: it is here that a whole series of texts emerge or well up in "Telepathy," a series that begins with *Glas* and then expands to cover an entire corpus within the corpus of Derrida, from *Lac arte postale* to *Feu LA Cendre* to the entire limping corpus of *la psychanalyse* (a word that itself encrypts, as if by fate, another proper name, and not the least significant, beginning in *lac*). Like the logic of the container and the contained that Jacques Derrida demonstrated the other day—the day of the turning, his turning, the same and yet another—to be at work in Heidegger's *Being and Time*, one can read "Telepathy" either as a small part of the oeuvre of Derrida or as the singular place, the point source, in which, telepathically perhaps, a whole tradition—past, present, and future—comes to well up. All this in a text that treats Freud's ambivalence toward telepathy and the entire network of associations he "found" around the famous *Forsyte Saga*—the Foresight Saga.

I recall again the circumstances of this text "Telepathy": it begins on the ninth of July, a few days before the trip to Oxford and the revelation of the *Fortune-Telling Book*. Derrida writes, "As you will see, our entire account of Freud also writes itself in English, it happens crossing the Channel. . . . I am leafing through the *Saga* rather absent-mindedly, without seeing very clearly whether I'll get anything out of it on the side of—of what? Let us say the England of Freud in the second half of the last century" ("T," 8–10). Is it simply a coincidence that it was precisely at the end of the nineteenth century that interest in psychic research really took off—especially in England, and especially around telepathy and, of course, the divining rod?

Now, the *Forsyte Saga* ends in 1926, the moment, says Derrida, that Freud "moved with regard to telepathy." It is an at once important and disquieting moment for psychoanalysis—a significant moment for the Cause [*la Cause*]. For it is the Cause of psychoanalysis that is put into question by telepathy, causality itself that becomes suspect. The kernel of the argument, the core, the *noyau*, a word that appears several times in this text ("T," 32, 36)—so close in French to *noyade*, to drowning—is that the categories of activity and passivity are seriously threatened by telepathy. Derrida demonstrates Freud's concern—whether conscious, unconscious, or indeed telepathic—over the question of the source of telepathy. To save or protect the theory of dreams, Freud wished to distinguish between the inner, psychic causality of dreams and the external causality of telepathy; if telepathy exists, it would be a warning or sign related to some external event. The dream as such, then, would not be telepathic; there might be a telepathic event that occurs while one sleeps, but it wouldn't be a dream. (One would have to awaken and say, like Derrida in the Bodleian Library when he finally sees Socrates and Plato, "I hadn't dreamed!") As with the divining rod, therefore, an attempt is made to understand telepathy as a physical or mechanistic phenomenon so that we might have at our disposal, to use Derrida's phrase, a "technē telepatikē" ("T," 20).[15] Telepathy would be but a more complex and refined version of the telegraph, or the telephone, except that the receiver could never really be taken off the hook.

So in the middle of this text about and entitled "Telepathy" Derrida is transformed or transforms himself into Freud, speaking in his voice, with his voice, as if during a séance. Not long after a reference to decapitation and to walking, like Saint Denis, with one's own head under one's arm, Derrida says: "Imagine that I am walking like him, to his rhythm" ("T," 20). Hence, he begins to walk like him, at his rhythm, and to imagine, to read in the thoughts of Freud, his belief or nonbelief with regard to telepathy. Speaking as Freud, Derrida says: "If there is any, our relation to Telepathy must not be of the family of 'knowledge' or 'non-knowledge' but of another type" ("T," 22). This time *Telepathy* is capitalized, like the *Turn* on the very next page. Why this change? Thanks to a certain telepathy between Freud's text and Derrida's, it appears that the very meaning of telepathy has changed or is in the process of changing because of the supplement of Derrida's envois. Through a kind of thought transference—or telepathy—between Freud's writing and Derrida's, "Telepathy" is no longer simply opposed to the activity of the psyche or the unconscious; it is now neither a merely physical process that can be scientifically known nor a purely occult phenomenon. Rather, it now seems to refer to a complex "system" or fathomless "source" of referrals and deferrals—of *décalages*—that in effect precedes and constitutes the addressers and addressees of these referrals, a "Telepathy" that comes *before* both the origin and the reception, that is truly "other" or "exterior" to both. "Telepathy" now means not the correspondence between an interior psychic event and an external "reality" but the welling up of both that event and that reality from a wholly other source—from the wholly other within: an other that could even go by the name "the unconscious." As Derrida writes early on in "Telepathy," "It's difficult to imagine a theory of what they still call the unconscious without a theory of telepathy" ("T," 14), that is, without thinking the relationship between consciousness and that which must remain wholly other to consciousness, beyond the simple opposition of knowledge and nonknowledge. Telepathy produces these pairs, these correspondences, although it itself can be understood from neither side.

At the very beginning of "Telepathy" we read: "Others would conclude: a letter thus *finds* [*trouve*] its addressee, him or her. No, one cannot say of the addressee that s/he exists before the letter" ("T," 6). The word *finds* is underscored here, no doubt, to show that it was not simply "found" in a lexicon but reinvented in this new context. For is it absolutely clear what "to find" means?[16] Although the divining rod, I hasten to add, is said to "find" the source, it could equally be said that the source "finds" it, acting on it, according to the traditional interpretations, by either an external magnetism or an internal, psychic force. And what about *The Post Card* itself, in which "Telepathy" was supposed to be found? Does it simply reproduce postcards or letters sent from an identifiable addresser to a cryptic although identifiable addressee, does it simply make a private correspondence public, or does it stage the simulacrum or fiction of a correspondence that then, later, in being published, finds its addresser and addressee? Is *The Post Card* the reproduction in writing of the spoken speech act, with a fully present and serious addresser and addressee, or is it an example of the performativity of a "speech act" proper to writing? Derrida continues: "All that, of course, according to a properly performative causality, if there is such a thing, and which is pure, not dependent on any other consequentiality extrinsic to the act of writing. I admit I'm not very sure what I mean by that; the unforeseeable should not be able to form part of a performative structure *stricto sensu*, and yet . . ." ("T," 7). It is just such a notion of "properly performative causality," of telepathy or telanalysis, that leads me, running all the "risks of obscurantism," to speak here of *writing as telepathy*. For example, right here, how can this writing not be attracted or magnetized by the essay "Telepathy"? How can it not turn like it, round it, thanks to it? Perhaps writing or even reading never simply finds or deciphers what a text means, never simply passively receives some original source or force. Rather, the source animates, moves, and attracts a reading and a writing that will then move it, reanimate and set it in motion.

The source can thus *never* be unequivocally located and determined. There is attraction in every direction: for example, here, between Freud and Derrida, Derrida and us, Derrida and the addressee of the envois. It is no doubt for this reason that in many places in the envois of "Telepathy" the addresser turns toward the addressee to ask *her* what *he* means, or what he says without meaning it, or better yet, what he cannot say because he does not know it. "Do you think that I am speaking here of the unconscious, guess [*devine*]" ("T," 4); "You know it yourself, tell me the truth, o you the seer [*la voyante*], you the soothsayer [*la devine*]" ("T," 11–12; see 38); and in Freud's voice, "soothsayer [*devine*], you know everything in advance" ("T," 24). That is why the addresser at one point apostrophizes his addressee, his *reader*, with the words, "Tell me, the truth, my little comma [*ma petite virgule*]" ("T," 23)—thereby suggesting that the addressee of the apostrophe is the very source, the very truth, of the apostrophe, the very source of the turning as telepathy. (And it just so happens—another coincidence?—that the divining rod is also called a virgula, the *virgula divinatoria* or *virgula divina*. Cicero speaks of it to evoke "things that fall upon you already cooked, so to speak, from the sky"—or that, we could say, well up from the ground or surface from the bottom of a lake.)

Everything comes to pass, then, between telepathies, as all the reassuring categories between activity and passivity, source and reception, get confused, and that which is radically exterior comes to haunt or communicate from "within":

*Fort: Da, tele*pathy against tele*pathy*, distance against menacing immediacy, but also the contrary, feeling (always close to oneself, one believes) against the suffering of distance that would also go by the name telepathy

I pass on to the second and last great epoch today, the turn [*le tournant*] has begun. . . . ("T," 35–36)

Yes, *Fort/Da*—but also *fore/cla*: two different readings of fortune, of destiny, one that foresees in advance, that sees at a distance, and one that forecloses that distance or resists such foreclosure by resisting all vision; *for*tune-telling and apo*cal*ypse.

What or who, then, animates what or whom? Can this ever be said with certainty? I cite, finally, Freud's letter of 1926, where he speaks of his conversion to telepathy, that is, of his own big Turn:

Our friend [Ernst] Jones seems to me to be too happy about the sensation that my conversion to telepathy has made in English periodicals. He will recollect how near to such a conversion I came in the communication I had the occasion to make during our Harz travels. Considerations of external policy since that time held me back long enough, but finally one must show one's colors and need bother about the scandal this time as little as on earlier, perhaps still more important occasions. ("T," 10)

As destiny would have it, it was also in the Harz mountain region of Germany that the modern history of the divining rod really got moving, according to the authorities. It was in the Harz that the rod was used in the sixteenth century to seek out not water but minerals—veins of iron and, yes, gold, which plays such a major role in the essay "Telepathy."

It is important to note here that Freud speaks *publicly* on this subject ("T," 34). The history of psychic or occult phenomena always involves witnessing, testimony. The convert must always recount his or her path to belief, and the conversion in belief must always be accompanied by a conversion of rhetoric, as autobiography becomes testimony.[17] Just a couple of paragraphs after citing this letter, Derrida himself confesses or bears witness to dreams that might be taken as telepathic—and telepathic not because they will have foreseen the future but because they will have already been moved by the very emergence or welling up of this text, its themes, words, and syllables:

I have just linked it [this dream] to that photograph by Erich Salomon which I talked to you about yesterday, *The Class of Professor W. Khal* (almost "bald" [*kahl*] in German). . . . Already a long time I drowned myself. Remember. Why, in my reveries of suicide, is it always drowning which imposes itself, and most often in a *lake* [*lac*], sometimes a pond [*étang*] but usually a lake? Nothing is stranger [*étranger*] to me than a lake: too far from the landscapes of my childhood. Maybe it's literary instead? I think it's more the force of the word [*lac*]. Something in it overturns or precipitates (*cla*, *alc*), plunging down head first. . . . Had I spoken to you about "Claude"? You will remind me, I must tell you who this name is for me. You will note that it is androgynous, like "*poste*" [post]. I missed it in *Glas* but it has never been far away, *it* has not missed me. The catastrophe is of this name. ("T," 10–11).[18]

Where to begin with such a passage? One doesn't just want to dive in head-first, but sometimes, as Derrida says in "Ulysses Gramophone," one cannot avoid throwing oneself in—especially when the key perhaps lies in the precipitation: "To throw oneself in the water, I was saying. I was, to be specific, thinking of the water of a lake. But, knowing Joyce's word, you may have thought that I was referring to the bottle in the sea. But lakes [*lacs*] were not so foreign [*étranger*] to him, as I shall presently demonstrate."[19] And just a couple of paragraphs later: "I was looking for postcards that would show Japanese lakes, or let's call them inland seas. It has crossed my mind to follow the edges of lakes in *Ulysses*, to venture out on a grand lakeside tour between the lake of life which is the Mediterranean Sea and the

Lacus Mortis" ("UG," 259). Lake of life, lake of death, lake of milk, lake of ashes, water of life and of death. Here's something a bit strange: lakes are not so foreign to Joyce, while nothing is more foreign to Derrida, as Derrida himself says. But can one simply declare such a thing to be so foreign? Might this declaration be in fact the first sign of resistance? In "Telepathy" Derrida shows himself quite aware of the eventuality of such an interpretation, since this phrase from July 9 already communicates with another from Freud cited five days earlier: "The theme of telepathy is in essence foreign [*étranger*] to psychoanalysis." And Derrida then remarks, "Who would be satisfied with such a declaration coming from him?" It thus seems quite justified to pose the same question concerning Derrida's declaration about lakes. If Freud says that his "conversion to telepathy is my private affair" ("T," 33), something irrelevant [*hors sujet*], a foreign body [*Fremdkörper*] for psychoanalysis—a word used by Freud to distance himself from any telepathic interpretation concerning the appearance of a particular piece of gold [*Goldstück*] in the course of an analysis—what is to be done with this other reflecting surface, this piece of water [*pièce d'eau*], this lake, that Derrida declares to be so foreign to him?

Like the piece of gold, the lake is perhaps that which can never be awaited or expected in a system, never *foreseen*, only seen as it surfaces in a dream. It would be precisely that which can never be declared irrelevant, since the very de*cla*ration would itself reflect the source of the foreign body, a source that, however, can never be revealed as anything other than a vibration, other than resistance itself, and so can never be revealed as such. One begins to feel the vibrations not of some particular source or other, some vein or other—of gold, iron, or blood—but of the turning itself, between our two hands, or multiplied across the surface of the body: "The 'conversion' is not a resolution nor a solution, it is still the speaking scar of the foreign body" ("T," 38). We thus see why Freud wanted to resist this foreign body called telepathy, why he wished not to "admit a foreign body . . . into the ego of psychoanalysis. Me psychoanalysis, I have a foreign body in my head" ("T," 35). We see why Freud, through Telepathy, just had to resist it.

Derrida remarks in "Telepathy" that the Foresight Saga had been forgotten by Freud in an earlier version of "Dream and Telepathy" through— and this is Freud's word—"resistance." At the beginning of "Telepathy," at the moment of explaining the place his text would have occupied in *The Post Card*, Derrida writes, "There will perhaps be talk of omission through

'resistance' and other such things. Certainly, but resistance to what?" ("T,"
39). I will not attempt to answer this question. I will simply let this word
resistance vibrate so as to indicate a whole range of phenomena and then to
ask, following Freud, how one can ever know for certain *what* one is resisting or even *that* one is resisting? Would we not always have to "detect"
resistance by means of a kind of divining rod—or mental detector—that
begins to rotate when a source or underground lake is not far away, when
some word gets upset and begins to go down, some word that wells up
from without within, some word like *caler*?

In a well-known passage from the *Dioptics* Descartes says that those
born blind see with their hands, in a manner of speaking, and that their
cane is the organ of a sort of sixth sense.[20] Light comes into the eyes of
those who see like the resistance of bodies comes into the hands of the
blind through their cane. And just as the colors of light vary, so do the
forms of resistance. It is thus possible to distinguish different bodies by
means of a cane—just as a good dowser can distinguish between water and
gold, or between water just beneath the surface and water deep down below, by the variations in movement and vibration in the divining rod. One
thus detects resistance not with the eyes but with the hands—a touching
at a distance. Derrida writes in "Telepathy":

Yes, touch, I sometimes think that thought . . . before "seeing" or "hearing," touch,
put your paws on it, or that seeing and hearing come back to touch at a distance—
a very old thought, but it takes some archaic to get to the archaic. So, touch with
both ends at once, touch in the area where science and so-called technical objec-
tivity are now taking hold of it instead of resisting it as they used to . . . touch in
the area of our immediate apprehensions, our pathies, our receptions. ("T," 13)

To put one's paws on it, or else to sniff out the territory,[21] to follow the
traces or *vibrations* in order to follow and "think" our resistances.[22] In
"Tympan" Derrida asks: "What is the specific resistance of philosophical
discourse to deconstruction?"[23] Two responses are proposed: hierarchy and
envelopment. But is there a resistance specific to a lake, to a *lac*, to all the
words in *l a c*? There are, no doubt, several, from the androgynous Claude,
who goes both ways, to something that resists at the center of all our *reflection*; for unlike a sea or ocean, one can often *see oneself* in a lake, see
one's own quasi-transparent image—at the risk of drowning, or wanting
to drown, at the risk of sinking right down to a unique source point. For
Freud too, we recall, the double was a sign of death. Although nothing is

more foreign to Derrida than a lake, there is, at the center of a lake, something even more foreign than the foreign, something caught in the *laces* of all these words in *l a c*, *une cale* or *un cal* in *le lac*, an original *calque*, an original tracing or transparency on the surface that ruins every origin by doubling it, every reflection by echoing it, a *cal* wedged into the eye of all foresight and all revelation: "the prophecy returning to itself from the future of its own to-come. The apo*caly*pse takes place at the moment when I write this, but a present of this type keeps a telepathic or premonitory affinity with itself (it senses itself at a distance and warns itself of itself) which loses me on the way [*me sème*] and makes me scared" ("T," 4; my emphasis).[24]

Une cale qui (se) cale, something that at once stabilizes and overturns itself, that at once uprights and upsets, that overturns itself from its own future. One can thus act like Theuth, who, we recall from "Plato's Pharmacy," "*turns* the word on its strange and invisible pivot, presenting it from a single one, the most reassuring, of its *poles*" ("PP," 97), or one can turn it in the opposite direction, which is a little less reassuring, or else one can make it turn not only on but toward this invisible pivot, toward the very turning of these poles, toward the vibration between source and reception—toward Telepathy itself. Here, in short, is my thesis—at the risk of obscurantism: deconstruction as rhabdomancy, the art of feeling the resistance, of letting oneself be moved, of feeling the vibrations through one's fingertips as they seek out the keys—like *l*, *a*, and *c*.

Deconstruction as rhabdomancy, as divining—hardly a philosophical connection, it will be objected. Yet how can we not recall everything Derrida said right here in Cerisy twelve years ago in "Of an Apocalyptic Tone Recently Adopted in Philosophy" concerning Kant's condemnation of the "supernatural communication" or "mystical illumination" of the mystagogues, "the death," according to Kant, "of all philosophy"? At the end of this text Derrida asks himself, asks us: "And what if this outside of apocalypse was *inside* the apocalypse?"[25] To which we might respond: and if this outside were a source, a source point, a lake that would not be some hidden source, something to unveil or discover, but a foreign body right on the surface of reflection?

This is why an essay on a text of Derrida "on" telepathy cannot avoid becoming itself telepathic, influenced, attracted, moved by the text being read. Derrida tells us, borrowing the voice of Freud: "I wanted to delay the arrival of the ghosts [*fantômes*] en masse. With you it was no longer possible to drag it out. Their martyrdom [*calvaire*] is very close to its end" ("T," 30–31). It is the passion of the *cal* that begins this foreign body called "Telepathy" with a *ver*, a verse, a worm that "would seek to reconstitute itself, slithering, something tainted which poisons life" ("T," 3): his—our—*cal-vaire*, our trial and our cross to bear. And that is why these words cannot but turn toward the source—a source that, this time, is nothing other than this turning, this version, this virgula. Which is why Telepathy can "happen without for all that being realized," why Telepathy is not simply the correspondence between an internal event and an external one, the foreseeing of an event and the event that is foreseen, but the animation of both source and reception from some unfathomable depth and distance already within. Borrowing once more the voice of Freud, unless it is Freud here borrowing Derrida, we read in "Telepathy": "An annunciation can be accomplished, something can happen without for all that being realized. An event can take place which is not real. My customary distinction between internal and external reality is perhaps not sufficient here" ("T," 25). What comes through Telepathy is not some thought or another, some theme, principle, or pathos or another, but *Telepathy itself.* Yet for this to "happen," one must follow a particular theme, however minimal, a particular concept, word, or syllable, the trace of some resistance. One must follow the borders between individuals and texts, between, say, Freud and Derrida, Derrida and us, between, for example, a telepathy on the side of England, of life, of foresight, of the syllable *for*, and a telepathy on the side of France, of death, of the apocalypse, and the syllable *cal*. We might even—for who knows how much was foreseen, how much calculated in advance?—follow the two of them over to the other side, Freud to *Clar*k University on the East Coast and Derrida to *Califor*nia on the West. One must follow both sides at once because inter*cal*ated between them, in their channel, their channeling, right there at the fork in the divining rod, the apocalypse happens without being realized—bifurcated from the very beginning, in Freud but already in Derrida, in Derrida but already in us, in us and so in Freud.

Perhaps this is what used to be called fate, or rather, already divided into past, present, and future, the Fates, who once went by the names *Lac*hesis, *Cl*otho, and *At*ropos.

The Phenomenon in Question

VIOLENCE, METAPHYSICS, AND THE LEVINASIAN THIRD

Derrida, the phenomenon: that, I believe, is still the question today, the phenomenon in question, the veritable phenomenon capable of raising anew a question that one might have thought decided or at least decidable for many years now. For do we really know, even today, the precise relationship between Derrida and the phenomenon, that is, between Derrida and phenomenology? Almost forty years after his introduction to Husserl's *The Origin of Geometry*, more than thirty years after *Speech and Phenomenon*,[1] the question of the relationship between deconstruction and phenomenology remains. It remains not simply because of the difficulty of the answer but, as we will see, precisely because it is a question. It persists, insists, and resists any attempt to provide a definitive answer, any attempt to declare or expose a clear line of influence or kinship, because the question of the phenomenon can never be asked without considering the phenomenon of the question.

If the question of the relationship between Derrida and phenomenology remains a question, it is no doubt in part because Derrida himself has never given up on the question, the question of the limits of phenomenology, certainly, but, more generally, the question of the limits of the question, the question of the question itself, even if and even when the priority of the question has itself been put into question. Derrida has always wanted, it seems, to reserve for himself the right—a right that perhaps responds to an obligation—to question. All the while recognizing the profound necessity of other forms of engagement in or with thought, Derrida has always claimed the necessity of the question, of the mode of questioning, which seems, for him, essentially related to philosophy, to so-called philosophical language and thus, in part, to the possibility of phenomenology.

For Derrida, then, the phenomenon is indeed the question, for there is no phenomenon without at least the possibility of the question, the possibility of posing questions about the phenomenon—including the phenomenon of the question—in a philosophical language, with its all terms, oppositions, and logical constraints. I thus propose to follow here what is to my eyes Derrida's unfailing fidelity to the question, a fidelity that can never be reduced to the question and yet cannot be expressed, translated, or analyzed without it. I will follow this fidelity to the question by asking about the way Derrida himself follows the question in another, that is, by following Derrida questioning Levinas on the role of the question and its relation to the phenomenon. We will see that from "Violence and Metaphysics" to *Adieu*, from 1964 to 1997, it is the question of the phenomenon and the phenomenon of the question that ceaselessly return. Oriented or driven each time by a new demand or concern within the work of Levinas, the question of the question always returns, the question of the relationship of philosophy as the realm or regimen of the question to that which exceeds philosophy, the relationship of ontology, if not phenomenology, to ethics. Each time, it is a question of the same and of something that resists both the question and the same, the possibility of philosophical language to receive or welcome what precedes or exceeds it. From "Violence and Metaphysics" to *Adieu* it is a question of the necessary violence of ontology, a question of the inevitable and perhaps salutary interruption of the ethical relation, a question of the hospitality that can ever be offered to the Other once this relation is interrupted, a question of the welcome that can ever be reserved for it.[2]

Reading Derrida over the course of the last three decades, we can today, in the light of *Adieu*, begin to read "Violence and Metaphysics" as a great text on hospitality, on a hospitality that is always granted by means of the question but can never be reduced to it. Yes, thirty years before *Adieu*, "Violence and Metaphysics" was, or will have been, a great text on hospitality, just as *Adieu*, as we will see, can be read as a great text on the relationship between violence and metaphysical language, *metaphysical* understood here in both its Levinasian and its more traditional sense. "Violence and Metaphysics" can today be read as a series of reservations or questions posed to Levinas concerning the relationship between philosophical language, the language in which Levinas never ceased to write, and its ability to accept, receive, or—and I'm now citing Derrida from 1964—"welcome" that which is wholly other within it.[3] How, Derrida was asking more than thirty years ago, can Levinas's language be hospitable to that which is foreign to it without posing serious questions, that is, without posing serious questions to this other, without requiring an answer that would translate the language of the foreigner or stranger—the question that *is* the stranger—into the language of the host, that would transform into a phenomenon that which exceeds and resists all light?

To circumscribe these questions of language and hospitality, Derrida spoke, already in 1964, of the relationship between inside and out, the dwelling and what comes to be lodged in it from the outside, the inscription or reception of what is beyond or otherwise than being in a philosophical language or political space. Already in 1964 Derrida was speaking about the possibility of welcoming what is radically foreign to the light into the midst of the biggest dwelling of them all, the Parmenidean well-rounded sphere of Being, the very sphere, and very thought of Being as one and not multiple, that Levinas repeatedly claims he must break with or indeed has already gone beyond. By contesting or questioning, by interrogating within a philosophical idiom that goes back to Parmenides, the meaning of this claim, "Violence and Metaphysics" asks about the necessity of breaking with a tradition from within, in other words, the necessity of a certain hospitality for this contestation, the necessity of being received and to some extent taken into and understood by the familial dwelling, by the Greek *polis*, before being able to discover, reactivate, or let oneself be visited by the stranger squatting within.

Near the beginning of "Violence and Metaphysics" Derrida questions Levinas's thesis that real multiplicity in eros—and particularly in paternity—must break with the Parmenidean notion of a single and unique Being. Although Plato himself in the *Sophist* had tried to make this break, allowing his Eleatic Stranger to "test the theory of my father Parmenides, and contend forcibly that after a fashion not-being is and on the other hand in a sense being is not," he could not complete it. Being Greek, Plato had to defer the act into a "hallucinatory murder" and make the Eleatic Stranger defend himself against the charge of being "a sort of parricide" ("VM," 89).[4] But how will Levinas, Derrida asks, fare any better in contesting the father,

Parmenides? It is just after this evocation of parricide—this "second parricide" to which Levinas "exhorts us"—that Derrida summarizes in a most striking and dramatic fashion the principal questions he will address to Levinas in the text that follows:

Will a non-Greek ever succeed in doing what a Greek in this case could not do, except by disguising himself as a Greek, by *speaking* Greek, by feigning to speak Greek in order to get near the king? And since it is a question of killing a speech, will we ever know who is the last victim of this stratagem? Can one feign speaking a language? The Eleatic stranger and disciple of Parmenides had to give language its due for having vanquished him: shaping non-Being according to Being, he had to "say farewell to an unnameable opposite of Being" and had to confine non-Being to its relativity to Being, that is to the movement of alterity. ("VM," 89)

Derrida asks, in short, whether one can be welcomed or taken in by the Greek language, the language of philosophy, without oneself becoming in some sense Greek, without giving oneself over to Greek terms, concepts, and oppositions—for example, the oppositions between inside and out, same and other, master and disciple, the Greek and the Stranger. Just as the Eleatic Stranger, in trying to show that nonbeing in some sense *is*, had to admit that nonbeing is shaped by Being, that is, in relation to it, must not the one who, like Levinas, wishes to shake the Greek *logos* at its foundation do so always as a relative nonstranger, that is, only after having accepted a certain Greek hospitality, with all its rites and reciprocal obligations—including, to borrow a word from the Eleatic Stranger, being put to the test of questioning?

It was in "Violence and Metaphysics," I recall, that Derrida spoke, in this now well-known phrase, of a "community of the question," "a community of the question about the possibility of the question" and "the origin of philosophy." Such questions, wrote Derrida in 1964, "should be the only [ones] today capable of founding the community, within the world, of those who are still called philosophers." Evoking a "discipline" and "tradition of the question remaining a question," a discipline and a community capable of safeguarding the question, Derrida seemed to be suggesting that such a community would always have to be a philosophical community, one whose discourse is dominated by the question, including, of course, the question of community ("VM," 79–80).[5]

Yet as philosophical, such a community of the question would always speak and pose questions within or in view of a certain horizon of understanding. Although that which calls for questioning might be beyond that horizon, a silent center at the heart of all discourse, all questions and responses would be formulated within or in view of it. In the very attempt to safeguard the question, therefore, questions that begin to determine or foreclose the question are inevitable. As Derrida argues, "the question is always enclosed; it never appears immediately as such, but only through the hermetism of a proposition in which the answer has already begun to determine the question" ("VM," 80). Hence Derrida recognizes that the originary question, the pure question or the question as such—if such phrases make any sense—the question before its inscription in a particular philosophical form, precedes philosophy. It can thus be indicated or, as Derrida will later say using Levinas's language, "traced" only through the "difference of a hermeneutical effort" ("VM," 80). Philosophy is thus defined in this text of 1964 as the "determined—finite and mortal—moment or mode of the question itself" ("VM," 81).[6]

These claims of Derrida concerning the status of the question in philosophy lay out the parameters or, indeed, the horizon for Derrida's own questions to Levinas concerning the status of Levinas's own language and, more or less explicitly, the status of the question within his language. As Derrida says near the end of "Violence and Metaphysics," all his questions are "questions of language: questions of language and the question of language" ("VM," 109). Such questions are not, however, Derrida clarifies, entirely foreign to Levinas himself, as if Derrida were himself a stranger come to enlighten this other stranger about just how much his language belongs to the light, to the tradition, just how much his language and his thought, despite all the claims to the contrary, are Greek. Borrowing another phrase from Plato's *Sophist*, where thought is defined as "silent inner dialogue of the soul with itself" (263e), Derrida says, "all our questions already belong to [Levinas's] own interior dialogue" ("VM," 109). The question will thus be to what extent these questions are posed explicitly by Levinas, to what extent the question of the question is formulated by Levinas with regard to his own language.

To recall briefly some already well-known theses, Derrida argues that since the concepts of philosophy are essentially Greek, it is difficult to speak and to be heard as speaking a philosophical discourse outside these concepts. Derrida thus asks whether a thought that "no longer seeks to be a thought of Being and phenomenality" ("VM," 82), a thought that nonetheless calls itself "metaphysics" ("VM," 83) and proposes to illuminate or clarify a relation with the absolutely Other that would free metaphysics as it is traditionally understood, can be expressed in a philosophical idiom. What is being put into question is the very use of philosophical language to criticize or question philosophy, to approach the other of philosophy. As Derrida succinctly puts it, "In question is a powerful will to *explication* of the history of Greek speech" ("VM," 83).

According to Levinas, Western philosophical language, and first of all Greek language, will have been struck from the very beginning by light, blinded by the light to that which eludes it—the (non)relation with the Other. All of philosophy since Plato and, Derrida writes summarizing Levinas, "more than any other philosophy, *phenomenology*, in the wake of Plato, was to be struck with light. Unable to reduce the last naïveté, the naïveté of the glance, it predetermined Being as object" ("VM," 85). Yet even if one were to acknowledge a certain truth in Levinas's diagnosis of philosophy in general and phenomenology in particular, and Derrida himself does, it seems, acknowledge such a truth—despite the reservations he expresses when he turns to Levinas's reading of Husserl and Heidegger—how is one to express or even understand this truth if not in and through a philosophical language? As Derrida remarks, playing the remedy off the diagnosis, "It is difficult to maintain a philosophical discourse against light" ("VM," 85), "for language in its entirety already has awakened as a fall into light"; "it arises with the sun" ("VM," 113). Derrida thus asks rhetorically, "How will the metaphysics of the face as the *epiphany* of the other free itself of light?" ("VM," 92). Can Levinas really maintain a discourse of radical separation or exteriority in a language of light, "in the medium of a traditional *logos* entirely governed by the structure 'inside-outside,' 'interior-exterior'" ("VM," 88)? Since one can only designate infinite exteriority as nonspatial, that is, negatively, must not Levinas "acknowledge that the infinite cannot be stated" ("VM," 113)—that is, stated positively? For when one attempts to think Infinity as "a positive plenitude," doesn't "the other become unthinkable, impossible, unutterable" ("VM," 114)?

If phenomenology and ontology are in fact philosophies of violence, as Levinas would claim and Derrida, with a caveat in each case, would agree, how would one escape such violence? How would one shed light on the limits of light, on what lies, so to speak, "beyond the light"? For light, Derrida suggests, perhaps has no opposite, since even its opposite can be understood only in terms of it, just as nonbeing could be understood in the *Sophist* only in terms of and in relation to Being, the Stranger supporting the hypothesis in his pursuit of the sophist as imitating dissembler who deals in the art of opinion that nonbeing in a certain sense *is*. Derrida thus calls into question what appears to be Levinas's attempt to develop a "positive movement" in the relation to the Other, the attempt to "open up classical conceptuality" in order to seek, through "concrete and subtle analyses" of the caress, death, fecundity, and work—analyses that bring phenomenology to its limit—"its own conceptuality between rejections" ("VM," 92). Indeed what could "its own conceptuality" possibly mean here, a conceptuality proper to Levinas or Levinasian discourse, when, for Derrida, a concept is not a concept unless it can be recognized in a language that is iterable, in other words, *readable*, by another, by a witness or, as we will see, a third?

Despite all these reservations and questions—or, actually, because of them—it could be argued that Derrida sees Levinas's attempt to dislodge his thinking from Greek thought all the while relying on Greek concepts and terms as a sort of deconstruction—or, indeed, as we will see again in Chapter 9, a kind of hospitality. It would be an attempt on Levinas's part to dislodge his own discourse from the philosophical discourse to which it is captive. Why else, Derrida asks, would Levinas return to concepts he had previously rejected, concepts such as Same and Other, if it were not because he recognized "the necessity of lodging oneself within traditional conceptuality in order to destroy it" ("VM," 111)? Did not Levinas recognize "some indestructible and unforeseeable resource of the Greek *logos*," "some unlimited power of envelopment, by which he who attempts to repel it would always already be *overtaken*?" ("VM," 112). Derrida writes, punctuating his sentence with a series of *it is necessary*s that he would like not only the reader but, it seems, Levinas himself to concede to, something Levinas will apparently do in later texts, although never without ambiguity:

That it is necessary to state infinity's *excess* over totality *in* the language of totality; that it is necessary to state the other in the language of the Same; that it is necessary to think *true* exteriority as non-*exteriority*, that is, still by means of the Inside-Outside structure and by spatial metaphor; and that it is necessary still to inhabit the metaphor in ruins, to dress oneself in tradition's shreds and the devil's patches—all this means, perhaps, that there is no philosophical logos which must not *first* let itself be expatriated into the structure Inside-Outside. ("VM," 112)

Indeed, for Levinas the rupture with philosophical language occurs, if it occurs, only from within or on the basis of that language. In fact, "the very energy of the break with tradition is precisely the adequation of Ego to the Same, and of Others to the Other" ("VM," 109). The very energy of a text such as *Totality and Infinity* is the result of the way it inscribes traditional terms so as to break with them, or break *within* them, and thereby release what is unthought and unthematizable within the system or the text.[7]

Attentive as always to questions of style, Derrida draws attention to the liberal use of metaphors in *Totality and Infinity*, "despite Levinas's disavowal or repudiation of poetry's enchantment," as well as to Levinas's use of negations to escape a traditional philosophical discourse dominated by the law of noncontradiction. Levinas's language would thus bring about a sort of "wounding of language," whereby, "in its opening, experience itself is silently revealed" ("VM," 90). Derrida thus sees in this thought that remains faithful to the point of infidelity to the phenomenological method a chance to shake the philosophical logos from within—even if Levinas did not himself formulate this in a sufficiently theoretical and explicit fashion, at least not in *Totality and Infinity*, the situation and the questions becoming radically modified, it seems, with the publication of *Otherwise Than Being*. The only thing, then, that really appears to be missing from this interior dialogue of Levinas with himself is, for Derrida in 1964, an explicit formulation of this attempt to work philosophical language from within. For "the attempt to achieve an opening toward the beyond of philosophical discourse, by means of philosophical discourse, which can never be shaken off completely, cannot possibly succeed *within language*—and Levinas recognizes that there is no thought before language and outside of it—except by *formally* and *thematically* posing *the question of the relations between belonging and the opening, the question of closure*" ("VM," 110). (I recall here in passing that it is in very similar terms that Derrida, during precisely the same period, poses his questions to Foucault concerning his history of madness. As we noted in Chapter 4, Derrida begins that text too with an explicit reference to a Platonic dialogue that stages a relationship between master and disciple, father and son, complete with its own parricide.)[8]

Although the Other escapes all philosophical understanding, all attempts by the Ego to grasp it, although there can be no "concept" of the Other, or rather, of *Autrui*, this word or this quasi concept can be thought or made intelligible only on the basis of the Greek *heteron*, and Levinas's attempts to communicate suggest that it is precisely by means of this that it *must* be thought. *Autrui* can be *read* only insofar as it communicates with the words and terms of the tradition, and the words and terms of the tradition can be reinvested or reactivated only by coming into contact with such quasi concepts as *Autrui*. Although *Autrui* cannot be thought positively as a concept, although it cannot be thought outside the Greek *heteron*, it provides the *heteron*, Derrida suggests, with "its irreducible center of meaning (the other *as* Other [*Autrui*])" ("VM," 105). It is as if Levinas were welcoming or reintroducing this perfectly good French word *Autrui* (the other as the other human being, the other as Other) back into the realm of the Greek logos, back into a language where it is always already understood in relation to otherness, to the French *autre* and the Greek *heteron*, so as then to reinvest these traditional terms with their "irreducible center" of otherness, a center that is unthinkable without these terms but cannot be reduced to them. This, it seems, is one of the deconstructive strategies Derrida sees at work in Levinas's engagement with the French language, a language that, in welcoming him, will have been profoundly transformed in turn by him. As Derrida will write some three decades later in *Adieu*:

> the idiom, an ambiguous chance, the *shibboleth* of the threshold, the preliminary chance of hospitality, one for which Levinas was grateful, a chance for his writing but also a chance granted by his philosophical writing to the French language . . . hospitality of a language and welcome extended to a language, language of the *hôte*, of the host, and language as *hôte*, as guest.[9]

Language, then, as *hôte*, as both "host" and "guest" (these English words appearing in *Adieu*, or being welcomed into *Adieu*, at the precise moment when it is a question of hospitality in and to language); language as both welcoming and welcomed. Language welcomes the thought of Levinas and makes available to him idioms such as *visage, autrui, adieu, me voici, hôte*, and *hôtage*; but because of Levinas's reinvestment of these words, his reactivation of their irreducible center, language is also welcomed by his thought, welcomed as foreign, these terms reinscribed so as to exceed both their traditional, nonspeculative meaning and the philosophical meaning that developed out of this nonspeculative origin.[10]

Derrida's questions in "Violence and Metaphysics" appear justified by the fact that Levinas never makes a complete break with a philosophical language that remains dominated although not completely controlled by the question, by questions of identity and conceptuality, by the law of non-contradiction. The question must dwell, then, within; it must dislodge from within by welcoming a stranger, a guest who is in turn immediately domesticated, having had to respond to the question of identity in the language of the same, but who, nonetheless, at the limit, in its irreducible center—foreign, strange, other—remains a guest whose nonpresence is a total question posed to my freedom, a total question that escapes all philosophical language. Derrida writes, "Without intermediary and without communion, neither mediate nor immediate, such is the truth of our relation to the other, the truth to which the traditional *logos* is forever *inhospitable*" ("VM," 90; my emphasis). One can thus thematize or conceptualize the encounter with the stranger, with the unforeseeable other, only by means of "the concept," which, like the question, always places the other within a certain horizon of the same, "a horizon within which alterity is amortized as soon as it is announced," wherein "eruptions and surprises are always *welcomed* [*accueillis*] by understanding and recognized" ("VM," 95; my emphasis).

It is in this sense that "Violence and Metaphysics" already raised, although discreetly and without really thematizing it, the question of hospitality. A traditional *logos* that is "inhospitable" and an understanding that "welcomes": these are more than simple tropes, analogies, or structural similarities, for we are speaking here of the very relationship between the traditional *logos* and that which institutes all language, in other words, the relationship between *logos* or understanding and the Other, *Autrui*. The traditional *logos* is inhospitable to the Other, to *Autrui*, because it poses questions to it rather than being put into question by it, because it poses questions always in view of a horizon that reduces the Other to my understanding.

We could follow this theme or question of the question in many other texts of Derrida, from "Violence and Metaphysics" to "At This Very Moment in This Work Here I Am" to *Of Spirit* and the famous footnote that speaks of a *gage* or an engagement that would be prior to the question, right up to Derrida's most recent work. We would see that the question is everywhere in question, the phenomenon of the question, the question as a phenomenon, and the question of whether it is possible to receive or be hospitable to that which exceeds the phenomenon. Nowhere is this clearer than in *Adieu to Emmanuel Levinas*.

In *Adieu* Derrida demonstrates how Levinas's thought of hospitality, usually understood in terms of the unconditional welcoming of the Other before all questions, seems also to require the figure of the third, and thus of the question, to make it possible for the Other to be effectively welcomed. Indeed what is at issue in *Adieu* is the necessity of the third—and, as we will see, of philosophical language—to receive or welcome the ethical moment into a discourse organized and determined by philosophical as well as political categories. It is less a question of translating some purely ethical moment into a political idiom than of inventing or negotiating a way between these moments, between the unconditional and the conditioned. Levinas's work would be the name of one such exemplary negotiation. It is in this sense that Derrida in *Adieu* would like us to read and receive Levinas as a great thinker of hospitality—not simply to embrace a Levinas who will have developed a powerful ethical thinking on the primordial welcoming of the Other before all questions but to accompany a Levinas who will have understood the aporias and undergone the questions of hospitality, both as a theme within his work and as the very form of his work.

Adieu is concerned most obviously with the problems and promises of the relationship between ethics and politics in Levinas's work. The book thus works chiasmatically to follow the political implications and interruptions of the ethical in Levinas's more overtly philosophical and ethical texts and the ethical implications or hesitations lodged within his more avowedly political texts. This chiasm is then set against the backdrop of some of the most pressing ethicopolitical questions of our time—all of them questions of hospitality: questions of immigration, exile, and asylum in France and elsewhere—and particularly in Israel, where Derrida follows Levinas as he tries to think the modern state of Israel in conjunction with a beyond of the state within the state, a messiancity without messianism, and so on.

But *Adieu* is also, like "Violence and Metaphysics," concerned with Levinas's language, with the very possibility of a philosophical language in Levinas. It is thus also written under the sign of the question—the question of the stranger or foreigner, no doubt, the question of ethics and politics in Levinas's work, certainly, but also the question as it imposes itself on Levinas and his writing. In the first part of *Adieu*, for example, where the theme of receptivity as welcoming and as hospitality is traced through Levinas's work, Derrida begins to relate the question of hospitality—the question of the stranger—to the question of the question, to everything that was so central to "Violence and Metaphysics." Derrida thus continues in *Adieu* his long, indeed lifelong, meditation on the question by trying to situate those places in Levinas that function as points of transition, or rupture, between ethics and politics, between my responsibility for the Other and my responsibility for the other of the Other, between an absolute relation to the Other and the relation to other others, points where the question of philosophical interrogation emerges for the first time. For Levinas this rupture occurs through the exemplary figure of the third or third party [*le tiers*], which we could follow from the section of *Totality and Infinity* entitled "The Other and the Others" up through certain passages from *Otherwise Than Being* or "Sociality and Money," and back to earlier essays such as "The Ego and the Totality."[11] This third comes to interrupt the face-to-face relation, not, as we might think, in order to bring an end to justice but precisely to introduce it, to institute a justice that can come only through deliberation, comparison, and, of course, questions. Derrida insists in his reading of Levinas that this second moment, the moment where the "uprightness of the *welcome* made to the face" is interrupted, is not secondary but, rather, a second moment that emerges with the first. Derrida writes in *Adieu*: "The third arrives without waiting. Without waiting, the third comes to affect the experience of the face in the face to face. . . . The illeity of the third is thus nothing less, for Levinas, than the beginning of justice, at once as law and beyond the law, in law beyond the law" (*A*, 29). It is here that the question emerges—the question as a theme, as a recognizable modality of thought, and the question as a rhetorical and, indeed, philosophical medium or instrument. Derrida continues, lending an ear to how the question in a passage from *Otherwise Than Being* is both mentioned and used:

> From pages where I have always thought I could make out a certain distress of the aporia, the complaints, attestations, and protestations, along with the outcries or objections, of a Job who would be tempted to appeal not *to* justice but *against* it, come to us the desperate questions of a just man. Of a just man who would like to be more just than justice. Another Job, unless this is the other of Job, asks what he has to do with justice, with just and unjust justice. These questions cry out a contradiction, one that is without equal and without precedent, the terrible contradiction of the Saying by the Saying, Contra-Diction itself. (*A*, 30)

Derrida then cites the passage from *Otherwise Than Being* to which he is referring:

> The third is other than the neighbor, but also another neighbor, and also a neighbor of the other, and not simply his fellow. What then are the other and the third

for one another? What have they done to one another? Which passes before the other? . . . The other and the third, my neighbors, contemporaries of one another, put distance between me and the other and the third. . . . The third introduces a contradiction in the Saying. . . . It is of itself the limit of responsibility and the birth of the question: What do I have to do with justice? A question of conscience, of consciousness. Justice is necessary, that is, comparison, coexistence, contemporaneousness, assembling. (*A*, 30)[12]

We see in this extraordinary passage exactly how the question emerges with the third, how it is used just before being mentioned. It emerges as an object or a theme within the text, in the voice, it would seem, of Levinas—"a question of conscience"—just after appearing through a voice that would be not necessarily Levinas's but that of just about anyone to whom the question of justice arises: "What then are the other and the third for one another? What have they done to one another?, etc." A singular "question of conscience," that is, a "matter of conscience," thus immediately gives rise to a plurality of questions, to multiple "questions of conscience," born in the very awakening of moral conscience. Questions of conscience but, at the same time, a conscience or consciousness of the question, the awakening of con-science as reason and knowledge, as a consciousness of oneself and of others. For with the question, within the horizon that always accompanies the question, come intentional consciousness, thematization, objectification, understanding, even calculation. Hence Levinas speaks in "Peace and Proximity" of "comparison . . . in view of equity and equality, a weighing, a thinking, a calculation, the *comparison of incomparables*, and, consequently, the neutrality—presence or representation—of being, the thematization and the visibility of the face" (*A*, 32). Such thematization can even lend itself, says Levinas in a short text entitled "Sociality and Money," to economic homogenization, to the reduction of human work and of the Other to the sole and unique value of money. Comparison, calculation, thematization—all these arrive at the same time as questions of conscience, questions about what to do, how to act justly, questions—in the plural—that themselves arrive at the same time as the question—the singular question—of conscience, the total question inscribed on the threshold, as the threshold question, the question that requires of me a response. And all this is indeed in the name of justice, a justice that interrupts and goes beyond the justice of the ethical relation, which itself interrupts and goes beyond the justice of the merely political. That's the contra-diction.

Question de conscience is thus indeed a "question of consciousness," as Alphonso Lingis translates it in *Otherwise Than Being*, for in what comes after it is a question of thematizing, objectivizing, intentional consciousness: "Justice is necessary, that is, comparison, coexistence, contemporaneousness, assembling, etc." To confirm the translation of *conscience* as "consciousness," we need only read another passage from the 1984 essay "Peace and Proximity": "The first question in the interhuman is the *question of justice. Henceforth it is necessary to know*, to become consciousness [*se faire une con-conscience*]." But before these assertions there is, as we just saw in *Otherwise Than Being*, a question of conscience, questions of conscience about what to do and how to act justly. The third is thus the birth not only of the question but of the difference between these two meanings of the French *conscience*, the difference between "conscience" and "consciousness," that is, between our coming to awareness of what we must do and our understanding or questioning of how we are to do it.

With the third, then, emerges the question—not only a being put into question by the Other but, without waiting, the necessity of taking up speech in order to ask questions about my responsibilities for the Other, and for the others of the Other. Already in "Violence and Metaphysics" Derrida spoke of the way in which language, for Levinas, is instituted by a relation that is an interrogation, "not a theoretical interrogation . . . but a total question, a distress and denuding, a supplication, a demanding prayer addressed to a freedom, that is, to a commandment" ("VM," 96). A total question that, without waiting, becomes partial, or becomes the question of partiality. Who shall go first? What are the other and the third for one another? We thus go from a total responsibility for the Other, one I cannot escape, to a responsibility for the others of the Other, a responsibility that is, this time, *understood* through, say, some universal concept like man or humanity.[13]

"Before" the third, there would be the total question that the Other "is," but not yet any questions to or about that Other, not yet any questions on the theme or subject of the Other, since the Other is not, or is not yet, a subject or object of thematization—a being on the subject of which questions can be posed. As Derrida remarks, "the ineluctability of the third is the law of the question" (*A*, 31).[14] It is the law of the question and, beyond the "ethics of ethics" that Derrida in "Violence and Metaphysics" says Levinas gives us, the question of justice, of law and of laws. Only with the third comes comparison, coexistence, contemporaneousness, in other words, the possibility—the necessity—of counting, of taking into account, of reckoning responsibilities. Only with the third comes the necessity of weighing responsibilities and adjudicating between various claims, of asking questions rather than being simply subject to a demand.

But—and here is the question of philosophical language that interests me most here—with the third also comes the very possibility of counting and taking into account in the first place, the possibility of addressing in a determined fashion not only other others but the Other itself—the "first" Other who faces us. Only with the third comes the possibility of counting and determining, perhaps even of recognizing, the I and the Other, the possibility of posing questions and speaking *philosophically* about them. As "the birth of the question," the third makes possible, as Derrida notes, not only the move to politics but the very philosophical discourse in which Levinas carries out his analysis of our ethical—and putatively prephilosophical—situation. Indeed, it is only with the third that we can *speak* of the first and the second, of the I and the Other, in texts such as *Totality and Infinity* and *Otherwise Than Being*. The third is, Derrida emphasizes in *Adieu*, the birth of the question(s) of conscience and of consciousness, but also—and Derrida marks this without insisting on it—the birth of an awareness, of a coming to consciousness, that responsibility to the Other and to the others of the Other requires a certain intelligibility, the possibility of a *philosophical* language, if not discipline, that would allow us to speak intelligibly of the Other and, so, avoid the violences of silence and mysticism. In this sense the third must always come first.

"The ineluctability of the third is the law of the question." "But also, as a result," Derrida continues—and here is where *Adieu* returns quite explicitly to the concerns of "Violence and Metaphysics"—"justice, philosophical intelligibility, knowledge, and even, announcing itself gradually from one person to the next, from neighbor to neighbor, the figure of the State" (*A*, 31). The question is located on the threshold between ethics and politics, between a being put into question and a taking up of speech so as to question, between two sorts of responsibility—unless responsibility consists precisely in negotiating this threshold. The question lies between "responsibility for the other human being," who is, as Levinas says, "in its *immediacy, anterior to every question*" (*A*, 32), and the juridical, political, and, I emphasize, *philosophical* responsibility that accompanies the emergence or birth of the third and, thus, of the question. In a first moment, then, a moment of immediacy wherein the Other is welcomed, we are put into question but are not yet questioning; as Levinas puts it, "to welcome the Other is to put in question my freedom" (*A*, 29). And elsewhere: "The subjectivity of a subject is responsibility or being-in-question in the form of the total exposure to offence in the cheek offered to the smiter. This responsibility is prior to dialogue, to the exchange of questions and answers" (*A*, 57).[15] But in a second moment, a moment that accompanies the first in the figure of the third, the being put into question, anterior in its immediacy to every question, takes up speech, takes up the question in a coming to conscience and consciousness. It is a question here, then, of an interruption of the interruption that the ethical relation to the Other already is, an interruption of the interruption of ontology and phenomenology in order to return, although wholly otherwise, perhaps, to ontology with all its terms and logic and to the possibility of phenomenological experience and analysis. This interruption occurs, Derrida insists, without waiting, not as some contingency that would interrupt the face to face by introducing an alien reflection into it but, ineluctably, as a "self-interruption" (*A*, 110).

Question de conscience—this phrase is itself a kind of threshold, a place of rupture between a responsibility that is prior to every question, prior even to questions of conscience, and a responsibility manifest in conscience, whose first question is the question of justice, a *conscience* that inevitably and immediately becomes *consciousness*, a consciousness where questions get multiplied, subject to calculating thought, political judgment, and, most important for my argument here, philosophical analysis. Although Derrida does not, as I said, insist on it, the analysis of the third in *Adieu* leads us right back to the very questions, including the question of the question, that were so central, more than three decades ago, to "Violence and Metaphysics." Derrida thus speaks of how Levinas in "Peace and Proximity" deduces

from this ineluctability of the third *at once* the origin of the question itself (and thus of philosophical discourse, whose status is governed and whose signature legitimated by the question: almost the entirety of Levinas's discourse, for example, almost the entire space of its intelligibility for us, appeals to this third) *and* justice *and* the "political structure of society." The leap without transition, the rupturing mutation of the "without question" at the birth of the "first question," defines at the same time the passage from ethical responsibility to juridical, political—and philosophical—responsibility. (*A*, 31)

Yes, "and philosophical," since the third is the birth of the question and, thus, of philosophy.[16]

In "Violence and Metaphysics" Derrida asked whether Levinas's ethics of ethics, "an Ethics without law and without concept, which maintains its non-violent purity only before being determined as concept and laws," does not have serious problems when it can "occasion neither a determined ethics nor determined laws without negating and forgetting itself" ("VM," 111). In *Adieu* these problems become, it seems, a sort of virtue, pointing out the need to negotiate (a word that runs throughout "At This Very Moment in This Work Here I Am") between two necessities, between Levinas's ethics of ethics and ethics in a determined sense, or between ethics and politics. Using the very tools and terms with which he earlier criticized—or at least questioned—this ethics of ethics, Derrida here defends Levinas against those who would see in the Levinasian ethical model no way to develop or even take into account a determined ethics let alone a politics.[17]

By highlighting Levinas's insistence on the necessity of the third, and of the question, Derrida shows that Levinas was perfectly aware or conscious—a word that now has both philosophical and ethical implications—of the dangers inherent in such an ethics devoid of law. He is conscious of both the violence the ethical relation can undergo at the hands of politics and the violence it itself might perpetrate without the third, what Derrida refers to as the "vertigo of ethical violence itself" (*A*, 33). The danger resides, says Derrida, writing at once for and against Levinas at this point, in the "impossibility of discerning here between good and evil, love and hate, giving and taking, the desire to live and the death drive, the hospitable welcome and the egoistic or narcissistic closing up within oneself" (*A*, 33). That is, the danger resides not only in a philosophical language that always neglects the radical exteriority of the Other, but in the suspension of this philosophical language and its Greek oppositions, including the opposition between welcoming the stranger and refusing him.

In this figure of the third, in the *question de conscience*, Derrida sees an attempt by Levinas to take into account the language in or through which ethics is couched, the very possibility of his own discourse as a philosophical discourse—even if such a discourse is being feigned to get closer to the king. The theoretical discourse on the third gives Levinas the resources to take into account the possibility of his own discourse as theoretical or philosophical. If, as Derrida says, "almost the entirety of Levinas's discourse, . . .

almost the entire space of its intelligibility for us, appeals to this third," we must begin to reread Levinas otherwise. One strategy, for example, would be to follow Levinas's own analysis in *Totality and Infinity* of Descartes's language and method in the *Meditations*, so as to distinguish between what might be called the chronological or descriptive order and the logical or deductive order of Levinas's own texts.[18] For it could be shown how, in texts like *Time and the Other*, which follow a more or less genetic phenomenology, we always encounter much later in the description of the ego that which logically precedes it and makes all description possible—namely, the idea of infinity or the Other. As in Descartes's *Meditations*, what comes first logically comes second chronologically. But it could also be shown how, in texts like *Totality and Infinity*, where the logical priority of the Other and of the ethical relation are given early on, we encounter only later—and sometimes much later—in the description of this logical order that which makes this description—and this chronology—possible or intelligible in the first place: not the language or the very opening onto language that the Other *is* but *philosophical language* in particular, the language made possible by the third.

Indeed, it could be argued that the justification for the very readability of a book such as *Totality and Infinity*, the intelligibility of its writing as bearing witness to the ethical relation, its opening to an other of the Other, to a third or a reader, is not really given before the section "The Other and the Others"—more than two thirds of the way through the book. It is not until this section that Levinas's entire discourse concerning the Other is philosophically legitimated as a series of claims or thematizations concerning that which is beyond all thematization. Only there, in the chronological or descriptive order, does Levinas justify a whole series of questions and thematizations he will have employed from the very beginning of the book to address that which logically precedes, so to speak, all questions and thematizations. Although *Totality and Infinity* speaks from the very beginning of this relation with the Other that is language, a language that expresses itself as Face but is perhaps not incompatible with writing, as Blanchot once claimed in a passage of *The Infinite Conversation* on *Totality and Infinity*, it is not before the section "The Other and the Others" that Levinas explains the possibility and the power, the capacity, to speak intelligibly *of* this language. We are thus faced with two origins on two different levels to which no absolute priority can be given—the Face or the ethical relation as Language that opens and makes possible all language, including the language of *Totality and Infinity*, and the philosophical language in which this other origin must be inscribed. Each origin is thus the origin of the other. Philosophical language only ever opens on the basis of the Other who is language, and the Other can be inscribed and made intelligible only through philosophical language. It is for this very reason that philosophy is defined in "Violence and Metaphysics" as a "determined—finite and mortal—moment or mode of the question itself" ("VM," 81). As "Violence and Metaphysics" makes clear, as the Stranger in Plato's *Sophist* confirms, language must be given its due, and one can twist free of it only from within it, only when already taken in by the *sumplokē*, where the term "Other," for example, has meaning only in relation to the Same, even though, in Levinas, it is explicitly denied as the Other of the Same. The origin, the origins, must be inscribed: language within language, justice within justice, the question within the question. But it is the divergence or difference between these two orders, between the Face as language and the language of the Face, that makes any welcoming possible.

Although the birth of the question does not wait, although there is no time before the third, one must guard against conflating these two moments or finding some point of transition or easy translation between them. To employ Lyotard's terminology in "Levinas's Logic," there remains a differend between the ethical phrase regimen in which the I is an addressee without ever being an addresser, in which the I is in question without ever being in a position to pose questions, and the cognitive phrase regimen where the I can take up speech in the position of an addresser, where the I arrogates for itself the power to state claims and pose questions.[19] Writing in a similar vein in "Violence and Metaphysics," Derrida identifies the ethical with an almost unheard-of vocative modality of speech, a modality that "is not a category, a *case* of speech, but rather a bursting forth, the very raising up of speech" ("VM," 103), a vocative with no accusative or attributive dimension. Derrida writes, "The dative or vocative dimension, which opens the original direction of language, cannot lend itself to inclusion in and modification by the accusative or attributive dimension of the object without violence" ("VM," 95).[20] There are thus two moments—although one does not precede the other; the moment of the direction of language, what Levinas will later identify with the Saying, and the moment of inclusion and attribution, later identified with the Said. Two moments that, as Derrida demonstrates in the essay that bears this title, are always to be found "at this very moment in this work." Although the attributive moment is ineluctable, although the Saying inevitably becomes included in the Said, there would be better and worse ways of negotiating—of practicing or inventing—the threshold between them, better and worse ways of being hospitable.[21]

Having begun with the first text of Derrida on Levinas, I would like to conclude with one of the last, for it is not with *Adieu* that Derrida's reflection on Levinas has ended. I am thinking, for example, of a little book apparently conceived and written at just about the same time as *Adieu*, a book that takes up many of its themes and so might fruitfully be read alongside it. This book, *Of Hospitality*, is in effect a transcript of a couple of sessions of Derrida's seminar of 1996 on the theme of the foreigner and hospitality.[22] It thus treats not only the question of hospitality but—and who would now be surprised by this?—the relationship between hospitality and the question. As Derrida says in a phrase that could have served as an exergue to all the texts of which I have been speaking: "The question of hospitality is thus also the question of the question" (*H*, 29). That is, the question of the role of the question in hospitality, the question of what interrupts the welcome without question as the only chance for an effective, receivable welcome—the only chance for *welcoming the stranger*. From "Violence and Metaphysics" to *Adieu* and *Of Hospitality* what is at issue is the question of knowing whether it is possible, or preferable, to welcome the Other without or before its name, before the question of identity has even been posed, to receive the Other in his or her purity as stranger, in the stranger's purity as a question posed to the very freedom of the host. Although hospitality must precede all questions, for it to be effective, for it to avoid the ethical violence such an unquestioning welcoming might entail, the justice of deliberation, calculating responsibility, and questioning is necessary. This is not simply some tragedy of human finitude but the only chance hospitality has for finite beings. For philosophical language to be intelligible, effective, it too must be inscribed, its idiom "received," already hosted by a tradition. *Adieu, Autrui, Visage, Sinai*—these are all figures of the threshold, particular inscriptions of the threshold, figures of reception and hospitality as such, threshold figures of the "total question" that precedes all language, but also, precisely because they are figures, inscriptions that have already been received and welcomed by a particular language, that have already crossed over the threshold.

It is thus surely no accident that Derrida begins this book on the question of hospitality with a question, a question on the subject of the question, and on the stranger as a question, which he then relates very quickly to Levinas and, thus, to everything that is at stake in *Adieu* and "Violence and Metaphysics." Derrida begins *Of Hospitality*:

The question of the stranger—is this not a stranger's question? Come from the stranger, from a foreign land? . . . Before being a question to treat, before designating a concept, theme, problem, or program, the question of the stranger is a question *of* the stranger, a question come *from* the stranger, from abroad, and a question to the stranger, addressed *to* the stranger. As if the stranger were first of all *the one who* poses the first question or *the one to whom* the first question is addressed . . . the one who, in posing the first question, puts me in question. One is reminded of the situation of the third and of justice, which Levinas analyzes as the "birth of the question." (*H*, 3–4)

A question *of* the stranger: that is, a question come *from*, a question posed *to*, and a question *about* the stranger. Once again, everything goes back and forth across this threshold of the question. The question posed to my freedom becomes, in a reversal that then gives meaning to all directions and determines the very difference between *from*, *to*, and *about*, the question or questions that the I poses to and about the other, the I being no longer what is put in question but, so to speak, the master and possessor of the question. Derrida asks later in *Of Hospitality*: "Does hospitality consist in questioning the one who arrives? Does it begin with the question addressed to the newcomer: what is your name? . . . [Or] does it begin with the unquestioning welcome, in a double effacement, the effacement of the question *and* the name?" (*H*, 27–29). The question of hospitality is thus inseparable from the question of the question, the question of what it means to ask the question of identity, or else to "welcome" the Other without or before their name, in their purity as foreigner, as a question posed to the freedom of a host.

Questions of hospitality in relation to language and philosophy are thus, we have seen, nothing new to Derrida. But they are also nothing new to philosophy. Indeed they go back at least as far as Plato's *Sophist*. Should we be surprised, then, that just after these initial remarks and questions on the relationship between the stranger and the question in *Of Hospitality*, just after the brief evocation of Levinas cited above, Derrida turns once again to the *Sophist*, to the very dialogue, and the very same place in that dialogue, to which he turned more than thirty years earlier in "Violence and Metaphysics"? He writes:

It is the Stranger who, by putting forward the intolerable question, the question of parricide, contests the Parmenidean thesis, puts in question the *logos* of our father, Parmenides. . . . As though the Stranger had to begin by contesting the authority of the chief or head, the father, the master of the family, the "master of the house," of the powers that be of hospitality. . . . He defends himself against the accusation of parricide by denial. He would not dream of defending himself if he did not feel deep down that he is, in truth, a parricide, virtually a parricide, and that to say "non-being is" remains a challenge to the paternal logic of Parmenides, a challenge that comes from the stranger, from foreign lands. Like every parricide, this one takes place in the family: a stranger can commit parricide only if he is, in some sense, among family. (*H*, 5–7)[23]

Hence the questions of 1964 return and are renewed in 1997, questions posed after the publication of *Totality and Infinity*, one of the great books of the master, and questions posed after the master's disappearance, questions of Jew and Greek, of being outside and inside a language or tradition, questions, then, of strangers and of family, of contestation and discipleship, parricide and paternity—this latter signifying, for Levinas, nothing less than time itself. We begin to see that Derrida has not ceased to weave a *sumplokē* of enormous complexity, inscribing the outside within, the whole in the part, the vocative that accuses in all the accusatives that call us, the ear in the eye, the total question in all the other determined questions, a *sumplokē* where, as in the *Sophist*, the terms and themes have meaning only in their imbrication and necessary mingling with one another, and where we, like him, are taken, taken up and taken on, but also taken by surprise, where we are called to appear in the light, called to be called into question but also called to question, so that we too might become, all the while being completely other, at once speech and phenomenon.

PART THREE

"OUR" LEGACIES

Better Believing It

TRANSLATING SKEPTICISM IN 'MEMOIRS OF THE BLIND'

Cowritten with Pascale-Anne Brault

. . .

—Well it all depends.

—Yes, but the question is whether it all depends on this? For I'll have you observe that from the very beginning of this conversation we've been going around in circles and keep on coming back to this same point. Indeed we've been doing just what I've been arguing *Memoirs of the Blind* does—returning to the origin, reflecting the beginning in the end, folding one edge back on the other. Just like *Memoirs of the Blind,* our conversation would seem to be reflecting the very structure of a draftsman or painter doing his self-portrait in front of a mirror. For just picture the scene of some painter or drafts-man—Fantin-Latour, for example—looking at himself in a mirror and do-ing his self-portrait: first you see the artist, then the canvas, then the mirror, then, reflected in the mirror, the canvas and the artist—an AB/BA structure with the mirror in the middle. It thus seems perfectly appropriate that Derrida should reflect this reflective structure in the beginning and end of *Mémoires d'aveugle* with the phrase "Vous croyez?" For you remember, surely, that the work begins with the words "Vous croyez?" and ends, or almost, with the phrase "Des larmes qui voient . . . Vous croyez?"[1]

—It's true that *Mémoires d'aveugle* begins and ends with the same words, with "Vous croyez?" and "Vous croyez?" but *Memoirs of the Blind* does not.

This wasn't an oversight or printer's error, you'll recall, but a more or less conscious decision—and, from my point of view, an essential one. Indeed this entire discussion is perhaps little more than an attempt to explain this decision and this difference. For the rather discreet disappearance of a direct object is at the very heart of our translation only because it is at the very heart of the question of faith or belief, be it in drawing or narrative or elsewhere, and because the question of faith or belief is, I believe, at the very heart of Derrida's work.

So although the genesis of this little dialogue on the translating dilemmas of *Memoirs of the Blind* is in fact rather complex, it might appear to some—and there would be some truth to this appearance—that we have fabricated the whole thing so as to do what every translator must at some point dream of doing, that is, to explain a seemingly idiosyncratic translation choice to a few sympathetic ears: in this case, to justify our rendering two identical sentences in French differently in English. The whole conversation would thus be, to paraphrase Milton, an attempt to justify the ways of translators to men.

You will recall that the framing lines of *Memoirs of the Blind* differ from the French insofar as they differ from each other. For while we translated the first "Vous croyez?" as "Do you believe this?," we translated the second as "Do you believe?" Right up until the last moment we hesitated, hand poised above the proof page, debating whether these two lines should remain the same. In the end, and this was the very final decision we made, we erased the "this" from the next-to-last line of the book, transforming "Do you believe this?" into "Do you believe?," saying something perhaps about the relationship between faith and the object of faith, the relationship between belief and the absence or disappearance of a direct object.

—But don't you remember that we erased the final *this* because we felt that there was an implied direct object in the antecedent, "Tears that see . . . Do you believe?" Don't you remember that we had enough faith in the reader to think that he or she would hear "tears that see . . . Do you really believe this? Do you really believe Andrew Marvell when he says that tears can see?" If the disappearance of the *this* had anything to do with faith, it had to do with our faith in the reader to understand the context, nothing more. And if there was any confusion caused by this, the first translators' footnote should have dispelled it. Don't you recall having written about "Vous croyez?":

This phrase, repeated on the next to the last line of the work, can be read in several ways, ranging from its everyday meaning, "Do you think so?," to the more literal, "Do you believe?," to the more incredulous, "Do you really believe this?" The phrase does not have a direct object [in the French], but we have given it one to indicate that it could be understood as a response to the epigraph or to the conversation in progress. (*MB*, 1)

—This is all true, but it's only half the truth, for the erasure at the end is not insignificant, and we did not really signal to the reader the fact that we omitted the direct object in the second rendering of this line. For what if the disappearance of the direct object, the disappearance, perhaps, of the object of faith, were still "visible" in some way after its disappearance, visible in its disappearance, so that there would open up a real difference between the beginning and the end of *Memoirs of the Blind*, transforming what you characterized as the circuit of return, the mirror's reflected image, into a line, into a linear narrative, into a story that ends with *real faith, real belief*, which is to say, a belief or a faith without object?

—You're making it sound as if "Vous croyez?" and "Vous croyez?" were the very beginning and end of the book so as to introduce this subtle and not very believable difference between beginning and end. But before the first "Vous croyez?" there is an ellipsis and, before that, a quote from one of Diderot's letters to Sophie Volland. So it is not absolutely clear what "Vous croyez?" is responding to. Is it provoked by a statement from the unknown interlocutor, or is it a response to the epigraph? And the final "Vous croyez?" is followed by the line "Je ne sais pas, il faut croire . . . ," "I don't know, one has to believe. . . ." So we have an ellipsis in the beginning and an ellipsis at the end, reflecting each other, as I said, or rather reflecting themselves, around an invisible mirror at the center of the book. And if you're now going to say that the epigraph from Diderot drastically alters this relationship since it is not repeated at the end, and so, being outside the circuit of the mirror, introduces the difference you are arguing for, let me read part of the letter and then ask you a question:

I write without seeing. I came. I wanted to kiss your hand. . . . This is the first time I have ever written in the dark . . . not knowing whether I am indeed forming letters. Wherever there will be nothing, read that I love you. (*MB*, 1)

Is it completely fanciful to think that this too is part of Derrida's own self-portrait in *Memoirs*, that we are supposed to hear the echoes of Diderot a few pages later when Derrida describes writing down a dream in the middle of the night, not knowing whether he is indeed forming letters? Doesn't the rest of the book draw this epigraph into it, so to speak, so that the book is indeed a sort of circle or ring or, as one says in French, an *alliance*? Derrida talks about the *alliance*, you remember, in *The Truth in Painting*.

—I can see that you are going to argue throughout for the circle, for the circular structure of *Memoirs of the Blind*, whereas I am going to push the line—the truth lying no doubt somewhere between us. But let me return to the question of the direct object for a moment; wasn't the point of translating "Vous croyez?" with a direct object in the beginning and without one in the end an attempt to show—in however discreet a way—that the object of drawing, and perhaps of translating, disappears in the process of drawing or translating, that it takes time and space to be able to get Sophie Volland or any reader to see or hear that "wherever there will be nothing, read that I love you?"

—Of course, but that is the point of the book from the very beginning, from Diderot's declaration of love to the conversions of St. Augustine and St. Paul: at the moment of faith or conversion the object of faith, or of drawing, disappears. So although the themes may change, it seems that Derrida's object remains the same throughout, to show that the object of drawing is always related to blindness. The point is that we must think belief or faith outside or at the limits of vision—at the limits of the direct object, as you say. But that's Derrida's thesis right from the start, and, if I understand you right, that's essentially your own thesis concerning translation. Like drawing, translation would have something to do with blindness, as if the original text always vanished at the moment of translation in the same way the model of drawing does at the moment of drawing. Couldn't Derrida's confessions about drawing be transposed—translated—into the terms of translation? For example, when he writes:

To this day I still think that I will never know *either* how to draw *or* how to look at a drawing. . . . I feel myself incapable of following with my hand the prescription of a model: it is as if, just as I was about to draw, I no longer saw the thing. For it immediately flees, drops out of sight, and almost nothing of it remains; it disappears before my eyes, which, in truth, no longer perceive anything but the mocking arrogance of this disappearing apparition. As long as it remains in front of me, the thing defies me, producing, as if by emanation, an invisibility that it reserves for me, a night of which I would be, in some way, the chosen one. (*MB*, 36)

Is it too much to say that this is also the experience of translation, that one cannot keep an eye on both the object or the original and the copy at the same time, that one inevitably disappears, that just as drawing traverses a certain invisibility, so translation always proceeds by way of a certain silence? "Vous croyez?" "Do you believe?" The passage between these is not a simple reflection, as if all one had to do to translate were to hold an English mirror up before the original French. But it seems to me that Derrida is saying nothing but this throughout *Memoirs of the Blind* so that the disappearance of the direct object in the next-to-the-last line is just another sign of the passage between the so-called original and the copy, in this case, between the French text and the translation. The point is that the *this*— the direct object, the object of drawing, or translation—is *always* disappearing, and from the very beginning.

—Yes, I too am suggesting that this is the point throughout, that in translation as in drawing there is a devouring power of invisibility that makes the book unreadable even for the author, as Blanchot would say, but then also for the translator. But I still can't help thinking that this happens because of or through the book, that the book, for lack of a better word, *progresses*, like a confession or conversion, from doubt and skepticism to faith, from sight to tears. Remember that the first drawing is Coypel's *Study of the Blind*, a drawing that evokes the fall, the moment of man's loss of vision, his paradise lost. And the book ends with DeVolterra's *Woman at the Foot of the Cross*, after passing by Jan Provost's *Sacred Allegory* of revelation. Isn't that not only a linear story but the paradigm of linear history itself, a line leading from the loss of Eden to Resurrection, from the Old Testament to the New? Why else would Derrida begin with all those stories from the Old Testament, Tobit and Tobias, Jacob and Esau, and end with St. Paul, Augustine, and Milton? Isn't Derrida writing himself into a certain line of history, a particular genealogy of Judeo-Christian culture? In other words, isn't *Memoirs of the Blind* a sort of *Via Dolorosa* or stations of the cross in seventy-one stages, beginning with the blindness of the fall and ending with the veiled tears of resurrection? Doesn't the book enact or put this conversion on the scene? And aren't we, as readers, supposed to follow this itinerary? Aren't we supposed to be transformed *in reading* the book, our eyes opened or, rather, veiled at the end by tears, moved to both tears and belief?

—But where do we end up in the end? Do you really believe that the book ends in faith? If so, then why does it come in the guise of a question, as close as possible to skepticism, as if all belief were ultimately to remain suspended or questionable? After all, the words immediately following the "Vous croyez?" at the very beginning of the book speak of the relationship between skepticism and belief: "But skepticism is precisely what I've been talking to you about: the difference between believing and seeing, between believing one sees [*croire voir*] and seeing between, catching a glimpse [*entrevoir*]—or not" (*MB*, 1). Doesn't the skepticism with which the book begins get repeated in the end, or rather, just as the two voices and two points of view cross and diverge throughout the book, doesn't skepticism itself become divided, undecidable, so that the last line could be a declaration or imperative to believe *as well as* a moment of hesitation? Derrida ends *Memoirs of the Blind*, recall, by citing the final lines of Andrew Marvell's poem *Eyes and Tears* and then expressing a certain incredulity about them:

> Thus let your streams o'erflow your springs,
> Till eyes and tears be the same things:
> And each the other's difference bears;
> These weeping eyes, those seeing tears.

To these lines one voice thus asks, "Des larmes qui voient . . . Vous croyez?" "Tears that see . . . Do you believe?" and the other responds, "Je ne sais pas, il faut croire . . . ," "I don't know, one has to believe . . ."

—Exactly, "I don't *know*, one has to *believe*." In other words, it is a question here of belief and not knowledge, of a belief before all knowledge. So whereas the question "Do you believe?" gets asked but not answered in the beginning, it is asked and then answered in the end. And answered with the classical opposition between knowing and believing. The last word, the final injunction, would express the imperative to believe rather than to know, to have faith rather than to see, to give oneself over to belief rather than to remain skeptical. This is a typical schema, a typical progression.

—But we've already noted that this is not the end of the book, that the ellipsis changes everything. First, it indicates that the interview between the two interlocutors—and there do seem to be two here and not, as in "Restitutions," $n + 1$—continues and that we have only a segment or portion of that interview. The ellipses at the beginning and the end make it clear that we are simply listening in on a conversation in progress, not watching a conversion or witnessing a profession of faith from beginning to end. So there is no true final word, no ultimate revelation, no closing imperative in the form "One has to believe!"

Second, the presence of the ellipsis makes your very literal interpretation or translation difficult to maintain. For rather than expressing the priority of belief over knowledge, the phrase "Je ne sais pas, il faut croire . . ." must also be heard—or rather must first and foremost be heard—as expressing skepticism, anything but an unreserved or unexamined faith. This rather colloquial formulation might best be heard as saying, "I don't know, so it seems . . . ," or "I don't know, maybe . . ."; that's a far cry from a declaration of faith. We thus have the same rhetoric in the end as in the beginning—a questioning of the relationship between faith and skepticism or faith and knowledge. So there's no real progression or transformation from beginning to end and certainly no conversion.

—All right, but let me come at this from a different angle. You'll no doubt think I'm groping in the dark here, but just at the level of the image, doesn't the line really take precedence over the circle in *Memoirs of the Blind*? I would see the outstretched arms of Coypel's blind men as a paradigm in this regard, reaching out into an unknown space but reaching out and moving forward nonetheless, or Derrida's hand reaching out to write down a dream in the middle of the night. Isn't the whole idea behind a prosthesis to touch or move beyond oneself, to get beyond the circle of self-reflection in order to move in a line, however crooked or wandering. When asked at the opening of the *Memoirs* exhibition in the fall of 1990 at the Louvre about the relationship between the text and the drawings, Derrida said that the text should be thought of as a sort of prosthesis for the drawings—a kind of blind man's cane. What I think he meant by this is that the text is something for the drawings to lean on, something they can rely on, something to support them. But it also suggests that the text is something that brings them out of themselves, sets them in motion, allows them to come into proximity to one another, to communicate. Without the prosthesis of the text there would be no communication whatsoever; without the prosthesis of rhetoric there would be no way *to read* these images or drawings. That's why I'm arguing for the priority of the prosthesis or the line, and just at the level of the image the line seems to win hands down over the circle: in addition to Coypel's *Error* look at Fragonard's *Blind Man's Buff* or the arm of Christ as it reaches out to heal the blind, the arm itself being a sort of originary prosthesis; and then look at the blind man's staff in Zuccaro and Lucas Van Leyde, Raphael's staff in the Bianchi drawing *Tobias Healing His Father's Blindness*, and the scalpel or styluslike instrument in Rembrandt's rendering of this same theme, and the shovel in the Passarotti drawing, and the wand or stick of Butades, and the pen of Fantin-Latour and the pointer in the drawing of Pieter Bruegel . . . and I could go on, but I think you get the point. Whenever Derrida touches on blindness, some sort of line, some piercing or probing instrument or prosthesis, is not very far away. Just look at the blinding of Samson by the Philistines or the burning stake with which Odysseus blinds Polyphemus, or . . .

—But you just said it yourself, whenever Derrida *touches* on blindness: what is it that these instruments are touching or touching on? Isn't it almost always the *eye*—the most helioform of all the sense organs, as Derrida says citing Plato? The rounded eye is clearly the most dominant image of the book . . . to say nothing of the sun, of Perseus's reflecting shield, and then all those ruins, archways, hollowed bones, eye sockets, glasses, and monocles. Whenever Derrida touches on blindness, it is the image of the circle and the theme of self-reflection that inevitably come up.

—Well *touché*. But even if I concede you the point at the level of the image, I still won't give up on the privilege of the line. I would still want to claim that the book progresses or develops—a bit like an instamatic snapshot, in fact—from the beginning to the end. Isn't it interesting that by far the most colorful drawings, or rather paintings, are found near the very end, as close as possible to revelation, in Jan Provost's *Sacred Allegory* and Clovio's *Saint Paul Striking Elymas with Blindness*. It is like the practice of certain Byzantine icon painters who begin with subdued earth tones and then lay successively brighter colors on these duller ones, moving up the spectrum, as it were, from earth to heaven. I realize that this is not quite so obvious in

Memoirs of the Blind, but when combined with the progress of themes from the fall to resurrection this movement toward color suggests to me that the book is a sort of icon that is supposed to open up a space for contemplation, for a type of religious vision, however that is to be understood.

—But let's look at another chronology, that of the paintings themselves. Although those marked off at the center of the book as self-portraits range in date from Chardin's self-portraits at the end of the eighteenth century to Fantin-Latour's self-portraits at the end of the nineteenth—as if Derrida could see himself most clearly in these more recent representations, as if the Fantin-Latour self-portrait reproduced on the front of the book were for Derrida an emblem for his own eye affliction as he recounts it in the course of the book, the experience, he says, of being unable to close a single, cycloptic eye—the paintings that frame these self-portraits are essentially from a different period. If the self-portraits are of a more recent date, most of the works at the beginning and end of the book are from the sixteenth and seventeenth centuries. So from the point of view of this chronology there would seem to be no movement, as we return in the end of the book to more or less the same period with which we began. This leads me to believe that Derrida is attempting to interrupt—to deconstruct, if you will—a certain tradition of drawing and of conceptualizing drawing by means of a series of hypotheses concerning self-portraiture that are located primarily at the center of the book. As I've been saying all along, the mirror or mirrors at the center of the book would, in effect, both reflect and fold the beginning onto the end and disrupt each and every image throughout. The book thus has the structure not of a line but of a series of concentric rings.

—I agree that the book does seem to return to its origin like the ring or *alliance* you mentioned earlier, but I still don't think it is a coincidence that the ring or *alliance* is, in this context, an image or a symbol drawn from the Judeo-Christian tradition. Is it a coincidence that the ring and all these images of circularity, the emphasis on the eye, on the circuit of reflection in the self-portrait, mark a lineage? I have already mentioned how the book moves from the Old Testament to the New, from the fall to resurrection. But what about the fact that it ends in tears, with the tears of a woman? As Derrida points out, there are very few great blind women in the Western tradition, as if the tradition has seen to it to remember only its great blind men. Yet for many, like Andrew Marvell, the essence of the eye, of man's eye, is not simply to see but to weep, to mourn, a function that has been traditionally assigned to women, so that although the tradition seems to privilege man over woman, it is a certain transformation of man into woman, or at least of vision into weeping, that is ultimately extolled. Although the self-portraits do, as you pointed out, occupy the center of the book,[2] as if they themselves were a series of mirrors around which the book unfolds, what surrounds or enframes these self-portraits are biblical references to the Old and New Testaments. Although *Christ's Healing of the Blind* is also found in the beginning of the book, what really dominates there are images and references to the Old Testament (notice I'm not saying the Hebrew Bible), so that if Christ finds a place among them, it is perhaps only because one can, after the appearance of Christ, which is to say, after the New Testament, begin to read the prophetic traces of him in the Old. But, and this is my point, the line is intact, running from the Old Testament to the New, from man to woman, from eyes to tears, so that, to return to the point of our discussion, it is only appropriate that this difference, this movement, be marked by a slight difference in translation. Don't you too believe this?

—No, because even though Derrida is indeed working in the line and tradition in which he finds himself, he is not simply reproducing them. A deconstructive reading of a text—even a text marked by a series of drawings or paintings—always works with the text and material it is given, but it does so only to question what it has received, the concepts as well as the chronology, the material as well as the modes of its reception. It would indeed be strange if, this late in the game, Derrida were simply accepting the chronology—or, to listen to you, the chromatology and the Christology—that leads from the fall to resurrection. Are you saying that Derrida is in a sense converting in this book or that we are supposed to be converted by him?

—Yes I suppose I am, but I'm also claiming that the whole notion of conversion is being turned around in the process. The traditional notion of conversion is itself being converted, so to speak, but this can take place only *through* or *by means of* the text, which is a sort of confession, autobiography, or self-portrait, a spiritual journey that questions the nature of the truth, the light, and the way. And speaking of the truth, don't forget that the themes of conversion and spirituality were already central to Derrida's

The Truth in Painting. There too the importance of bearing witness to the truth is clearly marked, for the rhetoric of progress or redemption emerges only at the point where the invisible point—the indirect object of faith, if you will—is inscribed, put into words. Remember Derrida's words in *Memoirs of the Blind* as he recalls the way in which the angel Raphael intervenes through Tobias to help cure Tobit's blindness: "It is from this 'vision' of the 'invisible' that he gives, immediately thereafter, the order to write: in order to give thanks, the memory of the event *must be inscribed*" (*MB*, 29).

—But you're confusing the point with the circle. I agree that writing proceeds only with the eclipse of the point or the invisible trait, but once writing begins, need it be characterized as a line, as some linear process? Since you mention Derrida's *The Truth in Painting*, perhaps it will be worth a short detour through it to bring us back to the ring or *alliance* I mentioned earlier.

Like *Memoirs of the Blind*, the essay "Restitutions" in *The Truth in Painting* is a polylogue that tries not so much to build a case and reach some definitive conclusion about Meyer Shapiro's reading of Heidegger's "The Origin of the Work of Art" as to put various points of view on the scene so as to lace and unlace a theory of correspondence. Rather than claim that the shoes that begin and end the essay, Van Gogh's famous pair of shoes, belong to someone other than a peasant woman, as Heidegger claims, or a male city dweller, as Shapiro claims, Derrida questions the theory of correspondence assumed in such attributions. What is there in a painting or drawing that would lead Heidegger or Shapiro to claim that the shoes belong or should be attributed or restituted to one party rather than another? What theory of reference is implied in their readings of painting? What contract or *alliance* is there between Heidegger and Shapiro that would allow them to disagree about who owns the shoes but allow them to agree about what it means to own something or restitute something from the world of art to a supposed world outside of art? All these questions are, I think, behind this seemingly surprising claim in *Memoirs of the Blind*:

This is why the status of the self-portrait of the self-portraitist will always retain a hypothetical character. It always depends on the juridical effect of the title, on this verbal event that does not belong to the inside of the work but only to its parergonal border. The juridical effect calls the third to witness, calls on him to give his word, calls upon his memory more than upon his perception. Like Memoirs, the

Self-Portrait always appears in the reverberation of several voices. And the voice of the other orders or commands, makes the portrait resound, calls it without symmetry or consonance. (*MB*, 64)

The Truth in Painting tries to analyze the contract of meaning on which such a juridical effect depends. It *begins* like this, and it *ends* like this. It does not try to outdo either Shapiro or Heidegger in order to give us the *truth* in painting but merely tries to undo the contract a bit so that we might see that there is no ultimate sanction for it.

—And that's exactly where we disagree—not over the terms or the nature of the contract but over the way in which we engage ourselves in it. I would say that Derrida uses Heidegger in "Restitutions" in much the same way he uses the theological tradition in *Memoirs*; in both cases he is trying to rethink faith, to convert it, by divorcing it from certain presuppositions concerning vision and language. Only through the spiritual progress of *Memoirs* can faith or belief be reinscribed along the lines of a faith that comes always in response to another, to the other of the self-portrait, and only through a rereading of the Heideggerian text can the concept of reliability be reinscribed as a sort of fidelity or faith that precedes any kind of symbolic assurance or contract. You will recall that Heidegger talks throughout "The Origin of the Work of Art" about the reliability of equipment—particularly the reliability of the pair of peasant shoes in the Van Gogh painting. But what is reliability, or what Heidegger calls *Verlässlichkeit*? Derrida writes—bearing witness to his own share of translator's woes:

The word is difficult to translate. I have laboriously specified "thanks to which," "by the force of which," "in virtue of which" because the relation (*Kraft*) is not that of a formal condition of possibility to its conditioned object or of a more profound foundation to what it founds, but of a sort of experience. An experience, let us say for the moment, of *reliability*: you can count on the product. The product is reliable. It is useful only if we can trust in its reliability.[3]

This reliability, if I understand Derrida, is a reliability not on this or that object—this or that direct object—for which we might give reasons for our trust or cite past experiences to justify our confidence. *Verlässlichkeit* is more open than that, more unlimited—indeed more blind. Imagine for a moment not a peasant relying on his or her shoes but a blind man counting on his outstretched hands or relying on his cane as he moves across the earth. Imagine the cane as an exemplary image of reliability, a sort of originary prosthesis that is not simply used within a world of equipment but that first opens up that world to use. Imagine that Derrida is referring to the blind man's cane when he writes in "Restitutions": "That which is *verlässig* deserves confidence, faith, or credit. In this case, the credit is anterior to any symbolic contract forming the object of an agreement signed (explicitly or not) by a nameable subject. It is not cultural any more than it is natural." (*TP*, 349)

—But if that's true, and I believe it is, then isn't your identification of the cane "as an exemplary image of reliability" already just a bit too handy, a bit too useful? I can see why you want to graft this "originary prosthesis" onto "Restitutions" at exactly this point in order to prove your case, in order to have it testify in favor of your argument concerning *Memoirs of the Blind*, but perhaps we need to be just a bit more faithful here to Derrida's text. For it is precisely at this point in "Restitutions" that Derrida begins speaking not of a cane but of a ring in the context of the *Arnolfini Marriage* by Van Eyck. After mentioning the mirror at the center of the scene representing a wedding *per fidem*, a wedding that requires no other witness than the painter himself, and after speaking of the ambivalent role the shoes play in this painting through a series of references to the value of shoes in the Old and New Testaments, one of the voices of "Restitutions" says:

The notion of reliability is here anterior to the opposition between the useful and the sacred. Without reliability there would be no useable product, but nor would there be any symbolic object. The ring, the "words and deeds" required for a hymen *per fidem*, must offer a minimum reliability for the commitment to take place, for the slightest exchange to be possible. This elementary reliability, this fidelity that predates everything, is a sort of ring (*Ring*, in the German), a sort of originary wedding ring. (*TP*, 351)

—And isn't it curious that Derrida takes this detour through the Van Eyck painting in order to bring in a whole series of Judeo-Christian themes right at the moment of speaking of reliability, as if reliability suggested a certain kind of Judeo-Christian faith? After all, Heidegger's examples in "The Origin of the Work of Art" are drawn essentially from either the nineteenth century (Hölderlin, Meyer, Van Gogh) or the ancient Greek world (the temple at Paestum, Sophocles' *Antigone*), yet Derrida brings in all these passages from the Old and New Testaments; he dedicates the essay to J. C. . . . sztejn, and, near the end of the piece, speaks of sin, of ghosts returning from the dead, and of apocalypse. Now I'm not claiming that Derrida is simply Judeo-Christianizing his material; after all it was Van Gogh who called himself J.C., and the debate between Shapiro and Heidegger surely cannot be divorced from the complex question of the relationship between Judaism and Christianity during the twentieth century. But isn't he converting conversion, as I said, trying to find a faith that would precede the opposition between the sacred and the useful, the sacred and the secular? Isn't he trying to get at a reliability that one could count on only insofar as it precedes anything useful, anything one could expect and anticipate, a reliability that is truly blind? In a passage not long after the one you just cited from "Restitutions" one of the voices says:

The *Verlässlichkeit* of the product, "before" its usefulness but as the condition of this usefulness, engages in the belonging to the earth and to the world. This belonging is no longer that of the shoes to the wearer or user, but of both to the world and to the earth, which are given to be thought in their very "combat," according to this engagement and no longer on the basis of the philosophical concepts to which we alluded above. "Thanks to" this reliability, and thanks to the product which presupposes it, the peasant woman is entrusted (says the French translation for *eingelassen*: received, welcomed, admitted into), accorded to the silent call of the earth, to that language without language of correspondence with the earth and the world. (*TP*, 351)

It is this welcoming that is the basis of the converted faith or reliability of which I'm speaking and believe Derrida to be speaking throughout *Memoirs of the Blind*.

—So you are arguing that Derrida is speaking of essentially the same thing in both "Restitutions" and *Memoirs of the Blind*, in which case, once again, there would be no real progress, no real conversion, as you are trying to claim. And I agree; compare what you just read from that 1978 essay to this passage from *Memoirs*: "At the origin of the *graphein* there is debt or gift rather than representational fidelity. More precisely, the fidelity of faith matters more than the representation, whose movement this fidelity commands and thus precedes. And faith, in the moment proper to it, is blind" (*MB*, 30). "The fidelity of faith matters more than the representation": isn't that similar to saying that the fidelity of reliability matters more than the usefulness of any product, and that, in the moment proper to it, reliability is unreliable—that is, that there can be no present reasons or arguments for relying on it? It would be like the moment when a blind man, relying, leaning, or counting solely on his cane, becomes a paradigm for all faith as it approaches a limit where it can no longer give itself reason for belief but must rely only, as you would say, on a reliance without object. But again, Derrida has *always* been saying this, so why do you want to see a linear movement; aren't you yourself relying too much on some myth of progress or some image of the spiritual journey?

—Perhaps, but let me try something more personal—the question of autobiography. What do you make of the fact that Derrida has written in recent years in a much more autobiographical way, for example, in *Memoirs of the Blind*, "Circumfession," and elsewhere? It is true that the theme of self-reflexivity has been in Derrida from the very beginning—just look at *Speech and Phenomenon*—but this autobiographical turn is certainly more pronounced in recent texts and suggests that the subjects of deconstruction now include not only Heidegger, Husserl, and others in the history of philosophy but Derrida himself, the name *Derrida*, and the institution of deconstruction. Isn't this turn to autobiography an attempt to question the image and meaning of a name like *Jacques Derrida*, and isn't this possible only because this name has become something significant for us, because it now has a certain history and tradition of its own to reflect on?

—On the one hand, I have to agree with you, and I won't be contentious by bringing up all the autobiographical elements of *La carte postale* or the constant deconstruction of Derrida's name from as early as *Signature événement contexte*, but why are you putting so much emphasis on the theme of self-portraiture and autobiography? I would agree that one would, in fact, need a certain life to reflect on—and a certain distance from that life—in order to make one's own life, along with the very mode of autobiography, subject for analysis; but in principle autobiography seems to be just another theme or place for the deconstruction of self-presence. If we accept Derrida's argument in *Memoirs* that the self-portrait can be distinguished from the heteroportrait only by means of a juridical effect, then couldn't one say that even *La voix et le phénomène*, which you just mentioned, was, in a certain sense, already a sort of autobiography or at least a work on the structure of autobiography? The very structure of *s'entendre parler* is very much like that of seeing oneself seeing in a mirror. Isn't the self that is posited through hearing oneself speak also always a hypothetical self? Isn't the claim that I myself am speaking similar in structure to the claim that a particular portrait is a self-portrait? Just look at the section "Mirror Writing" in Derrida's 1967 essay "Form and Meaning" in *Margins of Philosophy*, and you'll see what I mean. So, once again, I don't find any great progression or development between Derrida's early works and *Memoirs*. They all seem to turn on similar themes, and even if later works can be read as commentaries on earlier ones, I still don't see what would account for any conversion within the oeuvre itself. To return to the point with which we began, hasn't Derrida always been interested in the ways in which all direct objects, all thetic moments, all claims to self-presence—indeed, all autobiographical claims—are interrupted by blindness?

This helps explain, I think, why the drawings and paintings chosen for the *Memoirs* exhibition are so figurative and contain such clear thematic elements. The point for Derrida has always been to thematize the thematic in order to see what escapes thematization. So I see no real movement or progress from the very beginning of *Memoirs* to the end, or, for that matter, from *La voix et le phénomène* to *Mémoires d'aveugle*.

—Well let me try to illustrate what I mean with another self-portrait, one that Derrida mentions in *Memoirs* by an author he often evokes. It is said that Joyce, in writing *A Portrait of the Artist as a Young Man*, was influenced by accounts of Rembrandt doing his self-portraits and so tried in his writing to embody this circular or reflective structure that you mentioned in the very beginning. Like an artist sitting before his easel drawing a self-portrait by means of a mirror, Joyce tries to reproduce the AB/BA structure of which you spoke. *A Portrait of the Artist as a Young Man* thus begins with Stephen Dedalus's father telling Stephen his very first story as a child, and it ends with an invocation of Dedalus the artificer, who has become Stephen's patron for writing. It begins with Stephen's father saying, "Once upon a time and a very good time it was there was a moocow coming down along the road," and it ends with the hero of the novel writing, "27 April, Old father, old artificer, stand me now and ever in good stead. Dublin 1904/Trieste 1914."[4] But look at all the differences between these fathers. Whereas the first father, the biological one, tells the future artist his first story as a little boy, the second father, the spiritual Dedalus, the father of literary craft, no longer speaks but is spoken to, addressed or rather invoked in *writing* by a narrator who has now assumed the role and position of the artist. And whereas the first story is unmarked by the dates of historical, linear time, the book ends by speaking of the spiritual father in a sort of diary or memoirs. The story thus moves in a line from the time of myth to the time of history, from the time of the circle to that of the line—from Dublin to Trieste, from the fictional time and place of the child destined to become an artist to the times and places of the artist himself. Isn't that the transformation that occurs because of and through the self-portrait, by traversing the mirror, by moving through the invisibility that Derrida describes engulfing the object of the self-portrait, which in the case of the self-portrait is both subject and object? For what we begin to see in the end is that the impossibility of absolute self-presence in the self-portrait, the impossibility of drawing oneself looking at oneself drawing oneself, reveals the impossibility of absolute self-presence in perception itself. This is the insight made possible by the self-portrait. It is the prosthesis that makes the thesis of perception visible, and visible in its invisibility, for the first time. That's why I am insisting on the movement of *Memoirs of the Blind*. Even if the movement is effaced in the end, its fiction was necessary to its effacement, the line and progress of the book essential to seeing that there was no progress.

—Then aren't you coming around to my point of view? I never said there was no movement in the book, only that the movement turned back on itself, that the line you have been arguing for is really an *alliance*. And I agree that the *alliance* or ring is always open, that it never achieves closure, and that it is in the space between the beginning and the end that we would have the impossible and objectless belief with which we began. Between skepticism, "Do you believe this?" and faith, "Do you believe?" we would perhaps be able to glimpse the origin of both skepticism and faith, an origin that would itself be neither skepticism with object nor faith without object, neither transitive vision nor open declaration, but, to put it in other terms, the place of translation itself—impossible, silent, and yet giving rise to so many words, motivating a translation that would be at once impossible and endless. "Vous croyez?"—"Do you believe?" "Do you believe this?" "Do you really think so?" "Do you really believe?" . . .

And by the way—since you bring up Joyce—what do you make of the fact that the little poem about blindness at the beginning of *A Portrait of the Artist as a Young Man* itself has the AB/BA structure of which I've been talking?

—What little poem about blindness?

—Don't you remember?

> Pull out his eyes,
> Apologize,
> Apologize,
> Pull out his eyes.
> Apologize,
> Pull out his eyes,
> Pull out his eyes,
> Apologize.

—Maybe this has come to resemble a self-justification after all, an explanation or a confession. Or perhaps it has just been an attempt to keep the translation open, to open it up beyond an initial set of choices. And perhaps that would be justification enough for a justification in two voices, two voices that would, to cite Derrida, "cross paths, but without ever confirming each other, without the least bit of certainty, in a conjecture that is at once singular and general, the *hypothesis of sight*"—or, in this case, of translation—"and nothing less" (*MB*, 2). Perhaps there is, as I said in the beginning, a certain truth behind the suspicion that this whole dialogue was fabricated to explain to a few sympathetic ears why an identical phrase in French would be translated in two different ways in English. It was, in a certain sense, a chance both to say that we apologize and—to invoke the invocation of Milton once again—to justify the ways of translators to men. So to conclude, since I'm not willing to give up so easily on my thesis of the line, let me briefly recall Milton's *Paradise Lost* just to show how close *Memoirs of the Blind* is to the tradition and the lineage with which it is working. Just a couple of lines into *Paradise Lost* the poet invokes the divine Muses and asks for the gift of poetic sight or insight, praying:

> . . . what in me is dark
> Illumine, what is low raise and support;
> That to the highth of this great argument
> I may assert Eternal Providence,
> And justify the ways of God to men.[5]

And at the very end of the poem Eternal Providence returns, linking the end to the beginning—as you would no doubt notice—but Providence is now guiding not the poet telling the story of the Fall but the primordial couple, Adam and Eve, as they prepare to leave the protected circle of Eden and embark on their journey into the world:

> Some natural tears they dropped, but wiped them soon;
> The world was all before them, where to choose
> Their place of rest, and Providence their guide.
> They hand in hand with wand'ring steps and slow,
> Through Eden took their solitary way. (12.645–49)

From the illumined inner eyes of the poet in the beginning of the poem to the tears at the end, from eyes to hands, from the naked body to the prosthetic one—the fig leaves that are donned just after the Fall transforming the body itself into a prosthesis—and from the closed ring of Eden to the wand'ring steps of the couple after the Fall, are these not the ways of *Memoirs of the Blind*? To justify the ways of translators to men: would this not be, in the end, the endless or epic task of those who have left the natural world of Eden and who must now wander in a world of substitution, prosthesis, and difference, a world of fallen communication and translation, where all writing, all translation, must return endlessly to the place from which it set out so as to start all over, translate anew, relying always on other words, other prostheses?

—I can't believe my ears. Are you actually suggesting that having reached the end we should now return to the beginning—as I've been arguing throughout—so as to renew the contract like an *alliance*, pledge ourselves to it anew, and so do the whole thing over?

—Yes, but imagine for a moment that all we changed were *this*, that in retranslating all we did was reverse the order of the direct object so as to begin with "Vous croyez?" "Do you believe?" and end with "Vous croyez?" "Do you believe this?" beginning, therefore, with an open and unlimited belief, a belief without direct object, and ending in skepticism? Would that change anything in your view?

—Of course, if it all depends on *this* . . .

8

Just a Turn Away

APOSTROPHE AND THE 'POLITICS OF FRIENDSHIP'

> Greek *philia* is reciprocity, exchange of the Same with the Same, but never opening
> to the Other, never discovery of the *Other* inasmuch as I am responsible for him . . .
> never that extreme enjoyment in what makes him always closer to the Good than "I."
>   That is my salutation to Emmanuel Levinas, the only friend—O so distant
> friend—whom I address as "*tu*" and who says "*tu*" to me. This happened not be-
> cause we were young but by a deliberate decision, a pact I hope always to live up to.
> —Maurice Blanchot, *Pour l'amitié*

In the foreword to the *Politics of Friendship* Jacques Derrida recalls that during his 1988–89 seminar at the Ecole des Hautes Etudes, where many of the
ideas for this book were first presented, each session began with the famous
line attributed by Diogenes Laertes to Aristotle, "O my friends, there is no
friend."[1] Having faithfully attended that 1988–89 seminar, I clearly recall
how that line punctuated the entire year, signaling the beginning of each
class, the line not even recognized as a citation the first week, spoken, we
initially thought, by Derrida in his own name, but then later in the year
spoken precisely as a citation from the tradition, spoken to remind us—often with a smile—of what was done with the citation in previous classes, a
citation, then, of a citation, of one of the many previous variations on the
Aristotle line. Sometimes read within the context of another reinscription
of the line within the philosophical tradition, within, for example, Montaigne or Nietzsche or Blanchot, sometimes imaginatively presented in a
new and startling way—and, again, often with a smile—as a gunfight (the
sheriff draws, "O my friends," but the outlaw draws faster, "there is no
friend") or a silent movie in two frames (the romantic opening with the subtitle, "O my friends," and the dramatic conclusion, "there is no friend")—

this little line, this *petite phrase*, became, to paraphrase Proust's description in *Remembrance of Things Past* of a musical passage of Vinteuil, "the national anthem" of our seminar, marking the beginning of the seminar and calling us together as a seminar, allowing us to recall with each reinscription the long history of this phrase in the Western philosophical tradition on friendship. Spoken at the beginning of each class by Derrida, this citation reminded us of the tradition and repeated it, reinvoked it, redirected and readdressed it—to us, its heirs, to those who were, in some sense, constituted as its heirs precisely because it was to us that it was addressed.

For in addition to being a citation about friendship, this line attributed to Aristotle is also an address, an apostrophe, an address to an audience, one presumes, of friends; coming from the mouth of Derrida, it was never certain whether it was simply a citation of an address or an actual address, whether Derrida was citing it—citing it as an apostrophe, as an address—or using it to address us, whom we might have presumed to be, in some sense, his "friends." We were never certain whether Derrida was mentioning or using this line from Aristotle, and it was never certain—not for us and I presume not even for him—whether each subsequent iteration made things any clearer, whether the supplement of a smile indicated an additional set of quotation marks or an accompanying gesture for the address, the citation of an apostrophe or an apostrophe through citation. It would not be unfair to say that that entire seminar and the subsequent book *Politics of Friendship* do little more than unfold the essential ambivalence of this speech situation, of a phrase attributed to Aristotle that includes both an apostrophe—"O my friends"—and a claim about friendship—"there is no friend." At the beginning of each class, then, Derrida would both mention and use, so as to help demonstrate, so as to help perform, through this citation, that there is an essential relationship between friendship and address, between friendship and apostrophe, but also, as we will see, between friendship and mourning.

I thus hope to communicate in this chapter, and perhaps even to enact or perform through this communication, that, paradoxical as it may seem, friendship actually involves a kind of noninteraction and interruption of communication, that the lives of friends do not intersect but in fact diverge and distance themselves from one another the closer they come to one another. I will try to show that friendships exist always *between* individuals, at the limit of any context in which a friend may be identified. It is not that friends must remain indifferent to one another, or that friends become friends through mere geographical distance and isolation, but that friends are those who, in coming together, experience what Blanchot calls the "infinite distance" between them, a distance that proximity often only aggravates and makes more acute. Since friendships are thus to be found only at the very limits of any constituted identities, the only way to evoke the friend is to invoke them, that is, to call on or invite them in *turning toward* them.

Although I will try to keep the promise of the title of this chapter by addressing Derrida's analyses of friendship in the *Politics of Friendship*, I will do so by grafting onto his analyses a series of reflections on a text at the very limits of the Western tradition—namely, Homer. This is appropriate, if not called for, I believe, for at least two reasons: first, because a return to Homer is, as we will see, suggested if not actually called for by Derrida himself in *Politics of Friendship*; second, because the theme of return—and especially a return to the Greeks—has been central to much philosophical debate during the past few decades, debate that is intimately bound up with questions of friendship, guest-friendship, and, as we saw in Chapter 6 and will see again in the next chapter, hospitality. Heidegger, for example, wrote during his 1942 lecture course on *Hölderlin's Hymn "Der Ister"*: "The appropriation of one's own *is* only as the encounter and guest-like dialogue with the foreign."[2]

Thus even if the themes of friendship, guest-friendship, and hospitality might initially appear to be important but well delimited and circumscribed themes *within* the works of thinkers such as Heidegger and Derrida, Blanchot and Levinas, we might take to heart Heidegger's oft-repeated claim—which, with certain caveats and a multiplication of quotation marks, Derrida would probably accept—that a philosophical "reappropriation" of what is proper to one's "own" tradition and historical situation can take place only by means of an encounter with the foreign. From this perspective the themes of hospitality, return, homecoming, and guest-friendship appear not as localized themes or phenomena within Heidegger's or Derrida's corpus but as the very form or expression of Heidegger's rereading of the history of philosophy or Derrida's deconstruction of it. Homecoming would perhaps be the very task and motivation of philosophy itself after Nietzsche.

But what is the nature of homecoming? In *La trace de l'autre* Emmanuel Levinas suggests that already in the founding narrative of Greek culture, that is, in Homer's *Odyssey*, the West had given itself the model of philosophical speculation that would dominate for some two thousand years: philosophy as a speculative journey into the foreign whose passion is nourished by nostalgia and whose aim is always to close the circle of speculation by returning home. To this Greek model of return Levinas opposes the Jewish model of exile: "To the myth of Odysseus returning to Ithaca, we would prefer to oppose the story of Abraham leaving his country forever for an as yet unknown land, and forbidding his servant to take back even his son to the point of departure."[3] But although one may agree with Levinas's criticism of philosophical nostalgia, of an Odysseus who returns to Ithaca as a prototype of the Hegelian hero, it does not follow that any homecoming must be nostalgic or that any narrative—including Homer's—cannot contain within it resources that would forever frustrate this return to one's own or else reveal the foreignness of the home itself. Derrida thus responds in "Violence and Metaphysics" to the way Levinas had read this philosophical nostalgia in Heidegger: "The impossibility of the return doubtless was not overlooked by Heidegger: the original historicity of Being, the originality of difference, and irreducible wandering, all forbid the return to Being *itself* which is nothing. Therefore, Levinas here is in agreement with Heidegger" ("VM," 320 n. 92).

Both Heidegger and Derrida would want to claim that in rereading the ancient Greeks on hospitality and guest-friendship they are neither naively recovering the past nor nostalgically looking back toward it but enacting—perhaps in order to interrupt—a certain relationship or gesture of hospitality or friendship. For it just may be that one returns home always as a guest-friend, that homecoming never takes place without an "encounter and guest-like dialogue with the foreign" that transforms the very identity of the home itself.

With this encounter in mind we are, I believe, invited to read Derrida's *Politics of Friendship* as not only an extended rereading or exposition of the philosophical treatment of friendship from Plato and Aristotle to Montaigne, Kant, Nietzsche, and Blanchot, but as a *call* or *invocation*: a call from those who, both now and in the past, have explicitly or implicitly challenged certain philosophical assumptions concerning friendship—for example, the privileging of sameness, presence, or proximity—and an invocation of those distant others who might receive or hear such a call. Derrida's deconstructive reading of the philosophical tradition surrounding friendship might thus itself be thought of as an *act* or *performance* of guest-friendship. By following both the arguments and strategies of his work, we will see that all speaking *of* the friend or *of* various texts on friendship is interrupted by an apostrophe coming from the friend or from these texts, an apostrophe from and to a limit of friendship where no knowledge of the friend is possible, where all speaking *of* the friend or *of* the various texts on friendship is interrupted by an apostrophe *to* and *out of* death, an apostrophe whose addresser and addressee must remain radically unknown.

It is thus not by chance that Derrida begins his text on friendship not with a statement or constative but with a performative, that is, with an apostrophe that is not exactly or not directly from Aristotle but from Montaigne's essay "De l'amitié," an apostrophe in French, therefore, but one that is itself a citation and a translation, that is itself, then, *as* an apostrophe, already turned toward an entire tradition of speaking of friendship that goes back to the Greeks. This apostrophe—"O mes amis, il n'y a nul amy," which might be rendered, "O my friends, there is no friend"—was originally attributed by Diogenes Laertes to Aristotle, as Montaigne himself recalls, but has been repeated or reworked throughout the entire tradition from Kant to Nietzsche to Blanchot and, now, Derrida. If the very structure of friendship is more like a vocation, invocation, or invitation than a statement or constative, then it is significant that Derrida begins with this apostrophe, punctuates his entire work with its various modifications and inflections, and ends with a final apostrophe or invocation— "O my democratic friends."[4]

This strange apostrophe—"O my friends, there is no friend"—interests Derrida because of both its aporetic structure (a performative or vocative to "friends" before the comma or virgula, a constative or claim that there is no friend after) and its form *as* an apostrophe. For it will be the very values associated with the vocative (performativity, singularity, absence, withdrawal, and so on) that will disrupt any attempt to produce a coherent and systematic discourse on the nature of friendship. Derrida's "deconstruction" of the concept or category of "friendship" thus proceeds by sketching out a series of aporias encountered in the concepts traditionally used to define the nature or essence of friendship or the friend, concepts such as presence, communication, likeness (the friend as another self) and proximity. In his reading of the *Nicomachean Ethics*, for example, Derrida shows the aporias that arise when Aristotle tries to distinguish true friendship, friendship based on virtue, from friendships grounded in pleasure or utility. If the virtuous friend is, as Aristotle says, another self, then there would seem to be no need for such a friend, since such a friend would have nothing—not even virtue, since his virtue would be like his friend's—to offer. Unless, of course, such a friendship is best or highest precisely because, as Aristotle suggests, it is based not on exchange but mutual virtue, being an end in itself and not a means. But then what would one friend see in the other except his own mirror image, himself as another, making friendship into a sort of narcissistic circuit of self-reflection? Although Aristotle explicitly encounters and recognizes these aporias, he still seems to think that a quasi-systematic analysis of friendship can be carried out, that three different species of friendship can be distinguished and defined.

Such a tradition of speaking *of* friendship or *of* the friend would remain more or less intact, it seems, right up through Nietzsche, who reverses many of the values of friendship (privileging the enemy over the friend, absence over presence) but remains nonetheless beholden to the same oppositional logic. But in the work of Maurice Blanchot, Derrida appears to find a radical break with this tradition, a break that consists not only in the terms used to describe friendship but in the mode or voice in which friendship or the friend is to be addressed. Derrida thus lets himself be guided in *Politics of Friendship* by Blanchot so as to interrupt a tradition bent on defining the nature or essence of friendship and the friend. For Blanchot it is important that the friend not be analyzed, compared, or defined; indeed, the friend "is" someone who cannot be spoken *of* but only *to*—and spoken to *as* the very apostrophe or turning of an invocation. Derrida writes before citing Blanchot:

What happens politically when the "Who?" of friendship then distances itself from all these determinations? In its "infinite imminence"—let us listen to Blanchot—the "who" exceeds even the interest in knowledge, all forms of knowledge, truth, proximity, even as far as life itself, and the memory of life. It is not yet an identifiable, private or public "I." Above all, as we are going to hear, it is some "one" *to whom* one speaks (even only to tell him or her that there is no friend), but *of whom* one does not speak. (*PF*, 294)

Derrida's *Politics of Friendship* lets itself be oriented or drawn by this Blanchotian notion of friendship *in* or *as* apostrophe so as to subvert and displace the terms traditionally privileged in discourses on friendship: proximity, presence, self-identification, and so on. Although it is at the end of Blanchot's book *Friendship* that the apostrophic nature of the friend finds its most precise articulation, Blanchot himself uses the very apostrophe attributed to Aristotle by Diogenes Laertes at the very end of another text on friendship, his little book *Michel Foucault tel que je l'imagine*. Before turning, then, to

Friendship, let us listen to the final words addressed by Blanchot about—or perhaps *to*—Michel Foucault in the book written about or destined *for* him:

Philia, which for the Greeks and even for the Romans remains the model of what is excellent in human relations (with the enigmatic character that opposing demands gives it, at once pure reciprocity and generosity without return), can be welcomed as a heritage that is always capable of being enriched. Friendship was perhaps promised to Foucault as a posthumous gift, beyond all the passions, all the problems of thought, all the dangers of life that he felt for others more than for himself. By bearing witness to a work that needs to be studied (read without bias) rather than praised, I hope to remain faithful, however awkwardly, to the intellectual friendship that his death, for me so painful, allows me to declare to him today: while I recall the phrase attributed by Diogenes Laertes to Aristotle: "O my friends, there is no friend."[5]

Notice, first, that it is friendship or *philia* itself, in its "enigmatic character," that is to be welcomed as a heritage to be enriched. It is *philia* itself that must be welcomed, received, (re)admitted into our midst by a friendly gesture so that we may give to and enrich it. But does this mean that in so doing we ever really receive friendship into our lives, that we ever really make it present? In the case of Foucault, friendship seems to have been promised to him, says Blanchot, as a *posthumous* gift. Friendship would appear to be that which is welcomed from the past and promised to the future, received from out of death and given to it, borne witness to, declared, and recalled only in and from out of the death of the friend.

To confirm this, I turn now to "Friendship," to the few pages that bear this title in a book of the same name. These pages of Blanchot's are truly extraordinary for the way they drain a kind of eulogy of all its pathos, while still conveying a remarkable if enigmatic force. The essay is written, as we say, "on the occasion" of George Bataille's death—whose proper name appears only once in the essay, about halfway through; whose books are mentioned, although none by name; and whose life, much of which Blanchot shared, is evoked in only the vaguest terms. If this is a eulogy—and I believe it is—then it is as close as possible to a eulogy without object, as close as possible, to paraphrase the previous chapter, to eulogizing without a direct object. Blanchot begins:

How could one agree to speak of this friend? Neither in praise nor in the interest of some truth. The traits of his character, the forms of his existence, the episodes of his life, even in keeping with the search for which he felt himself responsible to the point of irresponsibility, belong to no one. There are no witnesses. Those who were closest say only what was close to them, not the distance that affirmed itself in this proximity, and distance ceases as soon as presence ceases. . . . Everything we say tends to veil the one affirmation: that everything must fade and that we can remain loyal only so long as we watch over this fading movement, to which something in us that rejects all memory already belongs.[6]

Near the very end of a book entitled *Friendship*, on its edge, Blanchot remembers Bataille by speaking of a fidelity that would consist in forgetting. He goes on to speak of the press there will be in the wake of Bataille's death to recuperate and gather his work, to publish the complete edition, to remember him and rewrite his life and work according to the dictates of a literary history. Such would be the betrayal of the one who would have asked himself who he was and would have received as a response "the openness of a 'Who?' without answer," an "'indefinite 'Who?'" We must, says Blanchot, "give up trying to know those to whom we are linked by something essential" and "greet them in the relation with the unknown in which they greet us as well, in our estrangement" (*F*, 291).

   Blanchot then offers at this point in his "eulogy" of Bataille what might be considered his most explicit "definition" of friendship, even if such a definition of the friend and of friendship threatens all our knowledge of the friend, all our speaking of the friend, and, as a result, the possibility of any stable, theoretical discourse about the friend and about friendship. Blanchot writes, at the very limit, it seems, of the philosophical tradition that has spoken of friendship since Plato's *Lysis* and Aristotle's treatises on ethics:

Friendship, this relation without dependence, without episode, yet into which all the simplicity of life enters, passes by way of the recognition of the common strangeness that does not allow us to speak of our friends but only to speak to them, not to make of them a topic of conversations (or essays), but the movement of understanding in which, speaking to us, they reserve, even on the most familiar terms, an infinite distance, the fundamental separation on the basis of which what separates becomes relation. (*F*, 291)

It is separation and not union that the friend brings us, distance and not proximity, a worklessness rather than an activity, a listening rather than a speech, a speaking *to* rather than a speaking *of*, a reserve rather than an openness, death rather than life. It might thus seem that the death of the friend, not their possible but their actual death, would be, contrary to all common sense, the accomplishment and fulfillment of friendship. Yet "when

the event itself comes, it brings this change: not the deepening of the separation but its erasure; not the widening of the caesura but its leveling out
and the dissipation of the void between us where formerly there developed
the frankness of a relation without history" (*F*, 292).

It is proximity, presence, and life that bring us distance, absence, and
death—a distance *in* proximity, an absence *through* presence, death as the
"frankness of a relation" *in* life. Hence when the event itself occurs, history
comes, along with the work of mourning, to inscribe the event, to speak *of*
the death and of the friend and no longer *to* them. This way of mourning,
of incorporating, of speaking of the friend in their death, may appear to
be an act of friendship but is in fact a betrayal. And so we must mourn differently, mourn without memory. Blanchot concludes his funeral oration
of?—to?—beyond?—George Bataille:

Undoubtably we will still be able to follow the same paths, we can let images come,
we can appeal to an absence that we will imagine, by deceptive consolation, to be
our own. We can, in a word, remember. But thought knows that one does not remember: without memory, without thought, it already struggles in the invisible
where everything sinks back to indifference. This is thought's profound grief. It
must accompany friendship into oblivion.

To think the friend, and perhaps to think friendship, would be to accompany it into forgetting. Blanchot is speaking here, as the title of these pages
and of the book in which they are found would seem to suggest, not simply
about his friendship with George Bataille but about the entire tradition that
speaks of friendship. Must we not accompany it, in what it already knows
and has thought, into forgetting? Are we already in fact approaching the end
of the history of friendship, the end of a certain philosophical discourse
and thought concerning friendship? It might appear that in *Politics of Friendship* Derrida is tracing just such a discourse as it develops from Plato and
Aristotle to Blanchot, from an attempt to define or describe the nature or
essence of friendship in terms of presence and proximity to the final realization that friendship cannot be so defined and so must be invoked in
other ways, through other forms of "writing," other modes of address.

Yet, as always, things are never so simple in Derrida. Indeed, most of
the three hundred pages of the *Politics of Friendship* are devoted to finding
elements or gestures within Plato, Aristotle, Cicero, Montaigne, Kant, Nietzsche, Schmitt, and Heidegger that do not fit so neatly into this attempt to
define the nature of friendship, elements that suggest, sometimes appar-

ently against the author's intent, a friendship that always exceeds thematization, that interrupts proximity, presence, and self-identity, gestures that interrupt the theoretical discourse on friendship and seem to accompany it into oblivion. Derrida does not simply oppose Blanchot's discourse concerning friendship to the more traditional discourses of Aristotle, Montaigne, and Kant; for there are, in these latter, gestures that resemble those of Blanchot, gestures that are the result of the aporias that emerge when one tries to understand friendship in a thematic way. In this sense Derrida's reading of Plato, Aristotle, Cicero, and others constitutes a return not to some stable and identifiable tradition of friendship to work with or against, a tradition to be constantly confronted or "taken on," but a return to the very elements of friendship that Derrida will find most clearly articulated in Blanchot.

In the spirit of such a return I here propose to supplement the canonical texts on friendship that Derrida analyzes with an even earlier—indeed the earliest—"account" of friendship in the West, one that, to my eyes, presents just as powerful a critique of the understanding of friendship in terms of presence, self-identification, and proximity as any other in *Politics of Friendship*. Derrida himself provides for this transition. About a third of the way through *Politics of Friendship*, in the context of a discussion of the exemplary nature of the "fraternal relation" in the Western tradition on friendship, Derrida cites the conclusion of Emile Benveniste's article on *philos* in his celebrated work *Indo-European Language and Society*. After a rather detailed and highly suggestive reading of the adjective *philos* in Homer, Benveniste writes, "All this wealth of concepts was smothered and lost to view once *philos* was reduced to a vague notion of friendship or wrongly interpreted as a possessive adjective. It is high time we learned again how to read Homer."[7]

I thus suggest taking up this invitation or challenge of Benveniste via Derrida by looking at the semantic field surrounding what is usually considered friendship or friendly relations in Homer's *Iliad*. As we will see, contrary to what the lexicons would have us believe, the verb *philein*, the adjective *philos*, and the noun *hē philotēs* do not first and foremost *refer* to some relation of propriety or ownness or else to some personal sentiment or affection but, rather, *mark* or inscribe a limit between proximity and distance. These words in Homer do not so much *describe* some relation of possession or personal sentiment but *enact* or *inscribe* a relation of proximity that is in the process of being either interrupted or recuperated, destroyed or reaffirmed. As in Blanchot, then, the Homeric friend is not so much spoken *of* but *to*, and spoken *to* only at the limits of proximity, presence, and life.

According to Liddell and Scott, *philos* or *philein* would initially refer to a kind of affective relation between the members of a family, clan, community, or army. A son, wife, uncle, or comrade might thus all be called *philos*, that is, loved or cherished or thought dear by one or many people. The verb *philein* would refer to this act of loving or cherishing or holding dear, or else to the sentiment or affection for the loved or cherished one. The verb can thus be used to designate a whole range of amicable relations, from simple consideration to hospitality to sexual love, this latter often being described as the result of some form of bewitchment or seduction.

Now, as Liddell and Scott and many others have noted, the adjective *philos* is often used in Homer to express relations where no apparent sentiment or affection is present, where the context suggests a relation that is often quite the opposite. In these cases it would seem to express not some "subjective" relation of affection but a more "objective" relation of propriety, kinship, or possession. Instead of translating *philos huios* as "dear son" or "cherished son," one would translate it simply as "my son," instead of "dear wife," "my wife," rather than "beloved comrade," "my comrade." There are, of course, many cases in Homer where it is more or less impossible to decide between these two renderings, between a relation of sentiment and one of possession. This is especially true when a relationship between the body and itself is being described. One cannot decide whether the Homeric character is speaking of an affective relation with a part of his body or a relation of possession with his body or thoughts. Homer translators thus opt for "my heart" in one case, "dear heart" in another, "my thought" here, "the thought that is dear or close to me" there, "dear clothing" at one point, "my clothing" in another.

Finally, the verb *philein* can be used to refer to the immortals' love of humans, a love that is emblematic, I will contend, of all the other relations of *philein* and *philos* insofar as it almost always explicitly translates a relation of proximity—even though we do not yet quite know what *proximity* means. This use of *philein* seems to reveal most clearly the common denominator of all the others, a proximity that depends on no objective measure but, rather, on a *turning*. In the *Iliad* Diomedes prays to Athena: "If ever with kindly [friendly] thought thou stoodest by my father's side [*phila phroneousa parestēs*] amid the fury of battle, even so do thou now be likewise kind to me [*eme philai*]" (5.116–17). Later in the same book Athena herself says to Diomedes: "I verily stand by thy side and guard thee [*soi d'ē toi men egō para th'histamai ēde phylassō*]" (5.809). Five books later Odysseus addresses a similar prayer to this same goddess: "Hear me . . . thou that dost ever stand by my side [*paristasai*] in all manner of toils, nor am I unseen of thee where'er I move [*oude se lēthō kinumenos*]; now again be thou my friend [*me philai*], Athena" (10.278–80). It appears here that the love of gods for mortals does not simply manifest itself by proximity but *is* this very proximity. To love is to be close to, to stand by [*paristēmi*], to watch over [*phylassō*]. Proximity is neither the result nor the cause of love or affection but its equivalent or translation. Moreover, the verb *philein* is used not simply to *refer* to some relation in the past but to *invoke* it in the present, to put it to work. Odysseus and Diomedes are not simply referring to Athena's love but asking for it, calling on her to be close to them in the present as she has been in the past. As for the precise limits and boundaries of this proximity, the distances that are involved, the only adequate response can be: to be proximate is to be just a turn away, distanced by just a turn or turning of prayer, persuasion, or hospitality, by an invocation or apostrophe.[8]

All the other uses of *philein* in Homer can be read on the basis of this proximity that is called on in times of danger. Indeed, it is remarkable just how many times this network is deployed when something or someone is being threatened or is in the process of being lost. A son, for example, is often called dear or close just before—indeed, almost exclusively just before—being killed. Priam calls Paris his "dear son [*philon huion*]" (3.307) just before the duel with Menelaus that he cannot bear to watch. Polydorus is said to be the youngest of Priam's sons and "dearest [*philtatos*] in his eyes" (20.410) at the very moment when Achilles slays him and a relationship of proximity is severed. Hector is called "dear son" and "dear child [*philon tekos*]" by Priam (22.35, 38), "my child [*teknon emon*]," "dear child [*phile teknon*]," even "dear plant [*philon thalos*], born of mine own self," by Hecuba (22.82, 84, 87), as they beseech him not to do battle with Achilles. In mourning for Hector just two books later, Hecuba calls him "far dearest [*polu philtate*] to my heart of all my children" (24.748). The *pathos* of these scenes thus comes from watching the proximity or dearness between parents and sons interrupted. It comes from witnessing the failed efforts of Priam and Hecuba to "persuade the heart of Hector" not to face Achilles (22.90–91). It comes from a limit of proximity that is at once invoked in the pleas for obedience and interrupted in disobedience. As the fates of Patroclus and Hector both show, death and glory are the tragic results of not heeding the counsels of those who are near and dear.

One thus often calls a comrade "dear" just before or right at the moment of the comrade's demise. There are literally scores of examples of this phenomenon, but I will restrict myself here, for reasons that will become clear shortly, to Achilles' relation to Patroclus—perhaps the *locus classicus* of *philia* in the Western tradition. In book 17, for example, we learn that although Achilles' mother, Thetis, had often spoken with her son in private of Zeus's purpose, she had not told him "how great an evil had been brought to pass, that his comrade, far the dearest [*philtatos*], had been slain" (17.409–11). Later in the same book Antilochus is sent to Achilles to tell him the "woeful tale" that "his comrade, far the dearest [*philtatos*], is slain" (17.641–42, 655). The pathos of Achilles discovering Patroclus's death is thus put on display through this intimacy established between the purpose of Zeus, Thetis's knowledge, and the narrator's revelation of this purpose and knowledge to the reader or listener. Patroclus's death is thus initially known to all but the one to whom Patroclus was most dear—the one to whom he was closest. Achilles' discovery is thus made all the more striking to us, as we in effect watch Achilles lose Patroclus right before our eyes, the relation of proximity severed in full view. Finally learning of Patroclus's death, Achilles cries out, "my dear comrade is dead, even Patroclus, whom I honored above all my comrades, even as mine own self [*ison emē kephalē*]" (18.80–82); thus he vows to seek out Hector, "the slayer of the man I loved [*philēs kephalēs*]" (18.114).

One could multiply examples in Homer of this relationship between dearness and death, examples of someone being called *philos* right at the moment a relation of dearness is being threatened or lost. Even events and things are sometimes called dear only at the precise moment they risk being taken away. A "return," for example, can be said to be dear but is said to be so only when threatened. Achilles says as he prepares for battle that he will "not return to [his] dear [*philēn*] native land" (18.101), and he worries that the Greeks will be robbed of their "desired return [*philon . . . noston*]" (16.82).

The strategy or effect here is not, it seems, simply to generate sympathy for the one who is at the point of losing someone or something. The words connected with *philein* mark the "place" or "moment" where proximity is interrupted, where death or sleep comes to turn someone toward its fold. In almost every case such words are invoked at extreme moments of suffering or misfortune, moments when proximity itself risks being lost. The parts of the body are thus called *philos* when the self is in dialogue with itself, when it is fearful and so must gather itself, pull itself together, regain self-control. Hence the word *philos* marks a limit between inside and outside, integrity and fragmentation, possession and loss, life and death. This is why it is often impossible in translating *philos* to choose between "dear heart" and "my heart," "dear return" and "my return." These words mark the text like a kind of tomb or sign, a *sēina* at the limits of life and death, immortals and mortals, one mortal and another or one mortal and himself. They inscribe either the last moment of gathering and the first moment of fragmentation and loss, or else the final attempt to stave off such fragmentation and loss. And that is why, finally, there are so many instances where life or spirit itself is said to be "dear" at the very moment of being lost. Priam cries to Hector to come within the Trojan walls lest he be "reft of [his] dear life [*philēs aiōnos*]" (22.58), and two books later Apollo announces that Achilles "reft goodly Hector of [dear] life [*philon ētor*]" (24.50). Death is thus conceived as a distancing of what is close, not necessarily the distancing of what adheres inside but the *loss of proximity itself*.

In death one is beyond relations of proximity, which is to say, no longer just a turn away. So it is with Agastrophus, who "lost *philon . . . thumon*"—that is, who lost his life, dear life, his own dear life (11.342). Having been hit by Aias, Hector says that he thought he would go down to Hades after having "gasped forth . . . *philon aion etor*" (15.252)—that is, his *dear* life, *his* dear life, both that which is "subjectively" *dear* to him and that which is "objectively" *his*. At this crucial turning point it is impossible to choose between the two translations: Hector is about to lose the life that is dear to him, dear because close, close because his, and his because it is leaving him, going down into Hades—in a word, a single word, a life that is *philos*.

We have, I recall, indulged in this extended digression under the pretext of answering an invitation and a challenge in order to show that at the very beginning of Western literature there may be a thought of the friend, indeed of all friendly or amicable relations, that is founded not on relations of affection or possession but on the withdrawal of such relations. Indeed, the traces of friendship in Homer do not designate a nature or essence of friendship as either affection or possession but, rather, mark a *limit*—a limit that is, as such, always in withdrawal. Such a rereading of Homer demonstrates that Homeric friendship is not something to be described but only marked, not a quality to be evoked but a relation or limit to be invoked, performed, in Homer's case, *sung*.

Perhaps we can now draw together the previous insights concerning vocation or apostrophe with those concerning *philos* and *philein* to show why Derrida's *Politics of Friendship* must be read not only as an analysis of friendship but as an enactment or performance of it, to show how the interpretative aspects of Derrida's text are constantly working with this performative aspect, this invocation of, by, and in the tradition of thought about friendship from Aristotle through Blanchot. We saw above many instances in which sons or comrades were not simply *referred to* as *philos* at the moment they were threatened with death but directly called *philos*, *apostrophied* as such. There are, however, other, very strange apostrophes where it is not some actor in the narrative who apostrophes another but the poet himself who apostrophes or addresses one of the actors. This invariably happens when the personage is in danger of being wounded or killed, thereby revealing an at least structural connection between *philos* or *philein* and the vocative. It is as if vocative relations, like the relations of *philein*, always mark the withdrawal of the one who is dear or close or one's own, since it is only *on the basis of this withdrawal* that one ever is dear or close or one's own: a friend is indeed someone to whom you can always turn, although this someone turns away from every determinate relation or attempt at identification and so essentially is only as this perpetual withdrawal. Significantly, then, the vast majority of these apostrophes concern Patroclus and are gathered around the scenes of his death. When describing, for example, the events of Patroclus's death, the poet occasionally breaks out of his detached role as narrator to inform Patroclus of something he could have never known on his own. Having earlier asked Patroclus—in a question that resembles those sometimes asked of the Muses—to tell him whom he slew, the poet turns to the injured Patroclus to tell him whom it was who first tried to slay him: "[Euphorbus] it was that first hurled his spear at thee, knight Patroclus, yet subdued thee not" (16.812–15). Or again, at the very moment of Patroclus's death the poet turns one last time, as if to mark the fold of death that is coming to take his favorite away: "Then, thy strength all spent, didst thou answer [Hector], knight Patroclus: . . . . Even as he thus spake the end of death enfolded him [*telos thanatoio kalypse*]" (16.844, 855).

What are we to make of these curious vocatives or apostrophes? Because of their proximity to Achilles' apostrophes of Patroclus an implicit identification is established between Achilles and the poet. Because Patroclus is asked questions similar in form to those asked the Muses, there is an identification of Patroclus and the Muses. And because Patroclus seems to take over an important simile at one point for the narrator, there is an identification of Patroclus and the poet. As such, the name *Patroclus* comes to mark a limit between the living and the dead, between what can be put into narrative and what cannot. It is as if the proper name *Patroclus*, like all proper names, although in an exemplary fashion, marks the place where the unique and singular gets put into language, able thereafter to be compared, repeated, no longer a unique expression of the unique but a mere figure of it. The arrival of the proper name would thus be part of the work of mourning; it would mark both the faithful inscription and the betrayal of a friend who must always remain unique, singular, incomparable. Montaigne already said of Etienne de la Boétie, to whose memory the essay "On Friendship" is dedicated: "If you press me to tell why I loved him, I feel that this cannot be expressed, except by answering: Because it was he, because it was I [*Par ce que c'estoit luy; par ce que c'estoit moy*]." (He says this, interestingly, just lines after evoking the relationship between Patroclus and Achilles.)

If every friendship is incomparable, how is one to speak of it? If every friend is unique and singular, how is one to speak of the friend without betraying that singularity, without using a language that would be understood, used, and repeated by others? The proper name would thus mark a limit here. Derrida writes in *Signsponge*, "The proper name . . . should have no meaning and should spend itself in immediate reference," but "its inscription in language always affects it with a potential for meaning, and for no longer being proper."[9]

It is perhaps not insignificant, then, that in book 19 of the *Iliad*, after Patroclus's death, Achilles at first calls on Patroclus in his death in the second person singular—calling him "you" or "thou": "Ah verily of old, thou too, O hapless one, dearest of my comrades" (19.314–15). Even in his dreams, when the spirit of Patroclus comes to admonish him, saying, "Thou sleepest, and hast forgotten me, Achilles" (23.69), Achilles responds, apostrophes, "Wherefore, O head beloved, art thou come hither, and thus givest me charge about each thing?" (23.94–95). But when a limit has to be set to mourning, when the Trojan youths have been sacrificed and the funeral games for Patroclus are set to begin, the poet remarks: "Then [Achilles] uttered a groan, and called on his dear comrade by name [*philon d'onomēnen hetairon*]: 'Hail, I bid thee, O Patroclus, even in the house of Hades'" (23.178–79). Hence the proper name returns in a vocative as a sign of the work of mourning. The vocative with a personal pronoun and not yet a proper name thus seems to mark that moment of extreme pain, extreme loss, where the friend is momentarily lost before becoming reidentified and reintegrated into narrative—even if the possibility of calling someone by the vocative form of a personal pronoun perhaps implies that mourning is already underway, that incorporation, however preliminary, is already beginning to take place, that what Blanchot called the "infinite distance" between friends is already beginning to be eclipsed.

The vocative, the pure vocative, would thus mark an impossibility—the impossibility of addressing a unique other uniquely, an impossibility that, I am arguing, is nonetheless traced out in every vocative, in every inscription of *philein*. The vocative would mark the impossibility of speaking without the possibility of repetition and, thus, without the possibility of betrayal. Derrida writes in *Politics of Friendship* before referring us in a footnote to his essay "Signature Event Context," "it is impossible to address only one person, only one man, only one woman. To put it bluntly and without pathos, such an address would have to be *each time one single time*, and all iterability would have to be excluded from the structure of the trace" (*PF*, 215).[10] This would be the promise of every vocative, a promise that will never be accomplished in a present but will always remain to come, as a promise to and from the friend. That is why Derrida's *Politics of Friendship* is and must be not only an explication but an invocation, an extended apostrophe. The friend is someone who essentially *is*, as in Homer, "just a turn away"—that is, someone who is not simply waiting there to be turned to but someone whose very being as a friend consists in being just a turn away, perpetually turned to and in withdrawal.

Friendship is thus not so much a relation of affection or possession but a line of separation, a boundary between proximity and distance, a limit that would perhaps itself be the mark of an infinite distance between friends, between ourselves and what is dear. The closer we come to this boundary, the more we interpret, scrutinize, or define it as either a subjective relation of affection or an objective relation of possession, the more it

recedes. For this is not simply some abstract limit between binary oppositions; it is the trace of the friend, of the one who is betrayed in being
brought near, beyond all ruse or indifference. It is the trace of the friend's
withdrawal or disappearance, of his or her constant retreat into what is beyond any conceptual grasp, beyond any text through which we might come
to terms with such a death, beyond the power even of our mourning—even
if it is always only this trace that we mourn.

Friendship begins in mourning, as does the tradition that speaks of
friendship. Derrida's *Politics of Friendship* is thus itself a work of mourning
as well as of friendship. Derrida himself turns toward the tradition that
speaks of friendship throughout *Politics of Friendship* because there is something within this tradition that is always in withdrawal, a limit that cannot
be thematized but only inscribed, marked, or enacted, that cannot be spoken *of* but only *to*, opened up to what exceeds all knowledge and all memory. If there is something within the tradition of friendship that does not
strictly speaking belong to it, that is always in withdrawal, whether it be in
Plato or Aristotle, Nietzsche or Heidegger, or, indeed, in Homer, then reading the tradition as an act of friendship would involve not appropriating
this relation or this limit but, I would suggest, turning like it, repeating or
inscribing it as the only way of marking its singularity. This is why *Politics
of Friendship* is a work of mourning, not simply a work *on* mourning but
a work *of* mourning, and it is why we can never know but can only begin
to mourn the guest-friend, why perhaps, in Homer, one can never know
whether the guest-friend is a mortal or a god, and why the guest-friend is,
in the end, neither simply present nor absent but, between sentiment and
the interruption of this sentiment, between possession and the loss of this
possession, always just a turn away.

9

Hospitality as an Open Question

DECONSTRUCTION'S WELCOME POLITICS

> Hospitality has its laws. They are not written, but they help make up the values
> and principles of a civilization. They sometimes imply rights, sometimes duties. . . .
> The industrialized nations, obedient to a cold rationality, must have unlearned
> hospitality. Time is precious, space limited. There reigns in these countries a lack
> of availability, that is, of generosity and of freedom, since everything is calculated,
> everything measured. Doors are closed. As are hearts.
> —Tahar Ben Jelloun, *Hospitalité française*

Before rushing into an analysis of Derrida's recent work on hospitality, let
me linger here a bit on the threshold. For it is always on or from a threshold, from a limit between inside and out, that hospitality is offered or given
or, as we say, *extended*. We extend our hospitality by opening our arms,
doors, or borders, always from a threshold, from a limit marking what is
our own—or what we take to be our own—from what is not. Although
the threshold marks the limits of one's own, and so is always exclusionary,
selective, oftentimes harsh and implacable, there would be no hospitality
without it. We would thus always do well, in considering hospitality, to
linger a while on the threshold, on this place of transition that is so easily
overlooked as we rush from one community, experience, or way of life to
another. One can never really understand hospitality without considering
the phenomenon of the threshold, even if, as we will see, our understanding of hospitality as a concept will always be frustrated by the fact that it is
precisely a threshold phenomenon—another way of saying that it is and
must remain, in its very conceptuality, an *open question*.

I begin, then, still on the threshold, by asking the good Platonic question of the essence or concept of hospitality itself. What is hospitality? *Ti*

esti hē xenia; What is it and what should it be? Can it be recognized, realized, accomplished? When we speak, say, of "Greek hospitality," and then again in the United States of "southern hospitality," we are, it seems, implicitly referring to some idea or essence that would be common to the rituals and practices of these two very different cultures. But what is this common trait or characteristic that would define the essence of hospitality? In what follows I will try to argue not only that deconstruction allows us to approach this question, and that deconstruction in fact does much to provide us with an answer, but that deconstruction itself is in some sense the answer, for deconstruction is itself a kind of hospitality and hospitality, as an open question, always a kind of deconstruction.

Deconstruction and hospitality, deconstruction as hospitality, deconstructive hospitality—these are phrases to make the critics laugh. For those who know of the term *deconstruction* only from newspaper articles, ads, comics, or titles like *Deconstructing Harry*, deconstructive hospitality would sound like the ultimate oxymoron or contradiction in terms, suggesting not some determined form of hospitality but the undoing or dismantling, even the destruction, of it, a form of nihilism that would signal the end of Western culture and so the end of hospitality as we know it. But beyond this popular misunderstanding, one might hear in the phrase *deconstructive hospitality* something like an inversion or perversion of hospitality. A deconstructive parody or send-up of hospitality proper: imagine, for example, to indulge in fancy for a moment, a guest arriving at the home of someone whom he believes to be his host, only to find himself being invited in not as a guest to be offered hospitality by his host but as one expected to provide hospitality to his host, invited in—to stretch the limits of inversion—not as a guest to be offered hospitality by the host but *as* the hospitality to be offered to his host, invited in not to partake in a meal offered to him by the host but to *be* the meal for his host. Imagine further, to stretch things to the point of the ridiculous, that having seen the laws of reception so transgressed, the tables of hospitality so dramatically turned, the guest transformed into an intended victim feels justified in effecting a reversal of his own, giving the hospitality he should have received from his host *to* his host, but now pushing that hospitality to the point of retaliation, the guest offering his host not only a little something to drink but enough to get him drunk, enough even to get him to pass out, so that he, the guest, might escape this abode of perverted hospitality unhindered, although not before, to give the story away, shoving a sharp stick in his host's eye. Such a story could easily be written off as a deconstructive parody were it not for the fact that it comes, as you will have recognized, not from Derrida or some other latecomer to the Western tradition but from book 9 of Homer's *Odyssey*. Odysseus's turning of the tables of hospitality on the one who had turned them on him, giving the Cyclops Polyphemus wine to drink when Polyphemus should have given food and drink to him, is indeed a parody of sorts of the rites of hospitality, an inversion of roles that appears licensed by Polyphemus's total disregard for the laws of hospitality, his contempt for the tacit prohibition against cannibalism, and his inhospitable if not inhuman practice of inviting strangers into his cave only to consume them.

But deconstruction is neither parody nor simple reversal, although such a parody or reversal as the one I just recalled can sometimes tell us a good deal about deconstruction and might even be one of its strategies. Yet in order to see the salient features of hospitality brought out by its parody or inversion, it is essential first to become acquainted with the noninverted version, the conventions, codes, and contexts of hospitality as it is usually practiced. Recall, then, to return to our shared example, Odysseus as he washed up onto the island of the Phaecians, the wretched refuse of a teeming shore, to paraphrase the inscription of France's other great gift to the United States besides deconstruction. Tired, poor, yearning to breathe free after seven years of captivity with Calypso, seven years of a divine but oppressive hospitality, Odysseus is the archetypal refugee. Homeless, tempest-tossed, naked and vulnerable, Odysseus is found washed ashore by the Princess Nausicaa and brought to the palace of Alcinoos, her father. Without asking any questions of the stranger, without even asking him his name, Alcinoos invites him to eat, drink, and restore himself. Without first knowing who he is—*unconditionally*, we might say—Alcinoos offers hospitality to Odysseus. Only after having been thus entertained is Odysseus expected, although not required, it seems, to tell the king and those around him who he is and from where he has come. At this point Odysseus recounts his adventures, including his confrontation with the Cyclops Polyphemus. Having just seen how Odysseus was treated by Alcinoos, the inversion of hospitality recounted by Odysseus in the land of the Cyclops is striking, right down to the request and offering of a name. For unlike Alcinoos, Polyphemus wants to know who Odysseus is before giving, or promising to give, anything to him. He wants to see Odysseus's I.D., his passport, before extending any invitation or visa to him. Recognizing that something is amiss, that trust cannot be granted in a land where one asks names first and offers hospitality second, the man of many devices, the wily and ever-vigilant Odysseus, proves himself worthy of his epithets and reputation by inventing and offering a false name, a word made up of a negation and an indefinite pronoun that Polyphemus takes for a proper name. *Ou-tis*—No body—which, at the end of the episode, becomes *Me-tis*, another negation and the same indefinite pronoun, which too means Nobody but which can also be heard as the noun Metis, meaning cunning or ruse, the proper name of a goddess and an epithet proper to Odysseus.

This whole episode, this entire parody of hospitality embedded in the tale Odysseus is telling Alcinoos in exchange for his hospitable welcome, is thus framed by the asking and giving of names, by the request for identification and the masking of it. There on the border, before all else, identification is requested, and so a false passport is rendered, and then, back on the border, at the end of the episode, the false name by which Odysseus entered allows him to escape as Polyphemus blindly pursues him while crying out to the other Cyclopes that "Nobody" has harmed him. There on the border, names are requested, and if one has the right name, the right origin, one is allowed to come and go freely, but if not, one must sneak in and out, strapped onto the bottom of sheep—or else hidden in the bottom of a flatbed truck.

We can thus see how a custom or ethics of hospitality can easily turn into a politics of hospitality, complete with its own immigration policy. There on the border, names are asked, identities verified, origins checked, and intentions cleared. For when it comes to politics, to hospitality in or of the state, conditions are *always* stipulated. Names and borders—that is what would have to be central to any analysis of hospitality and to anything like a "deconstructive hospitality": names and borders, names on borders, names as borders. It is with precisely these two threshold concepts—the name and the border—that I would like now to enter into the work of Jacques Derrida, who, in the last few years has devoted two books to the theme of hospitality, one entitled *Adieu*, an analysis of hospitality in the work of the Lithuanian-born philosopher Emmanuel Levinas, and another entitled simply *Of Hospitality*.[1] It is in this latter work that Derrida asks the question that I have implicitly asked above: "Does hospitality consist in questioning the one who arrives? Does it begin with the question addressed to the newcomer:

what is your name? . . . [Or] does it begin with the unquestioning welcome, in a double effacement, the effacement of the question *and* the name?" (*H*, 27–29). Does hospitality consist in a welcoming gesture before all knowledge, all vision, and thus all potential prejudice, or does it consist in asking names, in deciding whom we are to invite before opening our arms to them? In other words, does hospitality consist in being more like Polyphemus or Alcinoos? Must we choose between these two alternatives? Does the inversion of hospitality tell us anything essential about hospitality as such, or does it simply reveal the lack of it?

We are here approaching what I understand to be some of the themes or strategies of a deconstructive approach to hospitality. We got here, notice, by juxtaposing—and then trying to think together—two related but seemingly incompatible forms or variations of hospitality. Let us call them for the moment the conditioned and the unconditioned. Although Polyphemus pushes inhospitality or hostility to the extreme, consuming his guest rather than giving him to consume, one might imagine a slightly more lawful land of Cyclopes where once huddled masses of strangers and foreigners arrive on its shores and where the first question that is asked is the question of identity, where the stranger is greeted there on the border not with open arms but with an armed and very closed question: "Who are you?" Although the question would indeed bear witness to the otherness or foreignness of the one who has requested hospitality, the point of such a question would be to reduce such otherness or foreignness, to control and identify it by first understanding or simply recognizing it. For you can learn a lot from a proper name, a lot about the one who bears it. Name, rank, and serial number are often all that is needed to identify origins, languages, cultures, and classes. And all this, the practical-minded philosopher or statesman would tell us, is necessary.

On the other side, on another island, we might push the unconditionality of Alcinoos to another extreme. When Odysseus comes before Alcinoos in his palace, having been given grace and stature by Athena, it is evident that he is not just Nobody. Although Alcinoos does not know exactly who he is, although he gives hospitality before questioning, he was already in the process of identifying, of recognizing, of evaluating the status and rank of his guest. Imagine, then, to offset our slightly more sympathetic, civilized, and vigilant Polyphemus, a completely blind Alcinoos, who would welcome without even seeing, without evaluating his guest to any degree, knowing nothing about him at all, an absolutely unconditional welcoming. (I would add here parenthetically that Nausicaa's hospitality might be a better candidate for this unconditional welcoming since she welcomes a naked and as yet unglorified Odysseus. The princess welcomes Odysseus to her father's island before having any hint of who he is. This raises the complex question of the relationship between gender and hospitality, a question I leave open and unresolved here.) Now, such hospitality, such unconditional hospitality, such an absolute welcome, does indeed tell us something about the essence of hospitality, but would it *be* that essence? The essence of hospitality surely involves welcoming a stranger or foreigner and not someone with whom we are already fairly familiar, who is already family, into the home or the state, for one does not usually call a family dinner hospitality. But does this mean that the essence of hospitality consists in welcoming someone of whom we know *nothing*, someone for or to whom we can only, blindly, open our arms? In other words, isn't one of the conditions of hospitality that it have certain conditions, that it have a specific context and be extended to someone in particular? Without such conditions wouldn't we be welcoming not some particular someone, Odysseus or some other, but, precisely, some vague or indiscriminate Nobody?

I think we can begin to see the dilemma—what Derrida would call the aporia or double bind—of hospitality. On the one hand, hospitality does not seem to be hospitality if what we are welcoming is not a stranger, a real guest, someone whom we have not already identified or identified with. The guest to be received must always be a stranger. On the other hand, the stranger must be welcomed—in a particular way, by means of particular conventions, within a particular language. To be effective, that is, to have a genuine effect, to be a real welcome, the guest must be identified, and if not called out to or greeted by name at least selected, picked out, *invited*. Yet such an identification always risks negating the hospitality that is extended; for in inviting, recognizing, or identifying the stranger, in subjecting him or her to our suppositions or our knowledge if not our prejudices, the stranger always risks becoming a relative nonstranger so that hospitality, which should be granted only to strangers, would then be granted only to relative relatives, to those who look, sound, and smell like us, to those who share our tastes.

In an interview published a few years ago in *Le Monde* Derrida was asked to elaborate on the question from *Of Hospitality* that I recalled earlier.

He was asked whether hospitality consists in "questioning the one who arrives, and first of all by asking him his name," or whether it begins "with the welcome that is without question." He was asked, in other words, the question of the conditions of hospitality. Here is his response:

The decision must be made at the heart of what looks like an absurdity, impossibility itself (an antinomy, a tension between two equally imperative laws that are nonetheless without opposition). Pure hospitality consists in welcoming the one who arrives even before asking him questions, before knowing or asking anything of him, whether this be a name or a piece of identification. But this pure hospitality also assumes that one address oneself to him, singularly so, and that one thus call him by name and acknowledge a proper name for him. "Hey you there, what's your name?" Hospitality consists in doing everything to address oneself to the other; it consists in granting him, indeed in asking him, his name, all the while trying to prevent this question from becoming a "condition," a police interrogation, an inquest or an investigation, or a simple border check. The difference is subtle and yet fundamental, a question that is asked on the threshold of one's home [*chez soi*] and on the threshold between inflections.[2]

In both *Adieu* and *Of Hospitality* Derrida at once analyzes various readings or inscriptions of hospitality in literature and philosophy and repeatedly poses the question of what hospitality is or should be *for us today*, what we are and should be doing today for those who have been displaced by wars or famines, what our ethical responsibility is to those who are called illegal immigrants, in France or elsewhere, and what such responsibility should tell us about the framing of policy and law. In both of these texts Derrida attempts to think the passage from ethics to politics not only within Kant or Levinas, Sophocles or Plato, but, by means of them, in our own ethical and political situation, with our own *inflections*. Deconstruction would thus be not only a means of questioning the passage between ethics and politics within the history of philosophy but a way of practicing that passage. Derrida's work, or the work of deconstruction, offers us the means of asking these questions of hospitality, ethics, and politics within the tradition at the same time as it keeps us attentive and open to the future, to the unexpected or unprecedented within a rigorously determined context where the traditional laws and protocols of reading and interpretation are respected so as to prepare the way for what exceeds them.

But how does this happen? Let's step away from the theme of hospitality as such for a moment in order to make some more general observations about Derrida's work and deconstruction. First, notice in the passage just cited that Derrida speaks of "two equally imperative laws" at the heart of which a decision is to be made. It is not a question of *choosing* between two imperatives but of inventing a way of negotiating the tension between them. Already in some of his earliest texts from the 1960s, Derrida spoke of the necessity of a double reading of texts or of a double gesture with regard to them. To be brief and schematic, the first gesture would consist of reading within the rules and terms established by the text; it would consist of asking what the author means or meant in the most traditional and rigorous way possible, taking into account, among other things, the social, political, and historical circumstances in which a text was written; it would attempt to comprehend the text's self-avowed logic, its system or systematicity. All the rules for valid argumentation, beginning with the law of noncontradiction, are in force and must be heeded in an attempt to understand and clarify the author's intentions.

The second reading in a deconstructive approach, which is carried out always in conjunction with the first, seeks what is not apparent in a text, what is not explicitly argued for, what is at the limits of the text. One thus looks on the periphery of the text—sometimes, quite literally, in notes or margins, asides, examples, or slips—in an attempt to show that something else is at work in the text, something that was not and could not be captured by its logic, brought into its system, made present on the page or in the argument. This something would be more like a force than a concept, which would or could show up in the text, and thus become codified; it would be more like a gesture than a hidden argument, an impetus or an ambivalence rather than a discrete possibility or possible meaning to be set alongside others. Since no text can inscribe, circumscribe, and encode its own event, the force of its emergence, every text is open to this second reading.

Hence, whereas the first reading would be directed toward the systematicity of a text, the second would aim at articulating or tracing or simply gesturing toward the force or gesture that cannot become a present part of the text without becoming part of its systematicity, its readability. These two readings would then be brought together in a deconstructive approach to demonstrate where and how a text exceeds itself or is open to something beyond itself. The conjunction or juxtaposition of these two moments or readings, one inside the text and one at its limits, would be more than just strategic—although it would be strategic as well. For what is pointed to in the second reading actually makes the first reading possible; that is, a text can present itself, become effective, readable, only on the basis of this force or founding gesture that is traced out in a text but is immediately forgotten, deferred, or repressed. Conversely, the force of this ambivalence, of something that escapes the logic of noncontradiction, can itself become "part" of a text only on the condition of being received within the text's language and oppositions, of succumbing to its codes and protocols of readability. It can become part of a text, or, let us say, be *welcomed* into text, only by being questioned, by becoming questionable and, in principle if not in fact, understandable. Only by being opened up to a text's logic can the openness that gives a text its force be *received*. One gesture, one reading, thus calls for another.

Now, although I do not wish to claim that the two readings of a double reading, as Derrida has spoken of them from the 1960s onward, are the *same* thing as the two imperative laws mentioned earlier in relation to hospitality, there is an undeniable structural similarity. Just as Derrida would characterize both readings as necessary, so the two laws of hospitality—the law of unconditional or unlimited hospitality and the law of conditioned hospitality—are necessary. Just as it is necessary in a first reading to obey the conventions and contexts of reading, so it is necessary to take into account the current ethical and political practices and contexts through which the foreigner is *effectively* welcomed in our customs, laws, and institutions.

In hospitality, as in reading, limits must always be set—and not simply for the sake of practicality, not simply because we cannot invite everyone to our table, although that too is true. Limits and conditions must be established—as well as questioned, contested, and, when necessary, changed—so that particular others, particular strangers and not some general other might be welcomed. Although Kant proposes in *Perpetual Peace* what at first seems to be an unlimited because universal right of hospitality, which, he says, "means the right of a stranger not to be treated as an enemy when he arrives in the land of another," this right is nonetheless conditioned.[3] One may arrive in a foreign land and claim a right to hospitality, to being welcomed, but no one has a right to overstay that welcome. Thus Kant specifies that the universal right of hospitality does not include "the right to be a permanent visitor." The universal right of hospitality is, says Kant, "only a right of temporary sojourn," based on the fact that—and Kant's Judeo-Christian heritage here lends a hand in the formulation of his cosmopolitics—"originally, no one had more right than another to a particular part of the earth." You can visit, therefore; that is or should be your right based on this original situation. You can even make yourself at home. But something extra would be required on the part of the state you are visiting to give you the right to move in. Thus even in this most seemingly universal application of hospitality, conditions are laid down.

Just as Derrida in *Adieu* and *Of Hospitality* looks at his own country's more and more restrictive policies on granting citizenship, at new governmental measures aimed at securing national borders and controlling what are called "les sans papiers," those without the proper papers to be in France as *welcomed* guests, so we in the United States would have to analyze and question our own policies of hospitality, our own laws of immigration and citizenship, and what it means to say that we are, as we like to say, a nation of immigrants, or, to risk a more radical formulation, one that is not totally foreign to the spirit of Kant, who understands that "originally, no one had more right than another to a particular part of the earth," a nation of *guests*, of guests in our own home—from the beginning, originally and for always, no exceptions allowed. We would have to look at the national and international conventions governing movement to, within, and among states, for example, the different policies on political or religious asylum, the different governmental and nongovernmental structures in place to welcome those suffering persecution or the effects of war, poverty, or natural disasters. And we would want to look not only at general laws and policies but at specific examples and exceptions of hospitality, whether from our courts, our newspapers, or our literature. To think, for example, this Kantian theme of an original dispossession of the earth, an original wandering, in its Jewish rather than Christian incarnation, and in conjunction with the politics of modern states, we might reread the famous rewriting of the parody of hospitality I analyzed earlier from the *Odyssey*, namely, the Cyclops chapter of James Joyce's *Ulysses*. In this parody of a parody of hospitality, the chauvinist and hypernationalistic Citizen sits in the den or cave that goes by the name of Barney Kiernan's pub and, inebriated, utters invectives against the invasion of Ireland by foreigners, and particularly Jews, all within the earshot of Leopold Bloom—a born Jew of Hungarian descent sojourning in a foreign land. When Bloom, guest of the country and the pub, does not offer his host, the Citizen, a drink, he is expelled or deported from the pub and, symbolically, from the country, from the island of Ireland, cursed by the other citizens as he narrowly escapes in the guise of Elijah, or rather the second Elijah, the lamb of God—a parody, it seems, of Odysseus's escape from

Polyphemus on the bottom of sheep. To take into account the codes and customs of hospitality, the right to citizenship and exile, would clearly take us into the thick of some of the most pressing issues of our time, from the question of Zionism and the state of Israel to the mass migrations of peoples that have become all too common in our world, for example, in the former Yugoslavia, in Rwanda, or, closer to home, on our own southern border.

This first reading, then, would take all these contexts into account; constantly changing, perpetually calling out to be deciphered and understood—patiently, rigorously—the contexts of social practices must always be read and analyzed by deconstruction. But turning to the second gesture, just as the second reading in deconstruction looks for what escapes the first reading yet makes that reading possible, so a deconstructive hospitality, or a deconstructive approach to hospitality, would look to what escapes political practices and contexts yet makes them possible. Hospitality, I recall, must always consist in welcoming the one who arrives, the guest, before posing "him" or "her" any questions; it would consist in welcoming the other *unconditionally*—before any identification. This means, it would seem, that the host must be open to welcoming the very worst, a guest who may actually expel him from his own home, and the guest, who would not recognize his host either, open to receiving the very worst, like being consumed rather than being given to consume by his host. Neither hosts nor guests can know with any assurance what awaits them; that is the first condition of hospitality. The first condition—the first of many—is that the guest must always be unconditionally welcomed.

Such openness to the unforeseeable would thus be an essential part of hospitality, although, as we have seen, it alone would not constitute the essence of hospitality. The essence of hospitality—"real" hospitality—would consist of *both* this *and* the necessity of welcoming someone in particular, someone with a proper name and not just some vague Nobody. The problem is not that we can never live up to absolute, unconditional hospitality because we can never welcome everyone, because we must set limits to our hospitality. Obeying the law of conditions is not simply a concession to our finitude, to our limited capacities and resources, or else simply a concession to political expediency. It is a recognition that hospitality, "real" hospitality, consists in welcoming particular guests and not just anybody, particular guests and, as a result, *not* others. To make hospitality effective, one imperative would have to respond to *and* interrupt the other; the door would always open with the question "Hey you there, what's your name?" the question being both a response to and an interruption of the imperative to welcome without question or condition. One must welcome the other who washes up on shore—just as Alcinoos welcomes Odysseus—but in order to welcome this one and not some vague somebody, some indiscriminate "other," one must have just a little Polyphemus within.

Deconstruction, then, would put us to the test of maintaining without reducing these two imperatives. Between the welcoming question, "Hey you there, what's your name?" and the police interrogation, "Hey you there, what's your name?," the difference is subtle but fundamental—a difference between two *inflections*. The difference is fundamental yet unmasterable, impossible to regulate or determine once and for all by any science or law. Welcoming some particular other, calling him or her by name, can thus always turn into an identification that would allow one to exclude that other, or at the very least to make sure in advance that this other is not going to abuse our hospitality. No code or context can ever prevent the welcoming gesture from turning ugly. Yet for this gesture to become effective, the other as stranger—as essentially vulnerable and destitute—must be identified, and so never welcomed as a stranger, always reduced, and, as such, welcomed as one stranger rather than another. The double imperative prevents one from ever achieving good conscience, from ever saying "I do enough," since, by definition, "doing enough" is never enough. Between our responsibility and our actions, the passage is never given in advance but must be reinvented with each welcome—right there on the threshold.[4]

In the *Le Monde* interview cited above Derrida suggests that asking the question of identity in such a way that it remains a welcome, an invitation, and not a police inquisition or interrogation, is "an art and a poetics," a play between two inflections. Derrida seems to suggest here a new ethical-political practice or else a new role, a new meaning, for deconstruction. Always in danger of turning into an interrogation, into a simple controlling of the other, of the newcomer, deconstruction, like hospitality, deconstruction as hospitality, would be neither a science nor a method but, to use Derrida's words, an art or a poetics that attempts to invent new ways of inviting or welcoming the unexpected into a particular language and context without immediately subjugating it to them, without immediately making it conform to them, without initially asking anything from it but a proper name.

The first question of hospitality is always, says Derrida, "What is your name?" Although not exactly what he calls in *Of Grammatology* the philosophical question par excellence, that is, the "ti esti" or "what is?" question with which we began, the first question of hospitality is essentially the question of identity: "Who are you? What is your name?" Between the question as a welcoming gesture and the question as an interrogation, the difference is subtle and tenuous. Derrida thus encourages us not to do away with questioning but to negotiate between these two forms of questions, between the unconditional welcome and the conditioned one, between the ethical realm where one is put in question and the philosophical or political realm where one takes up speech to ask questions and to welcome into language, into the well-rounded sphere of our own domestic space, where the foreigner risks being controlled or repressed and yet might also be allowed to wander. By welcoming such a stranger or foreigner into "our space," we, as host, always run not only the grave risk of being expelled from our home by the guest but also the salutary risk of being reminded that we too are essentially guests in our own home, migrants in our own homeland.

The question of identity or identification is asked, says Derrida, on the threshold between two inflections, on the threshold and thus not on one side or the other, neither simply inside, in the space of a pure domesticity, if there is such a thing, nor simply outside in the public sphere. A gesture of welcoming, of open arms, takes place always on the threshold, between the unconditional welcome and the conditioned one. It takes place always on the threshold of the home, the *chez soi*, on the threshold of what is one's own—country, island, state, city, home, cave, whatever one calls and identifies as home.

Deconstruction would thus be, perhaps before all else, a thoroughgoing critique of the proper, of claims to ownership, propriety, and purity. This is already implied in the very notion of double reading, where a text always remains open to something it can never inscribe, appropriate, identify, or identify with—call it the other or the stranger of the text. Indeed, identity is actually constituted, Derrida argues, by means of this alterity that is forgotten and repressed even as it continues to exert its force. For identity always comes from the other, as an effect of the languages and codes that allow one to say, either in response to the question we have been repeating or as an affirmation, "My name is X," or "I am X, a real, genuine, native-born, honest-to-goodness, born and bred, dyed-in-the-wool X."

This affirmation always comes as an effect of language—and thus always from the other. To say "My name is X," "I am X," is to bear witness to a more originary dispossession, a more originary event or donation of identity, a more originary *invitation*. For we are welcomed before welcoming, Derrida maintains in both *Adieu* and *Of Hospitality*, a guest before ever being a host, a host *capable* of welcoming only insofar as we are a guest—a guest, therefore, in our own home, a guest who has simply overstayed his or her welcome to the point of thinking he or she owns the place—the cave, the home, the city, the state, and, why not, the world. We are who we are, our identities constituted, only through others—others who recognize, welcome, and name us in the first place. To return to the *Odyssey* for a moment, it is surely no accident that at the very moment the disguised Odysseus is about to be recognized by the nurse who raised him as she prepares to give him a bath, Homer interrupts the narrative to tell the story of Odysseus's name and the origin of his identity. Our proper name is, we there learn, never proper to us; even if it is inscribed on flesh like a birthmark or, in the case of Odysseus, a scar, it is never natural. Insofar as it is readable, iterable, available to others, it is always a *given name*, and the same goes for all the other things and institutions by which we are identified and with which we identify. The border between inside and outside is not crossed once and for all but is multiplied across the surface of one's own. There are *only* thresholds—even if some of these become rigidified and others do not, even if some become in practice almost impossible to cross without the right passport while others remain relatively permeable. There on the threshold, identities are not simply revealed but given, established, claimed, creating a difference between what is inside and what is out, what belongs and what does not. Although identities *must* be given and established, they are never natural, neutral, or innocent. Deconstruction would remind us of this law; it would remind us that we are never simply and naturally given to ourselves. It would remind us that we are always guests in our own home and that our home is not only a place from which we might extend our hospitality but a place that is and must remain open—open to the stranger and open to deconstruction.

Hospitality thus is and must remain an open question. We can never know whether there *is* hospitality as such, since pure hospitality is always impure, that is, always compromised insofar as it is achieved, real, made effective. The question of whether there *is* hospitality in a given situation must thus always remain open. The essence of hospitality is only as an open question, one that can always be read in at least two ways, so that if I were to give or grant it a name—here on the threshold, as a phenomenon of the threshold—I would have to call it a form of deconstruction, a form that could not be distinguished from the whole.

Yes, in the end hospitality is deconstruction and deconstruction hospitality. Because deconstruction is not some master name but simply a way of speaking of the relationship between the conditional and the unconditional, the determined and the open, it goes by many names. One of them, I would suggest in light of Derrida's recent work, is hospitality, and that is why I have risked shifting the emphasis and terminology away from deconstruction toward hospitality and the openness it entails. For deconstruction would be, in the sense I have tried to develop here, a certain form of openness. Openness to something other or unprecedented, to surprise or the unknown. Openness—but not without preparation and not without purpose. As we saw in Derrida's understanding of double reading, the protocols and codes of rigorous analysis preclude saying just anything and preparing in just any way. As with all careful argumentation, one is obliged to be clear, to make sense—even if what is ultimately welcomed does not. Philosophical rigor is necessary to prepare the way for what cannot be prepared for, expected, or awaited. As paradoxical as it may seem, the unanticipatable openness to the other is prepared by the work of the same, by the codes and practices of what we might think of as a determinate and conditioned form of hospitality. This, for me, is what was truly unanticipatable, although the history of philosophy had in a sense prepared the way: the fact that in the works of Emmanuel Levinas, and now Derrida reading Levinas, the philosophical concept of receptivity should have been understood not only in terms of hospitality but *as* hospitality. For having seen how hospitality has been treated by Derrida in his recent work, having seen how hospitality has become a theme *for* deconstruction, we now come to see, in a reversal of the container/contained relationship that often accompanies a deconstructive analysis, that deconstruction itself perhaps *is* hospitality. Deconstruction *as* hospitality—that is an identification I had never really expected, an idea I had never adequately entertained, a genuine guest for thought. Instead of thinking of deconstruction within the more general field of philosophy, and hospitality as just one theme deconstruction might treat, deconstruction might actually *be* hospitality, a hospitality, then, that will have received the theme of hospitality—a double hospitality, therefore, one within the codes and contexts of hospitality as it is usually understood and one at their limits, one received and the other receiving. The open door of hospitality, the possibility of a surprise guest, a guest who would prove to us once again just how much we are guests in our own home, would thus be that which assures deconstruction a future, even if that future is to be found in rereading the theme of hospitality in the oldest book of the Western tradition, Homer's *Odyssey*. That is why deconstruction, despite all the proclamations of its death or demise, despite the fact that its name, like that of postmodernity, is perhaps already a thing of the postmodern past, that is why deconstruction—this threshold phenomenon—still remains, I believe, so very inviting.

Conclusion

Passing on the Mantle

ELIJAH'S GLAS AND THE SECOND COMING
OF DR. JOHN ALEXANDER DOWIE

Q: Your name is Jackie. Did you yourself change your first name?

J.D.: You are asking in fact a very serious question. Yes, I changed my first name when I began to publish, at the moment I entered what is, in sum, the space of literary or philosophical legitimation, whose "good manners" I was practicing in my own way. In finding that Jackie was not possible as the first name of an author, by choosing what was in some way, to be sure, a semipseudonym but also very French, Christian, simple, I must have erased more things than I could say in a few words. . . .

Q: In *Circumfession* you indicate that you have another first name, Elie.

J.D.: Which is not inscribed in the civil record, I don't know why. I have a few theories about that.[1]

—Interview with Jacques Derrida, *Points . . . Interviews,* 1974–1994[1]

> So the two of them [Elijah and Elisha] went on. Fifty men of the company of prophets also went, and stood at some distance from them, as they both were standing by the Jordan. Then Elijah took his mantle and rolled it up, and struck the water; the water was parted to the one side and to the other, until the two of them crossed on dry ground.
>
> —(2 Kings 2:6–8)[2]

The mantle falls and two walls of water rise up, two columns or pillars between which the prophet and his successor walk. The mantle falls and Elijah walks to the other side, accompanied by the one to whom his mantle will fall, the one destined to follow in his wake. Elijah rolls up his mantle of sheep skin, strikes the water, and, in this *partage des eaux,* a legacy unfolds, an order of generations and a promise. Sustained by an invisible force, an almost unthinkable bead pressure, these columns remain erect just long enough for a future to be secured. For once they have passed over to the other side, Elijah, knowing that the end is near, asks Elisha what he may do for him before he is taken away. When Elisha asks to inherit a "double share of [Elijah's] spirit," Elijah proclaims that this shall be granted so long as Elisha sees him being taken away, that is, so long as he is able to witness Elijah's passage. And so, as they continued on, "a chariot of fire and horses of fire separated the two of them, and Elijah ascended in a whirlwind into heaven. Elisha kept watching and crying out, 'Father, father! The chariots of Israel and its horsemen!' But when he could no longer see him, he grasped his own clothes and tore them in two pieces" (2 Kings 2:9–12).

Hence the future is secured in the time of the passage, at the parting of two generations, between the parting of the river and the rending of clothes, between *two* partings of water. For to cross back over to the other side of the river, Elisha, having "picked up the mantle of Elijah that had fallen from him," repeats the gesture of his predecessor, and "the water was parted to the one side and to the other, and Elisha went over. When the company of prophets who were at Jericho saw him at a distance, they declared, 'The spirit of Elijah rests on Elisha'" (2 Kings 2:13–15). The mantle thus falls to Elisha in the time of the passage so that he may fulfill the promise of the passage, and Elijah then passes away, not dying but being taken up into the heavens—taken away but always with the promise of return. For it is written in the book of Malachi that God would "send the prophet Elijah before the great and terrible day of the Lord," the second coming of Elijah signaling the beginning of the end, the imminent arrival of the final judgment (Malachi 4:5–6).[3]

Elijah thus passes on the mantle to Elisha and is taken up in a chariot of fire into the heavens, only to return from out of the future. The one who is left behind somehow goes on ahead, ahead of time, so as to approach us from the future for a singular and unprecedented event whose signs we must now await. Elijah is coming . . . again, for the first time, coming from the future toward the passage he will have left in his wake.

"Today, for us, here, now"—and you will notice that this is already a citation, the "now" already not self-identical, having gone on ahead of itself, ahead of time—the question has been and will remain how to rethink and thus keep open the passage of *Glas*. The mantle falls and two columns rise up, and, between them, or within them, as we see at the base of the left hand column on the very first page, "two passages."[4] Reading Derrida today, we are all, in our own way, attempting to secure a future in this passage, a future for Hegel, for Genet, and for *Glas* but, most important, for the passage itself, for the opening between these two columns. Walking between these columns with different styles and at various rhythms, each one of us is attempting, more or less explicitly, to secure a certain future of deconstruction, not simply a future of the enterprise or enterprises called deconstruction but a future for one of the notions of the future that deconstruction has given or passed on to us. What is the future of this future, the future of this passage where a future is secured yet held open, however briefly or perilously, to the radically unforeseeable, to what is referred to near the end of *Glas* as "another legacy"? Indeed what will be the legacy of *Glas*? Can it be reduced to its radical reformatting of philosophical style and form, to its questioning of the relationship between philosophy and literature, primary and secondary texts? Can it be reduced to an experiment in the "deconstruction of the unity of the book,"[5] as Derrida himself once described it? Surely the legacy of *Glas* will have been all of this; but the form of my inquiry betrays yet another legacy, and that is the thinking of legacy itself, the thinking of tradition, of generations, of the future, and of mourning. For whenever we write on *Glas*, on this epoch-making text of 1974 that divides all our thinking about the nature and possibilities of philosophical writing into a before and an after, into the days before the coming of *Glas* and the days after its arrival, after its event, we cannot help but mourn the passage of *Glas*. Because *Glas* is itself, as Derrida says in "Two Words for Joyce," "a sort of wake,"[6] anyone writing today about *Glas* cannot help but be drawn into its wake, that is, not only into the wake *in Glas*, or into the wake that *is Glas*, but, almost thirty years—a full generation—later, into a wake *for Glas*. Any writing about the wake of *Glas* will thus be a work of mourning for *Glas*, a work of mourning that will have already been staged by *Glas* in every way *but for the passage*, which shall remain at once part of an immemorial past and always yet to come.

As Derrida has repeatedly said, there can be no metadiscourse on mourning since all work *on* mourning is also a work *of* mourning. My question will thus be, How does one commemorate, recall, celebrate, or mourn the passage wherein a future, or a new thinking of the future—and thus of mourning—is secured? Might this involve the mourning of all our moorings as we trace the passage between columns, shores, and generations, always risking the forgetting, preservation, cancellation, or lifting up of the passage itself? Might it involve a mourning of all our ways of mourning, a reinscription and an abandonment of the synthesis or dialectization of deaths, so that in moving from the mourning *in Glas* to the mourning *of Glas* we ourselves perform the unfaithful although unavoidable passage from one mourning to another, betraying the unique and irreplaceable passage that is *Glas*'s mourning, that *is Glas*, so as to secure it a future to come again, to sound again, as if in echo or fulfillment of its own prophetic passage?

In this conclusion I will attempt to remain as faithful as possible to this movement between fidelity and infidelity by trying not so much to digest and understand the two columns of *Glas* or any of Derrida's work but to be, in part, understood and digested by them. I will try to let these words—my little eucharist—float down between the two columns of *Glas*, to let them vibrate in its glottis or drift down its esophagus by a sort of peristaltic motion so as to touch both shores from time to time, so as to scan them here and there, without, I hope, becoming beached on either side. Nowhere will I really deviate from the digestive tract already laid out by Derrida in *Glas*; yet because the intestinal structure of this great "book" never remains internal but continually twists back toward past texts while anticipating future ones, because *Glas* is an essentially intertextual work, I too will zigzag between *Glas* and more recent texts of mourning, as well as another of Derrida's works on the author of "The Wake," his 1987 "Ulysses Gramophone." Everything will have been programmed in advance, everything except what does not appear here or in *Glas*—the passage between two shores, the parting of the waters, the movement of a throwaway, and the coming of another, unexpected Elijah.

Imagine, then, if you will, this text floating down between the columns of *Glas* like the throwaway Leopold Bloom received on June 16, 1904, promising the coming of Elijah, the throwaway he read and then threw away, into the Liffey, there to float down the river throughout the novel, returning from time to time to be seen from one side of the river or the other, returning like Elijah himself. Derrida himself, of course, already recalls this scene in "Ulysses Gramophone," but let me crank it up one more time just to remind you of it, this scene from the Lestrygonians chapter, the eating chapter, where Bloom receives the word of the second coming of Elijah and then sends it on its prophetic journey through Dublin,

securing for it a future that is at once predictable and open to an unprecedented event:

> A sombre Y.M.C.A. young man, watchful among the warm sweet fumes of
> Graham Lemon's, placed a throwaway in a hand of Mr. Bloom.
>> Heart to heart talks.
>> Bloo . . . Me? No.
>> Blood of the Lamb.
> His slow feet walked him riverward, reading. Are you saved? All are washed in
> the blood of the lamb. God wants blood victim. Birth, hymen, martyr, war, foun-
> dation of a building, sacrifice, kidney burntoffering, druid's altars. Elijah is coming.
> Dr. John Alexander Dowie, restorer of the church in Zion, is coming. Is coming! Is
> coming!! Is coming!!![7]

Like the little flyer or handout Bloom receives in Dublin on June 16, 1904,
this text too will be a throwaway text, one that moves between two shores,
between two languages (English and French), between two mantles, one
concealing and one revealing, between two texts of mourning, two forms
of the future perfect, two translations, two generations, between Elijah and
Elisha, or, even better, between Elijah and himself, between two Elijahs,
between two notions of legacy and the future, and, finally, between two
Zions, the one that can never be reached but must always remain promised
and the one that has already been established, whose foundation stone has
already been laid—and rather than keep you waiting until the end of time
I will proclaim to you in advance where it is to be found: just up the lake
from the place I am "now" writing, just a bit north of Chicago, Illinois. . . .

*

Derrida makes but a single allusion to Elijah in *Glas*, but already there he
is related, as he will be in later texts, to the rites and technologies of passage, transfer, and communication, to the necessary iteration of the past
and the possible coming of an unprecedented future. The reference occurs
in the context of a scene in Jean Genet's *Our Lady of the Flowers*, where
Darling is being arrested for shoplifting. Before Darling's arrest Genet provides a long description of the shoplifter's trade, the science or craft of seiz-
ing an object in a split second, slipping it up a sleeve, and making off with
it. We then see Darling in a store plying his trade, using his science. He
is active, and his activity confirms his place in a world of human agents
where the future is open but to some extent determinable by human action. Yet in a split second the tables are turned, or turned inside out, and

this very world of activity is itself stolen away from Darling when he is asked by a woman as he is leaving the store, "What have you stolen, young man?" In an instant one world is exchanged for another, the world of human activity and projects turned inside out. Genet writes:

Through the old woman's words and the man's gesture, a new universe instantaneously presented itself to Darling: the universe of the irremediable. It is the same as the one we were in, with one peculiar difference: instead of acting and knowing we are acting, we know we are acted upon. A gaze—and it may be of your own eyes—has the sudden, precise keenness of the extra-lucid, and the order of this world—seen inside out—appears so perfect in its inevitability that this world has only to disappear. That's what it does in the twinkling of an eye.[8]

It is at this precise point that Derrida picks up the narrative in *Glas*, citing Genet: "The world is turned inside out like a glove. It happens that I am the glove, and that I finally realize that on Judgment Day it will be with my own voice that God will call me: 'Jean, Jean!'" (*GL*, 196bi). We thus move from a world of activity, a world where the future is to some extent open and determinable, to one of total passivity, a world of irremediability and inevitability, to, finally, a world where one calls oneself with the voice of God to this inevitability, to a final Judgment. God calls Jean with Jean's own voice, calling him now not simply to some inevitability but, perhaps, to this self-relation between caller and called, God and man, Jean and Jean, John and John—and everything hinges precisely on how or whether these two Jeans or Johns are the "same."

Now, just before this reference in *Glas* to *Our Lady of the Flowers* comes a series of references to and from another Jean or John, the author of the gospel and of the final revelation and judgment. Derrida announces these references as a sort of complex telephonic exchange between one Jean and another, two Jeans speaking together on the subject of a third: "The Gospel and the Apocalypse, violently selected, fragmented, redistributed, with blanks, shifts of accent, lines skipped or moved out of place, as if they reached us over a broken-down teletype, a wiretap in an overloaded telephone exchange" (*GL*, 196bi). God speaking to Jean, Jean speaking to Jean, on the subject of another—and all this is relayed through a telephone exchange that, in "Ulysses Gramophone," goes by the name of Elijah. After this reference to the telephone exchange, then, and just before citing Jean Genet, Derrida cites Jean speaking of Jean, or John speaking of John, that is, John of the Gospels speaking of John the Baptist—just at the moment that this latter is himself predicting the coming of another: "And the light shines in the darkness, and the darkness did not find it . . . glory as of a single son from his father, full of grace and truth. John bears witness concerning him, and he cried out: This is he of whom I said: He who is coming behind me surpasses me, because he was before I was. . . . The world is turned inside out like a glove" (*GL*, 196bi). The world is now turned inside out because, as John the Baptist testifies, the one who is coming after him [*ho opisō mou erkhomenos*] has come before him [*emprosthen mou gegonen*]; the one who is coming after him was before [*hoti prōtos mou ēn*]. This seeming paradox can be resolved and the world restored, turned right side out, when we interpret or translate the coming before as a metaphorical "surpassing" or "ranking before." But it can also be resolved by understanding that the one who comes after *will have already* come or at least been announced in advance. Jesus will have already been announced in Moses; faith will have been what was always lacking in law, what was necessary to fulfill the law or lift it up. The next lines of John read: "From his fullness we have all received, grace upon grace. The law indeed was given through Moses; grace and truth came through Jesus Christ" (John 14:16–17). Although Mosaic law is here implicitly opposed to Christian truth, the opposition is sublatable, the grace and truth of Christ being the long-awaited fulfillment and overcoming of the law of Moses.

Hence the unique one who comes after will have come before; the one who comes after becomes iterable as the one who will have fulfilled what came before. The singular event thus becomes *repeatable* in the time of this future perfect. Jean calls out to Jean; Jean calls out to Jean to become what he will have already been. But everything depends on the *passage* between the call and its reception, that is, on whether the call must pass through an irremediable difference, just long enough for the singularity of an event to arrive, or whether this difference becomes mediated so that Jean and Jean become one and the same—Jean calling out to Jean without detour or difference, Moses calling out to John the Baptist, John the Baptist calling out to Christ—who will have fulfilled what already began in Moses. It all depends on who is coming, or who is coming again, on whether it is a radically unforeseeable Elijah coming for the first time or an Elijah coming again, coming this time in the guise of John the Baptist or even of Jesus Christ.

Just after citing these opening verses from the first book of John and then the scene from *Our Lady of the Flowers* where Darling is caught shoplifting and the world is turned inside out like a glove, just after the voice of Jean calls to Jean through God at the final Judgment, Derrida picks up the telephonic conversation with John the Evangelist a couple of lines later as John recalls how John was once confused with Elijah: "And some Pharisees were sent. And they questioned him: Why then do you immerse if you are not the Christ, nor Elijah [*Elie*] or the prophet? John answered them: I immerse only in water. In your midst stands one whom you do not know, who is coming after me, and I am not fit to untie the fastening of his shoes" (*GL*, 196bi). The Pharisees' uncertainty about the position or identity of John is repeated in other Gospels. Is he the Christ, or is he the second coming of Elijah who announces the coming of Christ? The singular event is understood or awaited by the Pharisees in terms of a repetition of the past, a fulfillment or return of past prophets—although everything turns here on what is meant by "fulfillment" or "return." But Christ too will be confused with John the Baptist, Elijah, and the other prophets by the people.[9] Moreover, he himself will identify, or will be interpreted by the disciples as identifying, John the Baptist with Elijah, the one who prepares the way for the second coming. When asked by the scribes why Elijah must come first, Jesus replies, "'Elijah is indeed coming and will restore all things; but I tell you that Elijah has already come, and they did not recognize him, but they did to him whatever they pleased. So also the Son of Man is about to suffer at their hands.' The disciples understood that he was speaking to them about John the Baptist" (Matthew 17:10–12).[10]

The arrival of John the Baptist, although unnoticed until after his departure, would thus be the fulfillment of the prophesy in Malachi. Elijah is indeed coming, but Elijah has already come. John the Baptist would be this second Elijah who came to prepare the Messiah's coming, a repetition that would prepare the way for a singular event, a repetition that would nonetheless always risk inscribing that singular event, putting it into a chronological sequence, subjecting it to the structures of iteration and, thus, making it no longer singular. That is why there are, for Derrida, always two Elijahs, each the condition of the other. The first Elijah would be the *iterable* one, the one who appears in time—and so always comes more than once: yes, yes, ja, ja, Elijah, Elijah, but then also, since this iterative structure has no determinate end, Elijah I, Elijah II (namely, Elisha or, better, John the Baptist), and then Elijah III (who, let me add here in parentheses, will have come from Zion, from Zion, Illinois . . .). In contrast to this first, repeatable, predictable Elijah is the second, *unforeseeable* one, the unrepeatable, uniterable one, the one who cannot come in time, whose coming is always betrayed even if it is also first made possible by all these iterative structures, the Elijah who never comes in some present but nonetheless leaves the mark of his passage, who first opens up a genuine difference between generations and makes all legacy possible.

In "Ulysses Gramophone" Derrida makes the connection explicit between these two Elijahs. There is, first, the Elijah who makes all the connections, "the great operator" of a "large telephone exchange,"[11] "the head of the megaprogramotelephonic network," the voice that assures the communication of all voices, the medium in which these voices move. Derrida writes: "In the second coming of Elijah after 'the end of the world,' Elijah's voice acts as a kind of telephone exchange or marshalling yard. All communication, transport, transfer, and translation networks go through him. Polytelephony goes through Elijah's programophony. . . . Elijah is just a voice, a skein of voices" ("UG," 277–78). This Elijah is in advance of even the cutting edge of communication technology, his network far ahead of any Internet, for he says to "those who are in the *vibration* (a key word in my view) that they can call him any time, straightaway, instantaneously, without using any technique or postal system, but going by the sun, by solar cables and rays, by the voice of the sun—we could say photophone or heliophone" ("UG," 278). To be in the vibration is a bit like being on the Net, one that is already solar-powered—and Elijah is always online.

But in addition to the Elijah who connects and makes all communication possible is the one who disconnects or is disconnected, "the other Elijah," "the name of the unforeseeable other for whom a place must be kept" ("UG," 295). From this Elijah to the other, from one future to another, from the "singularity of the event" to its iteration, programmation, and prediction, the passage is always precarious, precarious because so easily forgotten, so easily forgotten because so easily recalled. For "Elijah can always be one and the other at the same time, we cannot invite the one, without the risk of the other turning up. But this is a risk that must always be run" ("UG," 295). There is thus always the risk of inviting the wrong Elijah, the risk of "the parasiting of an Elijah, that is to say of a me, by the other" ("UG," 295).

Recall that we are still floating down the river between two columns, the two columns of *Glas*, this great text on religion, on the binding and unbinding of the hyphen between *Judeo* and *Christian*, between one Elijah and another, between Elijah and Elisha, between two columns of water around a strip of land or two strips of land surrounding water, depending on whether or not the river is turned inside out like a glove. Drifting along after an initial fall, we are in on another vibration, one that would be not a voice or medium of connection but, rather, the very movement between the two columns, the space of a passage between the two Elijahs. Derrida speaks near the end of "Ulysses Gramophone" of "two *yeses* that *must* gather together like twins, to the point of simulacrum, the one being the gramophony of the other. I hear this vibration as the very music of *Ulysses*" ("UG," 308). And I hear this vibration as the very music of *Glas*, another *Finnegans Wake*, the vibration between two columns, between Hegel and Genet, Shem and Shaun, between the two Elijahs, or between two futures, a tremor of the throat, a singular strain.

There is thus always the risk, as we just heard, of "the parasiting of an Elijah, that is to say of a *me*, by the other" ("UG," 295; my emphasis). But why "me"? As Derrida says in "Ulysses Gramophone," we are all Elijah, for we all always run the risk of being visited or parasited by our other—and always without expecting it. The *me* is thus general in this respect. But it is also quite specific, for as Derrida reminds us in "Ulysses Gramophone," he too—he especially—is Elijah: "Of course you do not believe a word of what I am saying to you at the moment. And even if it were true, and even if, yes, it is true, you would not believe me if I told you that I too am called Elijah: this name is not inscribed, no, on my official documents, but it was given to me on my seventh day. ("UG," 284).[12] The name was given, the name inscribed, on the same day that something else was taken away, another mark made. Indeed much could be said here about circumcision as symbolic castration in *Glas*. Derrida writes, for example, "the Jew effects (on) himself a simulacrum of castration in order to mark his ownness, his proper-ness, his property, his name" (*GL*, 46a). And Elijah, Derrida recalls in "Ulysses Gramophone," "is the name of the prophet present at *all* circumcisions. He is the patron, if we can put it like this, of circumcisions. The chair on which the new-born baby boy is held is called 'Elijah's chair'" ("UG," 284–85). Through the event of circumcision one enters into a community, into an alliance, a relationship of filiation and legitimation. Whether he is connecting or cutting off, therefore, Elijah brings one into a community, although he is, as such, never present. During the Passover Seder a chair is thus left empty for Elijah, and if he arrives—which he sometimes does, as an empty glass sometimes testifies—it is always unnoticed. Derrida continues in "Ulysses Gramophone": "You are awaiting the passing through or the second coming of Elijah. And, as in all good Jewish families, you always have a place set for him. Waiting for Elijah, even if his coming is already gramophoned in *Ulysses*, you are prepared to recognize, without too many illusions, I think, the external competence of writers, philosophers, psychoanalysts, linguists" ("UG," 284).

Derrida is speaking here to the scholars of a Joyce conference who have invited him to speak before them. He is asking, in effect, whether his arrival, whether the arrival of any guest, has not already been programmed, already understood, by the Joycean network of filiation and legitimation that, as we have seen, can go by the name of Elijah. For Elijah is not only the one who comes for the time of a passage through the community but the prophet who first brings one into a community, who renews the alliance, and who, as such, always risks being forgotten by being remembered, always risks being taken up into relations of filiation and succession, forgotten in advance, then, through anticipation. His arrival thus risks always being forgotten by the networks and machines of filiation that themselves go by the name of Elijah: "The machine of filiation—legitimate or illegitimate—functions well and is ready for anything, ready to domesticate, circumcise, circumvent everything; it lends itself to the encyclopedic reappropriation of absolute knowledge which gathers itself up close to itself, as Life of the Logos, that is, also in the truth of natural death" ("UG," 294). Elijah is thus received by Elijah; Elijah makes the arrival of Elijah first possible; one Elijah calls out to the other. And that is why "the figure of Elijah, whether it be that of the prophet or the circumciser, of polymathic competence or of telematic control, is only a synecdoche of Ulyssean narration, at once smaller and greater than the whole" ("UG," 286). Such Ulyssean narration is, as we know, always bent on returning home, on establishing a relation of filiation, on finding the absent father, and on ridding the home of parasites to ensure a legitimate succession. It would seem impossible, therefore, to surprise or even genuinely visit either the Joycean text or a society of Joyce scholars, since everything would seem to have been predicted in advance, awaited from the very beginning, reappropriated before the fact by the Joycean odyssey.

Yet, says Derrida, "the eschatological tone of this yes-laughter," of this encyclopedic reappropriation, seems to be "haunted" or "joyously ventriloquised by a completely different music." The machine would be haunted by the "yes-laughter of a gift without debt," by an "abandoned event," by a "lost signature without a proper name that reveals and names the cycle of reappropriation and domestication of all the paraphs only to delimit their phantasm, and does so in order to contrive the breach necessary for the coming of the other, whom one can always call Elijah, if Elijah is the name of the unforeseeable other for whom a place must be kept" ("UG," 294–95). Thus I return to the question of filiation and tradition in order to ask how a legacy can ever be established on the basis of this waiting, how the place for the unforeseeable other can ever be kept open, how one can ever keep the Elijah Chair empty.

Near the end of "Ulysses Gramophone" Derrida imagines a department of Joyce Studies that would decide, under the authority of an eminent scholar who holds the Elijah Chair, to put Derrida's reading of Joyce to the test by instituting a program that would begin by counting all the *yes*es in *Ulysses*. But who could ever hold or inherit such an endowed chair? What forms of election could ever make this possible or legitimate? How could those who are not Elijah ever determine to whom the mantle must fall? How could they ever prevent such a chair from being usurped? Must they not always have to risk filling such a chair, and so risk making a bad appointment, precisely in order to keep the chair from being usurped, or precisely in order to keep it empty, to ensure that the mantle falls to an Elijah who knows how to give way to another, an Elijah who always proclaims *ex cathedra* the coming of another, always another, to fill his chair? Must they not always run the risk of an Elijah passing on the mantle in order that another Elijah might pass it on, his very election being confirmed in the way he passes it on, in the way he takes it up so as to take a pass on it, in the way he passes it up as the only way of passing it on—another way, perhaps, of deconstructing or, let us say, *dismantling* a certain tradition of tradition, a certain tradition of determining filiation, legacy, and succession?

But what exactly is a mantle? For example, the mantle of Elijah? As we have already seen, it is that which anoints a successor, a sort of official garment or robe that helps designate or reveal the successor of Elijah to others.[13] Having heard the commandment of the Lord on Mount Horeb to "anoint Elisha" (1 Kings 19:16), Elijah "threw his mantle over him" (1 Kings 19:19), and Elisha followed him as his servant. The mantle thus reveals a successor, establishes a filiation, after having concealed and protected Elijah from the revelation of this revelation. For when he awaited the revelation of God on Mount Horeb, Elijah, having already withstood the winds, earthquakes, and fires in which God did not appear, "wrapped his face in his mantle and went out and stood at the entrance of the cave" as he heard "a sound of sheer silence" (1 Kings 19:13).

The mantle thus *conceals* Elijah from the sound of sheer silence at the same time as it *reveals* the one who is to follow in his wake. But follow me, if you will, for just a moment as I drift down between the columns of the *O.E.D.* in order to look more closely at this English word *mantle*, imitating *Glas* once again with this gesture. From the Latin *mantellum*, the word *mantle* refers to a cloak or covering of some sort, be it a garment that is worn, a covering on a standing body of water, or else the envelope or shade of a mechanical device. The word can also be used to describe the covering or envelope of a mollusk or the plumage of a bird's folded back wings. And, of course, it can refer to the passing on of a spirit, status, or legacy. As a verb, *to mantle* thus means to clothe, to wrap up or over, to envelop or cover with a coating, to spread back the wings of a bird, or to suffuse with blood, as in cheeks that become flushed or blushed—revealing as they conceal.

But just as the mantle of a shell, its outer envelope or covering, is typically a paired structure, the two halves meeting either just behind or in front and behind depending on whether the shell is bivalve or univalve, so this word *mantle* forms a pair—and this is the chance of English[14]—with another that sounds just like it, the difference, like *différance*, being visible in writing although not heard in speech. Paired with *mantle* in the adjoining column of the *O.E.D.*—itself a sort of *Glassary*—the "mantel" turns almost all the values of *mantle* inside out, suggesting display rather than concealment, a lifting up rather than a veiling, a putting into evidence rather than an enveloping. For the mantel, mantelshelf, or mantelpiece is almost always a place of display, a place for revelation, or else something that sustains, lifts, or holds up, like the mantel-tree, the wooden beam that supports the masonry of a fireplace. In each case the mantel supports, preserves, lifts up, displays, gives to be seen. And what is given to be seen on a mantel is more often than not a sign of the past: relics, mementos, souvenirs, trophies of past glories, family photos (including, of course, photos of the dead), sometimes even an urn containing the ashes of the dead. It is also the place where, in the famous scene from Genet's *A Thief's Journal* that Derrida recalls and reads in *Glas*, the narrator and Stilitano ceremoniously place the cluster of grapes that Stilitano had pinned inside his pants to fool or surprise the men trying to pick him up. The mantelpiece is there the altar on which this substitute penis, this substitute for the penis, is placed, the penis of the one-armed Stilitano being transformed into something that bears more of a resemblance to a mutated cluster of gonads or ovaries than a penis. Although the game abruptly ends when "one night Stilitano got up to throw it into the shithole," the ceremony lasts a number of days, the narrator unpinning the prosthesis from Stilitano and then laying it atop the mantelpiece supported by two columns, elevating and thus glorifying the offering.[15] The mantel, then, is a place of celebration and ceremony, memory and mourning, a place where the past is inscribed and incorporated. In an essay on the work and life of Louis Marin, Derrida makes explicit this passage between the mantelpiece and mourning. In the course of an analysis of Marin's claim that the force of representation lies in its ability to make the dead "re-appear with greater clarity or *enargeia*," Derrida cites an example from Marin: "Thus the photograph of someone who has passed away displayed on the mantel."[16]

Whereas the *mantle* thus conceals, covers over, or envelops, the *mantel* reveals and displays. Whereas the mantle is turned toward the future, toward an order of succession, the mantel is turned toward the past, toward remembrance—unless both of them are turned, and this is where the two mantles/mantels would cross, toward a certain notion of the future perfect. Derrida proceeds in this essay on Marin, this essay *on* and *in* mourning, to speak not simply of the way a photograph on a mantelpiece can make the dead reappear with greater clarity but of the way Marin himself indicates this, the way Marin, himself now dead, indicates, indicated, or will have indicated how the portrait or photograph of the dead makes the dead reappear with greater clarity. It is as if Marin were saying to those of us reading his last book, *Les pouvoirs de l'image*, not simply "This will have been me" or "I will have been dead," but "I am dead," telling or foretelling his death not simply in the future, and not even in the future perfect, but in a tense that is not a modification of some present. Derrida writes:

Louis not only saw death coming, as we all see it coming without seeing it, as we all expect it without expecting it. He approached death, which approached him, more and more quickly; he approached it in preceding it, and anticipated it with these images and glosses, for which the grammar of the future anterior no doubt does not suffice to convey their force and time, their tense. The future anterior is still a simplistic modalization of a fundamental present or representation; simplistic because still too simple to be able to translate the strange temporality that here gives its force to the mourning affect of which we are speaking. ("FM," 186)

And later:

To say "I died," "I am dead," is not simply a future anterior. . . . The "I died" is not a phenomenologico-grammatical monstrosity, a scandal of common sense or an impossible sentence with no meaning. It is the time or tense, the grapho-logical time, the implicit tempo of all writing, all painting, of every trace, and even of the presumed present of every *cogito ergo sum*. ("FM," 186)

Not "I will be dead" or "I will have been dead" but "I died," "I am dead"— the very sentence from Poe's "The Facts in the Case of M. Valdemar" that Derrida cited back in 1967 as one of the epigraphs to *Speech and Phenomenon*.

We already saw how the *mantle* that reveals a successor could be turned toward a future perfect, Elisha or John the Baptist being the one who *will have been* Elijah, Elijah truly returning. Now the photograph on the *mantel* risks enduring a similar fate, its subject saying, in effect, "The person you are looking at now was destined to die"; "The one you see living here *will have been* dead." In the case of both the mantle and the mantel Derrida wishes to oppose this future perfect as a modification or iteration of some present to another, perhaps apocalyptic time, a time of Elijah, where the catastrophe happens without taking place in some present, where the Messiah comes to Zion but never arrives, where the death that makes all our mourning possible does not simply happen on one fateful day.

In *Glas* the future perfect is invariably linked to the time of the *Phenomenology of Spirit*, and from the very first page on: "For us, here, now: these words are citations, already, always, we *will have* learned that from him" (*GL*, 7a; my emphasis). Later Derrida writes, "When a future is used for the student, it is a grammatical ruse of reason: the sense that reason will have meant (to say) is, in truth, the future perfect, the future anterior. The encyclopedic version of the greater *Logic* (circular pedagogy, for the student) narrates itself in the future perfect" (*GL*, 15ai). And again, "to be, matter will-already-have-become spirit" (*GL*, 23a). For Hegel, according to Derrida, the truth of religion itself would appear "only in philosophy, in the future perfect, the future anterior, of absolute religion" (*GL*, 92a). This future perfect is thus opposed by Derrida to the "I am dead," which, he says, is the graphological time of every trace. For every trace implies the death of its author not in some future present but already and structurally from the beginning. "This will have been me," "I will have died," conceals the fact that death comes from the very beginning to work over all writing, all photographs, all traces. The family photographs on the mantelpiece depicting the living thus already participate in mourning; they are already a shrine to the dead, the sounding of their *glas*. In leaving a trace, any trace at all, they are not simply announcing that their truth will have been their death, their being-toward-death, for example, but that the will-have-been of their deaths was already conditioned, and already from the beginning, by death.

All this is consistent, it seems, with everything Derrida says in *Speech and Phenomenon* or "Signature Event Context," as well as with another text of mourning, written some ten years before "By Force of Mourning," another text on another friend, "The Deaths of Roland Barthes." In this text photographs are once again on display, as Derrida follows Barthes in his attributing a special status to the photographic representation. Derrida writes in the context of Barthes's notion of the *punctum* that comes to strike, pierce, and wound me in the photograph: "But it is always the singularity of the other insofar as it comes to me without being directed towards me, without being present to me; and the other can even be 'me,' me having been or having had to be, me already dead in the future anterior and past anterior of my photograph."[17] Although the *punctum* of the photograph seems to strike me with a unique and irreplaceable death, with the "having-been of a unique and invariable referent," it cannot but compose with the *studium* and begin to pluralize itself: "If the photograph bespeaks the unique death, the death of the unique, this death immediately repeats itself, as such, and is itself elsewhere. . . . The *punctum* allows itself to be drawn into metonymy. Actually, it induces it, and this is its *force*, or rather than its force . . . its *dynamis*, in other words, its power, potentiality, virtuality, and even its dissimulation, its latency" ("DRB," 285–86).

From one mourning, then, the other, from "The Deaths of Roland Barthes," which was already plural, to "By Force of Mourning," from Roland Barthes to Louis Marin. This is the force of the singular other as it becomes repeated and dissimulated not just in the photographic trace but in all traces, all names. And that is why "even before the unqualifiable event called death, interiority (of the other in me, in you, in us) had already begun its work. With the first nomination, it preceded death as another death would have done. The name alone makes possible the plurality of deaths" ("DRB," 273). The name makes possible the plurality of deaths, to be sure, but it also sustains the plurality of lives and appearances, of generations. The iterability of the name makes not only possible but necessary the appearance of a future perfect that will link two times and appearances. Not only the Hegelian "to be, matter will-already-have-become spirit," a future anterior that allows one to identify a past determination and move beyond it, but the future anterior of "I will have died." In each case the unique death is forgotten in a plurality of deaths, the unique appearance repeated so as to become a multiplicity of appearances, each one implying both death and resurrection. And that is why, to return from the place we set out, Elijah—the unique other—always returns, why one Elijah always runs the risk of being parasited by another, why Elijah always calls out to Elijah.

As I recalled earlier, we encounter Elijah in chapter 8 of *Ulysses*, the Lestrygonians chapter, as Leopold Bloom receives a throwaway announcing the coming of Dr. John Alexander Dowie, restorer of the church in Zion. Moments later, Bloom "threw down among [the seagulls] a crumpled paper ball. Elijah thirtytwo feet per sec is com. Not a bit. The ball bobbed unheeded on the wake of swells, floated under by the bridge piers" (*U*, 152). As the throwaway floats down the Liffey, as it is digested by it, the figure of Elijah returns several times throughout the novel, either through mention of the "crumpled throwaway," which is seen from one side or the other of the river, or through a series of identifications of Bloom with Elijah.[18] This culminates when Bloom is forced to leave Barney Kiernan's pub at the end of chapter 12, a Jew expelled from a den of Christians, disgraced yet glorified; for as he leaves,

there came about them all a great brightness and they beheld the chariot wherein He stood ascend to heaven. And they beheld Him in the chariot, clothed upon in the glory of the brightness, having raiment as of the sun, fair as the moon and terrible that for awe they durst not look upon Him. And there came a voice out of heaven, calling: *Elijah! Elijah!* And he answered with a main cry: *Abba! Adonai!* And they beheld Him even Him, ben Bloom Elijah, amid clouds of angels ascend to the glory of the brightness. (*U*, 345)

As a combination of the ascension of Elijah in 2 Kings with the transfiguration of Christ—at which, it should not be forgotten, Elijah was, along with Moses, present[19]—this passage reveals just perfectly the possibilities of the future perfect: like Elisha in 2 Kings, the denizens of Barney Kiernan's pub witness the elevation or the rapture of ben Bloom Elijah, a Jew turned Christian, a Jew who will have been, who will have revealed himself to be, Elijah, either the old one or the new, or perhaps even the newest of the new. For Elijah always returns. Even when the one and only Jesus Christ was on the cross, bystanders thought that with his last words he was calling out not to God, his Father, but to the prophet Elijah. Matthew writes: "And about three o'clock Jesus cried with a loud voice, 'Eli, Eli, lema sabachthani?' that is, 'My God, my God, why have you forsaken me?' When some of the by-standers heard it, they said, 'This man is calling for Elijah. . . . Let us see whether Elijah will come to save him'" (Matthew 27:46–49; Mark 15:35, 36). Elijah thus always comes back to save us; he returns from out of the Old Testament to haunt the Gospels, and he returns to haunt the Circe chapter of *Ulysses*, the chapter Derrida makes so much reference to in "Ulysses Gramophone." Elijah returns there in the figure of A. J. Christ Dowie, as he is referred to in this scene (see *U*, 428). He returns to convert the world and restore Zion, preaching in a brothel to prostitutes and their clients of the second coming, and of himself as Elijah III, promising divine healing and peddling salvation like a miracle salve to restore body and soul:

Join on right here! Book through to eternity junction, the nonstop run. Just one word more. Are you a god or a doggone clod? If the second advent came to Coney Island are we ready? Florry Christ, Stephen Christ, Zoe Christ, Bloom Christ, Kitty Christ, Lynch Christ, it's up to you to sense that cosmic force. . . . It's just the cutest snappiest line out. It is immense, supersumptuous. It restores. It vibrates. I know and I am some vibrator. Joking apart and getting down to bedrock, A. J. Christ Dowie and the harmonial philosophy, have you got that? (*U*, 507–8; see *U*, 492)

With this nineteenth-century evangelist, Dr. John Alexander Dowie (another J.D.?), we return from Ireland or, like Stephen, from Paris, from Europe, from the Old World to the New, to the very place these words are "now" be-ing written—Chicago, Illinois. For it was in Chicago that Alexander J. Dowie, born in Edinburgh, Scotland, in 1847, truly made a name for him-self, taking on this other name, the name of the one whose second coming, or rather, if we count John the Baptist, whose third coming would signal the second coming of the Messiah, taking on the name, then, of the Messiah of the Messiah. Indeed it was just north of Chicago that Dowie founded the community of Zion, Illinois, proclaiming himself Elijah the Restorer. In a book of sermons from 1899 entitled *Zion's Holy War Against the Hosts of Hell in Chicago*, Dowie writes, in words that should give us pause in these

threshold years between not only centuries but millennia, "I have been keeping steadily before me the thought that God requires us to establish a number of Zion Cities. The first of these must be built near Chicago." And later,
in words that reach us almost one hundred years later over the Elijah-Net:

> The time will come when the reproduction of the voice of a speaker like myself,
> speaking now in tones which you all hear, and in which you are intensely inter-
> ested, will be heard clearly in every Tabernacle of Zion throughout the world. I
> mean the exact tone of that voice; the exact words. I do not mean the written page.
> But through the wonderful power of the phonograph Zion shall have the whole
> world for an audience. *That is what is coming*—when a word spoken from the
> headquarters of Zion can be reproduced throughout the world. . . . Our Officers
> even now can be reached in a moment by telephonic communication, or in an hour
> or so by telegraphic communication. I received cablegrams recently which, accord-
> ing to sun time, actually reached me an hour before they left, meaning, of course,
> that they outstripped the sun. . . . Yes, we are coming. Set your houses in order.[20]

Although Dowie failed in his attempt in 1903 to convert New York City
with three thousand of his followers, although he himself was ultimately
deposed from the community for "tyranny and injustice," for "polygamous
teaching and other grave charges," he was successful in founding Zion, a
community known today for little else than its controversial nuclear power
plant. But following Derrida and all his recent work on a messianicity that
must be thought at the limits of all messianism, it could be argued that
Dowie Elijah's greatest success, the founding of Zion, was his greatest failure, for it involved failing to see that Zion must not be found or founded,
that a place must always be promised or kept open for Zion as for Elijah,
for the passage between two inscriptions or two shores.

   Unless, of course, Dowie realized that only by repeating the origin,
only by laying down another foundation, could the coming of Elijah be
prepared. Unless he realized that there must never be just one Zion, one
holy and unique land, but always "a number of Zion Cities," all of them
preparing for the arrival of an unforeseeable guest, all of them laying down
a foundation stone—multiplying and scattering the foundation of Zion
across the surface of the earth—none of these cities being the privileged
site but each only the trace of all the others, each requiring yet another city,
yet another foundation stone, yet another inscription of the origin in order
to prepare the way for Elijah. That is, in order to prepare the way for a guest
whose coming will leave little more than a trace, who will be received with-

out our knowing it, without our consuming or digesting him, who will leave us with nothing more than a glorious vibration in the glottis and a throwaway announcing the coming of another, another unforeseeable other, another throwaway received by accident in the street, or stumbled upon in the library, another crumpled throwaway—even if immense, like the entire corpus of Derrida—which is then left to drift down between two columns, toward a future beyond all identifiable times and legacies, left to be read or refused from either shore, open always to chance, dependent always on who will get the drift, itself now taking on a history, itself now taking on tradition, as it goes, a tradition apart, already a part, already a way, away, along the riverrun. . . . [21]

Notes

INTRODUCTION

1. See, e.g., Derrida's early essay "Signature Event Context," in Jacques Derrida, *Margins of Philosophy*, trans. Alan Bass (Chicago: University of Chicago Press, 1982), 307–30, as well as the follow-up to that essay, *Limited Inc.*, trans. Samuel Weber (Evanston, Ill.: Northwestern University Press, 1988).

2. The goal of most scientific language, as I understand it, is to minimize this performativity, whereas the goal of much poetry and literature is to maximize it. Traditionally, philosophy has wished to be more like scientific writing than literature, although certain notable exceptions, such as Plato, complicate this claim. Derrida's understanding of language as performative has necessitated a new form of philosophical writing, one that looks as much at the gestures of argumentation as at the arguments themselves, at the way in which language actually *works* to produce the truths of which it speaks.

3. For a comprehensive bibliography of Derrida's work and of secondary sources on his work up through 1991 see William R. Schultz and Lewis L. B. Fried, *Jacques Derrida: An Annotated Primary and Secondary Bibliography* (New York: Garland, 1992). I would also recommend John Caputo's annotated bibliography in *Deconstruction in a Nutshell: A Conversation with Jacques Derrida*, edited and with a commentary by John D. Caputo (New York: Fordham University Press, 1997), 204–8. Caputo divides his recommended secondary sources into those related to literary theory, philosophy, hermeneutics, theology, religion, ethics, feminist theory, architecture, and pedagogy. I would add to Caputo's list Marian Hobson's very perceptive analysis of Derrida's language and modes of argumentation in *Jacques Derrida: Opening Lines* (New York: Routledge, 1998). On the question of politics see Richard Beardsworth's *Derrida and the Political* (New York: Routledge, 1996). I also recommend Bill Martin's important book *Matrix and Line: Derrida and the Possibilities of Postmodern Social Theory* (Albany: State University of New York Press, 1992); and its equally important sequel, *Humanism and Its Aftermath: The Shared Fate of Deconstruction and Politics* (Atlantic Highlands, N.J.: Humanities Press, 1995).

On the relationship between deconstruction and literary theory see Jeffrey Nealon's excellent *Double Reading* (Ithaca, N.Y.: Cornell University Press, 1993); and *Alterity Politics* (Durham, N.C.: Duke University Press, 1998), which take the notion of performativity in a different although related direction. See also Peggy Kamuf's *The Division of Literature: Or the University in Deconstruction* (Chicago: University of Chicago Press, 1997), which turns to the work of Derrida "for indications of how to continue to encounter the texts of *our tradition*" (5; my emphasis).

Other books that have been particularly helpful to me include Geoffrey Bennington's *Jacques Derrida* (Chicago: University of Chicago Press, 1993), esp. "The Signature" (148–66); Rodolphe Gasché's *Tain of the Mirror* (Cambridge: Harvard University Press, 1986), with its subtle reinterpretation of reflection and the relationship between philosophy and literature in Derrida's work; David Wood's *The Deconstruction of Time* (Atlantic Highlands, N.J.: Humanities Press, 1989), particularly its treatment of the future in deconstruction; and Herman Rapaport's *Heidegger and Derrida: Reflections on Time and Language* (Lincoln: University of Nebraska Press, 1989).

For works relevant to particular chapters in this book I would recommend, for Chapter 1, Jay Farness's *Missing Socrates: Problems of Plato's Writing* (University Park: Pennsylvania State University Press, 1991); and Jasper Neel's *Plato, Derrida, and Writing* (Carbondale: Southern Illinois University Press, 1988). For Chapter 2 see Caputo's *Deconstruction in a Nutshell*, particularly the section "*Khōra*: Being Serious with Plato"; for Chapter 5 see Nicholas Royle, *After Derrida* (Manchester, U.K.: Manchester University Press, 1995), particularly his chapter on "Telepathy." For Chapters 6 and 9, on hospitality and Derrida's reading of Levinas, see Hent de Vries's *Philosophy and the Turn to Religion* (Baltimore: Johns Hopkins University Press, 1999); and Simon Critchley's *The Ethics of Deconstruction: Derrida and Levinas* (Oxford: Blackwell, 1992). For Chapter 7 see David Krell's *The Purest of Bastards* (University Park: Pennsylvania State University Press, 2000), esp. chapter 2, "Echo, Narcissus, Echo"; John D. Caputo's *The Prayers and Tears of Jacques Derrida: Religion Without Religion* (Bloomington: Indiana University Press, 1997), esp. sec. 19, "These Weeping Eyes, Those Seeing Tears: The Faith of Jacques Derrida"; and on the theme of the prosthesis, David Wills's *Prosthesis* (Stanford, Calif.: Stanford University Press, 1995). For the Conclusion see again Caputo's *Prayers and Tears*, particularly sec. 16, "Circumcision"; and Geoffrey Hartman's *Saving the Text: Literature, Derrida, Philosophy* (Baltimore: Johns Hopkins University Press, 1981) for a reading of *Glas* in the light of *Finnegans Wake*.

4. Although much less attention has been paid to such "receptive" structures or strategies in Derrida's work than to its themes, claims, and arguments, these structures and strategies have not gone wholly neglected. To cite just two recent examples: In *The Division of Literature* Peggy Kamuf demonstrates through a Derridean-inspired reading of Melville's *Confidence-Man* precisely how the reader becomes implicated in Melville's text and why academic criticism has tended to avoid the

thesis that "any possible meaning depends on the reader's act, which the text describes as the act of extending confidence or credit" (38). I argue throughout this work that it is this extending of confidence or credit that not only sustains but first institutes the tradition.

There is also, it seems, an affinity or sympathy between what I am trying to do here and works such as Nicholas Royle's *After Derrida*. Through his own idiomatic supplements of Shakespeare and Beckett, among others, Royle resists making his work into a mere "labor of filial piety," an apologia of Derrida's work or a defense of its positions, by taking up and doing something else with Derrida's work, something that is nonetheless a result of his encounter with Derrida. As the translator of Derrida's "Telepathy," the text that is the focus of Chapter 5, Royle not only understands but appears to undergo the kind of "telepathy" Derrida evokes in that text. He sees how Derrida "takes on Freud's identity" in this work, "writing *as* Freud . . . telepathetically occupying Freud's thoughts and feelings" (9) so as to challenge us "to think telepathy (and indeed sympathy) no longer in terms of a relation between two or more subjects whose identity is already constituted and assured" (72). In other words, the tradition is not simply passed on but constituted through "Telepathy," through a kind of "reception" that will be the "focus" of several of the following chapters.

5. On the question of pedagogy in Derrida see *Derrida and Education*, ed. Gert J. J. Biesta and Denise Egéa-Kuehne (New York: Routledge, 2001). See in particular Didier Cahen's contribution to this volume, "Derrida and the Question of Education: A New Space for Philosophy," 12–31, which contains an excellent reading of Derrida's *Du droit à la philosophie* (Paris: Galilée, 1990). Cahen's question "How can we educate the Other as Other?" resonates throughout the present work.

6. See, e.g., "Freud's Legacy," in *The Post Card*, trans. Alan Bass (Chicago: University of Chicago Press, 1987), 292–337; *Specters of Marx: The State of the Debt, the Work of Mourning, and the New International*, trans. Peggy Kamuf (New York: Routledge, 1994); *Archive Fever: A Freudian Impression*, trans. Eric Prenowitz (Chicago: University of Chicago Press, 1996); and *Religion*, ed. Jacques Derrida and Gianni Vattimo (Stanford, Calif.: Stanford University Press, 1996), 1–78.

7. An entire chapter—indeed several chapters—could be added here to address the question of the relationship between Derrida and his "students," from Jean-Luc Nancy to Sarah Kofman, from Geoffrey Bennington to Serge Margel and Catherine Malabou, all of whom Derrida has written on in recent years.

8. Jacques Derrida, *Resistances of Psychoanalysis*, trans. Peggy Kamuf, Pascale-Anne Brault, and Michael Naas (Stanford, Calif.: Stanford University Press, 1998), 74. This line comes from a passage in which Derrida reaffirms his method of reading Descartes in his much earlier work on Foucault's *The History of Madness*, his 1963 text "Cogito and the History of Madness." The full passage is illuminating:

> In a protocol that laid out certain reading positions, I spoke of the way in which philosophical language is rooted in non-philosophical language and

I recalled a rule of hermeneutical method that still seems to me valid for the historian of philosophy as well as for the psychoanalyst, namely, the necessity of first ascertaining a surface or manifest meaning and, thus, of speaking the language of the patient to whom one is listening: the necessity of gaining a good understanding, in a quasi-scholastic way, philologically and grammatically, by taking into account the dominant and stable conventions, of what Descartes *meant* on the already so difficult surface of his text, such as it is interpretable according to classical norms of reading; the necessity of gaining this understanding *before* submitting this first reading to a symptomatic and historical interpretation regulated by other axioms or protocols, *before and in order to* destabilize, wherever this is possible and if it is necessary, the authority of canonical interpretations. Whatever one ends up doing with it, one must begin by listening to the canon. (74)

9. Jacques Derrida, *The Work of Mourning*, ed. Pascale-Anne Brault and Michael Naas (Chicago: University of Chicago Press, 2001), 162.

CHAPTER 1

An earlier version of this chapter was presented at the Collegium Phaenomenologicum in Perugia, Italy, in July 1993 and was published under the title "Receiving the Tradition," in *Interrogating the Tradition*, ed. John Sallis and Charles Scott (New York: State University of New York Press, 2000), 7–17.

1. Jacques Derrida, "Plato's Pharmacy," in *Dissemination*, trans. Barbara Johnson (Chicago: University of Chicago Press, 1981), 65. Hereafter abbreviated as "PP."

2. I use fore*fathers* advisedly here to echo Plato's use of such terms throughout the *Phaedrus*. I also speak throughout this work in terms of *a* tradition or *the* tradition, even though it is precisely the singularity, homogeneity, and exemplarity of this tradition that I am trying to question.

3. Jacques Derrida, "Force of Law: The 'Mystical Foundation of Authority,'" trans. Mary Quintance, *Cardozo Law Review* 11, nos. 5–6 (1990): 990–93. I will try in what follows to demonstrate the impossibility of receiving such a pure performative act—even when it has "taken place."

4. Jacques Derrida, *La dissémination* (Paris: Seuil, 1972), 93.

5. One might also say that Theuth's presentation of the *pharmakon* as a remedy already turns it toward the light, toward the revelation of technique and learning, toward a rational persuasion that is always male, related to speaking in full presence in the agora, and away from the darkness of seduction, away from the night of veils and perfumes, disguises and magic. Remedy—rather than, say, potion—already translates from the side of philosophy and, thus, already from the side of the king, which is also, as we will shortly see, the side of Theuth.

6. In *Spurs* Derrida makes a similar move, immobilizing the scene once again at the moment of donation: "I immobilize for the moment the play on 'to give'

and 'to give oneself' and 'to give oneself for'" (*Spurs: Nietzsche's Styles*, trans. Barbara Harlow [Chicago: University of Chicago Press, 1979], 70).

7. As we will see in subsequent chapters, just about every other text in which Derrida pays homage to a thinker or teacher can be read in a similar way. This is clear, for example, when Derrida pays homage to Levinas in "At This Very Moment in This Work Here I Am." But the relationship between reception and pedagogy can be found in more subtle ways, for example, in Derrida's "*Khōra*," an essay in honor of Jean-Pierre Vernant. As we will see in the following chapter, an astonishing resemblance becomes apparent in that essay between the *khōra* as the place of donation and reception, the place that precedes any particular donation or reception, and the teaching—or the figure—of Jean-Pierre Vernant, the point being, I take it, that what Derrida *received* from Vernant was not this or that teaching, this or that doctrine or idea, but a way of gesturing or turning toward the *khōra*, a way of receiving it, without making it out to be something determinate or present.

8. Jacques Derrida, *Positions*, trans. Alan Bass (Chicago: University of Chicago Press, 1981), 52.

CHAPTER 2

An earlier version of this chapter was presented at the annual meeting of the Society for Phenomenology and Existential Philosophy in October 1993 and subsequently published in the *Oxford Literary Review* 18 (1997): 67–86.

1. Jacques Derrida, "*Khōra*," trans. Ian McLeod, in *On the Name*, ed. Thomas Dutoit (Stanford, Calif.: Stanford University Press, 1995), 100; *Khōra* (Paris: Galilée, 1993). Hereafter abbreviated as "*K*."

2. I am excluding all those moments when we are *forced* to take a detour, even though we can often, if we are clever enough, recuperate or capitalize on these moments too and derive some benefit or advantage from them.

3. Jacques Derrida, *Given Time*, trans. Peggy Kamuf (Chicago: University of Chicago Press, 1992), 7; *Donner le temps* (Paris: Galilée, 1991), 19. Hereafter abbreviated as *GT*.

4. Jacques Derrida, *The Truth in Painting*, trans. Geoffrey Bennington and Ian McLeod (Chicago: University of Chicago Press, 1987), 320.

5. I use the term *autodonation* and not *self-donation* to suggest that the self cannot be taken for granted in this donation. The one who gives is not the same as the one who receives; this is not a simple reflexive giving in which everything comes back to some identifiable subject.

6. Martin Heidegger, "The Origin of the Work of Art," in *Basic Writings*, ed. David Farrell Krell (New York: Harper and Row, 1977), 163.

7. The theme of *khōra* as a place for retrospective hermeneutical interpretations—interpretations programmed from the start by Plato's text—runs throughout the "*Khōra*" piece.

8. One will recall that the second line of *De l'esprit* [*Of Spirit*] asks "what, for Heidegger, *avoiding* [*éviter*] means?" *Heidegger et la question: De l'esprit et autres essais* (Paris: Flammarion, 1990), 11; *Of Spirit*, trans. Geoffrey Bennington and Rachel Bowlby (Chicago: University of Chicago Press, 1989), 1. Derrida quotes from Marcel Detienne and Jean-Pierre Vernant, *Les ruses de l'intelligence: La mètis des Grecs* (Paris: Flammarion, 1974), 66.

9. It is precisely this precipitation that causes Heidegger to project the figure of a peasant woman into the shoes of Van Gogh's painting. An even greater precipitation, however, leads Shapiro to believe he has caught Heidegger at his game and encourages him to project what he believes to be the true referent into the shoes, namely, the male city dweller. For Shapiro, Heidegger has erred because he has failed to identify the referent. But for Derrida, Shapiro makes the even more egregious error of assuming that he knows what is at stake in a painting, that it is a question of identifying a referent before or beyond the painting. Shapiro thus appears to close the chasm of the shoes even more than Heidegger, the shoes that would open up the difference between reference and referent in the first place.

10. Derrida uses the phrase *bouche bée* to describe this gaping mouth, a mouth open, perhaps, in awe or amazement. Fancifully, the phrase can be heard to have both a subjective and an objective dimension—being astonished before that which is astonishing, standing openmouthed before the open mouth of *khōra*, as if the yawn of the abyss immediately provoked the yawn of the one beholding it. Perhaps we cannot avoid the pathetic fall of anthropocentrism, the identification, at the very least, of an orifice, a mouth, the basis of all future object relations.

11. Just as Derrida saw a certain programmation of the *khōra* in the interpretations that would come after it, he sees in the so-called frame dialogue a reflection or programmation of the discussion of *khōra* that comes later in the dialogue. The serious stakes of philosophy are thus already raised before we get to the philosophy as such, already in the mythological introduction to that philosophy. Here, as there, the question is what *dekhomai* means, that is, what it means "to receive."

12. The question of the relationship or "fit" between discourse and the subject of discourse is explicitly raised by Derrida in several places. This relation depends, says Derrida, "on a sort of metonymy . . . [that] would displace itself, by displacing the names, from types [*genres*] of being to types [*genres*] of discourse" ("*K,*" 91). To being, becoming, and the third kind that is *khōra* there would correspond logos, mythos, and the bastard discourse about *khōra*. But what legitimates this metonymy? Does the metonymy break down when it comes to *khōra*? Is it appropriate that a discourse about the spacing of space should take place as "the time of a detour"?

13. One must speak of *khōra*, says Derrida, not always with the same name but "*in the same manner*" (Derrida's emphasis). There is a difference here, it seems, between the repetition of a name and the iteration of a way or manner. But this is not the way the tradition has usually understood the *Timaeus*, for the line has tra-

ditionally been translated not just in the same way but with the same name, the phrase *tauton autēn aei prosrēteon* (50b) being typically translated as *khōra* must be "called always by the same name," rather than "always spoken of in the same manner." Derrida asks: "And if it is important that the *appellation*, rather than the *name*, should say the same, will we be able to replace, relay, translate *khōra* by other names . . . ?" ("*K*," 98). For example, will we be able—will we be required—to call or translate *khōra* by names such as *espacement*, *pharmakon*, or *différance*, speaking of it or her in the same manner but not always with the same name?

CHAPTER 3

An earlier version of this chapter was published in *Cultural Semiosis: Tracing the Signifier*, Continental Philosophy, vol. 6, ed. Hugh J. Silverman (New York: Routledge, 1998), 219–38.

1. Aristotle, *Physics*, trans. P. H. Wicksteed and F. M. Cornford (Cambridge, Mass.: Harvard University Press, 1957), 2.193a–b.

2. Jacques Derrida, "White Mythology," in Derrida, *Margins of Philosophy*, 209. Hereafter abbreviated as "WM."

3. In architecture a *socle* is the base of a column, in geology a layer of rock, the bedrock beneath the surface. It could also be used, however, to describe the base of a bed.

4. Homer, *Odyssey*, trans. A. T. Murray (Cambridge, Mass.: Harvard University Press, 1919), 14.213–15. Hereafter abbreviated as *Od.* In what follows I will also be using Murray's translation of the *Iliad* (Cambridge, Mass.: Harvard University Press, 1924), hereafter abbreviated as *Il.*

5. Jean Starobinski, "The Inside and the Outside," *Hudson Review* 28, no. 3 (autumn 1975): 346. Hereafter abbreviated as "IO." My thanks to Joel Shapiro for bringing this article to my attention.

6. Such a sign can be found either in the sky or on the earth. Odysseus puts a *sēma* along a path during the night raid of the *Iliad* so that he will not miss the place on his return (*Il.*, 10.466–68). The Greeks decide who will face Hector in man-to-man combat by casting lots, each man putting his own *sēma* on a stone—a mark known only to him (*Il.*, 7.189). A *sēma* is thus a distinguishing mark of some kind—for example, a "spot [*sēma*] of white" on a horse (*Il.*, 23.455) or an indentation marking the distance of a discus throw (*Il.*, 23.843; *Od.*, 8.192, 195). It can be a token that provides a guest-friend with his credentials (*Il.*, 6.176) or an "evil token [*sēma kakon*]" (*Il.*, 6.178) that marks the one who bears it, like the "baneful tokens [*sēmata lugra*]" of writing (*Il.*, 6.168). Zeus's thunder is a *sēma* for men, as is the appearance of certain snakes or birds (see *Il.*, 2.53, 2.308, 8.171, 9.236–37, 13.244, 22.30; and *Od.*, 20.111, 21.413). In book 4 of the *Iliad* "Zeus turned the [Myceneans'] minds by showing them tokens [*sēmata*] of ill" (*Il.*, 4.381). A *sēma* can thus be that which motivates action, whether it comes from the gods or men (*Od.*, 21.231).

A *sēma* is also a tomb, a mark on the earth that would seem to indicate the presence of buried bones and ashes. In the penultimate book of the *Iliad*—once again the penultimate book—a *sēma* functions as both an indication in speech and an external mark, both a mark on the earth and a tomb. Instead of indicating the linear flight of a discus, it marks the turning point of a chariot race. Nestor says to his son Antilochus: "Now will I tell thee a manifest sign [*sēma . . . ariphrades*] that will not escape thee. There standeth, as it were a fathom's height above the ground, a dry stump whether of oak or of pine, which rotteth not in the rain. . . . Haply it is a monument [*sēma*] of some man long ago dead, or haply was made the turning-post [*nussa*] of a race in days of men of old; and now hath . . . Achilles appointed it his turning-post [*termata*]" (*Il.*, 23.326–33). Once again the sign is manifest, can't be missed, although it still needs to be pointed out. The *sēma* seems to refer here to *both* the indications of Nestor *and* the tomb or monument that will serve as the turning point for the race, to both the manifest sign of a speaker and the seemingly exterior sign of an object, that is, to both the signifying process and the signified.

7. When in book 19 the disguised Odysseus describes in detail the clothes and manners of Odysseus, whom he feigns to have met in a foreign land, Penelope weeps "as she recognized the sure tokens [*sēmata . . . empeda*]" (*Od.*, 19.250)—the words of the beggar but also, it seems, the clothes, the fabrics, and brooch that she herself had given to her husband before his departure. Hence narrative seems to provide sure signs as long as they are anchored in experience or else woven into it. Indeed, the weaving of Penelope, the metaphor or emblem for narrative throughout the *Odyssey*, is perhaps the female counterpart of the crafting of the bedpost, the latter knitting its way through the fabric of the former, weaving and unweaving the narrative web, like the moon that waxes and wanes.

8. The verb *pēgnumi*, interestingly, is used in Homer to describe a spear when it sticks into the earth, a spear that is fixed but not actually rooted—a bit like Antiphon's bedpost.

9. Richard Wilbur, "Lying," in *New and Collected Poems* (New York: Harcourt Brace Jovanovich, 1988), 10.

CHAPTER 4

An earlier version of this chapter was delivered at the annual meeting of the Society for Phenomenology and Existential Philosophy in 1994 and subsequently published in *Philosophy Today* 22 (1997): 141–52.

1. This appendix was apparently withdrawn by Foucault from later editions. The second part of Foucault's response, "Une petite pédagogie," was published in *Le Monde*, June 14, 1973, 23.

2. Other events and texts could, of course, be evoked to complicate this scenario. For example, as Derrida writes at the end of "'To Do Justice to Freud,'" much of the analysis at the end of that essay "intersects a much longer treatment

of the subject in an unpublished paper entitled "Beyond the Power Principle," presented at a "conference at New York University organized by Thomas Bishop in April 1986." Jacques Derrida, "'To Do Justice to Freud': The History of Madness in the Age of Psychoanalysis," in *Resistances of Psychoanalysis*. Hereafter abbreviated as *RP*.

3. Michel Foucault, *Histoire de la folie à l'âge classique* (Paris: Gallimard, 1972), 57; my translation.

4. Jacques Derrida, "Cogito and the History of Madness," in *Writing and Difference*, trans. Alan Bass (Chicago: University of Chicago Press, 1978), 55–56 (Derrida's emphasis; translation slightly modified). Hereafter abbreviated as "C."

5. Michel Foucault, "My Body, This Paper, This Fire," trans. Geoff Bennington in *Oxford Literary Review* 4 (autumn 1975): 27. Hereafter abbreviated as "MBTP."

6. Michel Foucault, *The History of Sexuality*, vol. 1, *An Introduction*, trans. Robert Hurley (New York: Vintage, 1980), 45. Hereafter abbreviated as *HS*.

7. Such a strategy of applying the terms within the dialogue to the terms of the dialogue is not unrelated to Derrida's own way of proceeding in "'To Do Justice to Freud.'" Whereas Derrida in 1963 asks primarily about the possibility of writing a history of madness, he writes in 1991 about the conditions that made Foucault's attempt possible. In other words, Derrida looks not so much at the possibility of what Foucault wrote—that is, a history of madness—as at the possibility of his very writing, a writing that not only determines but is in some sense determined by the age or history of psychoanalysis. Derrida writes: "Were one to trust too readily in the opposition between subject and object, as well as in the category of objectification (something that I here believe to be neither possible nor just, and hardly faithful to Foucault's own intention), one would say for the sake of convenience that it is a question of considering the history of madness *a parte subjecti*, that is, from the side where it is written or inscribed and not from the side of what it describes" (*RP*, 76).

8. Other notions such as genius, repetition, interminability, and dialogue could be similarly analyzed.

9. *RP*, 85. Here is another example of Derrida's emphasis on mastery within Foucault's text: "But he also does this, more or less willingly, *as Descartes*, or, at least, as the Descartes whom he had accused of excluding madness by excluding, mastering, or dismissing—since these all come down to the same thing—the powers of the Evil Genius" (*RP*, 95; Derrida's emphasis).

10. There is much to say about the role that writing plays in this debate between Foucault and Derrida, about the mastery of language and the relationship between language and madness. I recall here that the first footnote of "Cogito and the History of Madness" relates the circumstances surrounding the oral presentation of the essay and its eventual publication to Plato's condemnation of writing in the *Phaedrus*. Derrida speaks of the way in which writing, according to Socrates in the *Phaedrus*, always needs "the assistance of its father," whereas living speech

is animated by the father within or behind it. Considering all that follows in the "Cogito" essay concerning the relationship between disciple and master, it would not be inappropriate to want to insert at this point the reading that Derrida would eventually devote to this dialogue in "Plato's Pharmacy," especially to the scene where Theuth, the inventor of writing—of *écriture*, let us say—gives to the king, Thamus, his newest invention for evaluation. Were we to follow out the implications of Derrida's reading, we would see, I think, that we are confronted in both the *Phaedrus* and the "Cogito" essay with a kind of parricidal scene, although one in which the figures of father and son *cannot* be definitively fixed or located. See Chapter 1.

11. In October 1984 Derrida wrote in the context of a debate over school reform and the teaching of philosophy in France, "How can the necessity of the presence [*avoir-lieu*] of a master and the necessity of his effacement [*non-lieu*] be reconciled? What unbelievable topology do we require to reconcile the heterodidact and the autodidact?" In *Du droit à la philosophie* (Paris: Galilée, 1990), 521. Translation from Didier Cahen, "Derrida and the Question of Education," in *Derrida and Education*, 24.

12. Michel Foucault, "A Discourse on Language," included as an appendix to *The Archeology of Knowledge*, trans. Rupert Swyer (New York: Pantheon, 1972), 237.

CHAPTER 5

An earlier version of this chapter was presented on July 19, 1992, during a ten-day colloquium at Cerisy devoted to Derrida's work. It was subsequently published in French in the proceedings of the conference, *Le passage des frontières: Autour du travail de Jacques Derrida* (Paris: Galilée, 1994), 467–75. The implicit agreement of the conference was that papers would focus essentially on works published by Derrida after 1980, the year of the first Cerisy conference on Derrida. I should also note for what follows that Derrida's own lecture at the conference, "Aporias," was delivered four days earlier, on July 15.

1. "Qual Quelle: Valéry's Sources," in Derrida, *Margins of Philosophy*, 273–306.

2. Socrates would have perhaps sympathized with the search for a nonphysical cause for the divining rod, for I recall that it is he who, in the *Phaedrus*, as Derrida puts it, "mockingly proposes a learned explanation of the myth in the rationalistic, physicalist style of the *sophoi*" ("PP," 69).

3. "Circumfession," in *Jacques Derrida*, by Geoffrey Bennington and Jacques Derrida, trans. Geoffrey Bennington (Chicago: University of Chicago Press, 1993), 6.

4. *Of Grammatology*, trans. Gayatri Chakravorty Spivak (Baltimore: Johns Hopkins University Press, 1976), 229–42; *Memoirs of the Blind*, trans. Pascale-Anne Brault and Michael Naas (Chicago: University of Chicago Press, 1993), 50–51. One might add here all the staffs and canes of the Old Testament, associated not only with blindness but, sometimes, with divining. It has thus been speculated that the story in Numbers 20:9–11, where Moses strikes a rock with his staff to find water for his people, is a reference to water divining.

5. See "PP," 93. The art of rhabdomancy is thought to go back to the time of the ancient Greeks. In Homer the *rhabdos* is associated with the magic of Circe, who uses her wand to transform the comrades of Odysseus into pigs (*Od.*, 10.237–38). Athena also uses a golden wand to transform Odysseus into a beggar (*Od.*, 13.429). But the magic wand is most closely associated with Hermes, who puts people to sleep and wakes them up with it (*Il.*, 24.343–44 = *Od.*, 5.47–48 = 24.2–4). Almost every book on the art of water divining refers to the caduceus or wand of Hermes.

6. E. W. Beaven, *Tales of the Divining Rod* (London: A. H. Stockwell, 1899), 183. Hereafter abbreviated as *TDR*. Of all the books written on this subject, I will cite only those written during the same period around which "Telepathy" revolves—the end of the nineteenth and beginning of the twentieth centuries. What interests me here, obviously, is less the "reality" or "truth" of the phenomenon of water dousing than the rhetoric around it at a given epoch and place.

7. Jacques Derrida, "Telepathy," trans. Nicholas Royle, *Oxford Literary Review* 10, nos. 1–2 (1988): 3–41. Hereafter abbreviated as "T."

8. Jacques Derrida, *The Post Card*, trans. Alan Bass (Chicago: University of Chicago Press, 1987), 208–9. Hereafter abbreviated as *PC*.

9. In John Mullins and Sons, *The Divining Rod: Its History, Truthfulness, and Practical Utility* (Colerne, Wiltshire: J. and H. W. Mullins, 1908). Hereafter abbreviated as *DR*. Mullins speaks of the importance of holding the divining rod with *both hands*. As for the use of the divining rod in France, Beaven says that "the French appear to have been of a more practical nature and less under superstitious influences than the British" (*TDR*, 185).

10. I recall here the well-known words of Merleau-Ponty in the chapter entitled "The Intertwining—The Chiasm," in *The Visible and the Invisible*, trans. Alphonso Lingis (Evanston, Ill.: Northwestern University Press, 1968), 139: "There is a fundamental narcissism of all vision; . . . as many painters have said, I feel myself looked at by the things, my activity is equally passivity."

11. For the correspondence between the discovery of water and the eliciting of tears see *TDR*, 112, 120. Beaven's strange and idiosyncratic book combines historical and scientific observations with fictional accounts, oftentimes moving with little transition from one to the other. In the beginning of the book, for example, two English aristocrats are taking a stroll, one with the aid of a cane. Engaged in a conversation about politics and, eventually, "revolution," Beaven uses this last word, combined with an ellipsis, to mark the transition between two registers. They are discussing revolution, and then there is "a revolution . . . of the walking stick" (*TDR*, 19). The language of revolution and turning is inscribed everywhere in this account, the stick "twisting" and "inclined" in such a way that its user is himself "converted" at this "turning point" in his life.

12. See the "Glossary" of the English translation of *The Post Card*, xvii. For an interesting reading of Derrida's relationship to Lacan see Herman Rapaport, *Between the Sign and the Gaze* (Ithaca: Cornell University Press, 1994), 184–201.

13. Cf. Arthur J. Ellis, *The Divining Rod: A History of Water Witching* (Washington, D.C.: Government Printing Office, 1917), 16. Ellis gives a long list of the past uses of divining rods. He ultimately tries to discredit this art and concludes his article for the American government by recommending that public funds no longer be used to support research into this phenomenon.

14. Is it a question here of a dream of the previous night—that is, of July 8? Derrida later writes concerning one of the two dreams that Freud thought might be telepathic: "All of these things, if it is really a question of the dream of 8 July 1915" ("T," 27).

15. Explanations of the movement of the divining rod are almost as diverse as the authors who have written on the subject; they range anywhere from an unconscious mental or muscular action to unconscious or involuntary (auto)suggestion, from electricity or electromagnetism to some kind of sympathetic affinity, from unknown forces of attraction and repulsion to demonic or satanic influence (so that wands sometimes had to be dipped in water—baptized—to ward off evil influences).

16. For the reinvention of this word *trouver* see the first essay of Derrida's *Psyché: Inventions de l'autre* (Paris: Galilée, 1987), 11–61.

17. This is the case of the book by John Mullins and sons, which is little more than a concatenation of testimonies designed to prove "the public utility of the divining-rod" (*DR*, ii) "by way of corroborative and independent testimony of the truthfulness, utility, and efficacy of the detective powers of the so-called 'Divining Rod'"(*DR*, 2). Testimonies are always necessary; one believes because one has seen with one's own eyes—or, perhaps, seen another who has discovered without seeing. Indeed, this scene is often described: a group of English aristocrats resort to calling on a diviner to discover a water source on one of their estates. When the divining seems to work and the rod begins to turn in a particular direction, someone suggests blindfolding the diviner (in "Telepathy," too, it is a question of walking without seeing ["T," 35]) to ensure that he is not judging the presence of a source by a particular form of grass or plant growing nearby. The diviner is thus transformed into a sort of blind man, moving along by means of a cane that is no longer passive in his hands but leads him where it will(s). The testimony almost always takes the same form: the witness—someone respectable and trustworthy—an aristocrat or scientist, perhaps even a geologist, begins by explaining that he has been skeptical all his life about such phenomena but that after having seen with his own eyes, and after having taken all the necessary precautions to guard against trickery and exclude other possible causes for the successful results, he now believes and so pronounces his faith in the rod and in the integrity of the diviner, concluding with the prediction that in spite of science's ignorance of the true cause of divination such a cause will one day be found.

18. On the name *Claude* see sec. 47 of "Circumfession," along with Hélène Cixous's *Portrait de Jacques Derrida en Jeune Saint Juif* (Paris: Galilée, 2001), 91–95.

19. "Ulysses Gramophone," trans. Tina Kendall, rev. Shari Benstock, in *Acts of Literature*, ed. Derek Attridge (New York: Routledge, 1991), 258. Hereafter abbreviated as "UG."

20. René Descartes, *La dioptrique* (Tours: Fayard, 1987), 73. If one did not know what *La dioptrique* was about, one might conclude from the drawings in the sixth discourse, which tries to explain how we understand the "situation" of the two sides of our body, that they depict a water diviner with his rod.

21. "And now we can pick up the scent of lots of things and give lectures on their stories and noses" ("T," 9); "any scent I can follow" ("T," 10); "one has to sniff around in that area" ("T," 37).

22. As for the word *vibration*, I cite "Ulysses Gramophone," 305: "We cannot separate the twin *yeses*, and yet they remain completely other. Like Shem and Shaun, like writing and the post. Such a coupling seems to me to ensure not so much the signature of *Ulysses* but the *vibration* of an event which *succeeds only in asking*" (Derrida's emphasis).

23. "Tympan," in Derrida, *Margins of Philosophy*, xix.

24. The delay or *décalage* of the message is a recurring theme in this text. "A telepathic message may not coincide with the event in time. . . . It will have needed the time it takes to reach consciousness. With the aid of psychic temporality, of its discrepant [*décalée*] heterogeneity, its time differences [*décalages horaires*], if you prefer" ("T," 33; see 36–37); "Suppose that an anachronism which resembles no other unwedges [*décale*] us, it lifts or displaces the blocks [*les cales*], brakes or accelerates as if we were late with respect to that which has already happened to us in the future" ("T," 3).

25. "Of an Apocalyptic Tone Recently Adopted in Philosophy," trans. John P. Leavey Jr., *Oxford Literary Review* 6, no. 2 (1984): 7, 35.

CHAPTER 6

An earlier version of this chapter was presented in Paris on June 18, 1999, at a colloquium organized by Jacob Rogozinski at the Collège international de philosophie on the theme "Derrida and Phenomenology." My thanks to Jacob Rogozinski for his kind invitation.

1. I have left out of this history Derrida's master's thesis, *Le problème de la genèse dans la philosophie de Husserl* (Paris: Presses Universitaires de France), because, although written in 1953–54, it was not published until 1990.

2. I will not even attempt to speak here of the question of woman and domesticity in Levinas nor of the related questions of fraternity and paternity. Although these questions too are already raised in "Violence and Metaphysics" and become more and more central to "At This Very Moment in This Work Here I Am" and *Adieu*, I have, for reasons of time and thematic coherence, restricted my analysis to the question of philosophical language in Levinas and have done little more than evoke "At This Very Moment in This Work Here I Am."

3. "Violence and Metaphysics," in *Writing and Difference*, 95. Hereafter abbreviated as "VM." This essay was first published in the *Revue de métaphysique et de morale* 3 and 4 (1964).

4. *Sophist*, 241d, trans. Harold North Fowler, Loeb Classical Library (Cambridge, Mass.: Harvard University Press, 1977).

5. Using a word that, in the context of an essay on the work of Levinas, might easily be heard as coming from that work, Derrida speaks of a "dwelling" for such a question, a "founded dwelling" ("VM," 80).

6. "The question itself": Derrida might perhaps hesitate to employ such a formulation today, but the risk of misunderstanding is reduced here since Derrida distinguishes this question "itself" from all determined questions, which lets it be understood, it seems, that the question "itself" cannot "itself" be posed, or posed *as such*.

7. For the structure Inside-Outside emerges, writes Derrida, only "on the basis of an *included* origin, an *inscribed* eastern horizon which is neither within nor without space" ("VM," 113). This would be the site or place of the origin of site and language, space and speech—an origin that Levinas calls the Face.

8. See Derrida's "Cogito and the History of Madness," 307 n. 1.

9. *Adieu to Emmanuel Levinas*, trans. Pascale-Anne Brault and Michael Naas (Stanford, Calif.: Stanford University Press, 1999), 35. Hereafter abbreviated as *A*.

10. As Derrida argues in "Violence and Metaphysics," "Philosophical language belongs to a system of language(s)" and so always brings its "nonspeculative ancestry" along with it ("VM," 34). Hegel's *Aufheben*, Heidegger's *es gibt*, Derrida's *différance*—these appear to be examples of what Levinas has done in and with the French language, accepting the hospitality of this language and returning that hospitality by reinscribing this language, reinvesting the idiom not with a surplus of meaning but with an irreducible center, letting the idiom receive and interrupt itself, on the subject, for example, of hospitality, on the subject *as* hospitality, on the *hôte* as *otage*, the host as hostage.

11. "Le Moi et la Totalité" was first published in *Revue de Métaphysique et de Morale* 59 (1954): 353–73, and then in *Entre nous: Essais sur le penser-à-l'autre* (Paris: Bernard Grasset, 1991), 25–52 ["The Ego and the Totality," in *Collected Philosophical Papers*, trans. Alphonso Lingis (Dordrecht: Martinus Nijhoff Publishers, 1987), 25–46]; "Socialité et argent" was first published in 1989 in the acts of a colloquium of Jewish intellectuals around the theme of *money* (*L'argent*, Paris: Denoël, 1989), and then in *Emmanuel Levinas*, ed. Catherine Chalier and Michel Abensour (Paris: Editions de l'Herne, 1991), 134–38.

12. From Emmanuel Levinas, *Otherwise Than Being*, trans. Alphonso Lingis (Dordrecht: Kluwer Academic Publishers, 1991), 157. In "Violence and Metaphysics" Derrida argues that space would be the "wound and finitude of *birth*"—"without which one could not even open language" ("VM," 112; my emphasis).

13. But between these two extremes, which are not on the same level, one might imagine an "ethics of partiality" that would take seriously questions such as

"who shall pass before the other?" without immediately jumping to some universal concept of the human or humanity. Levinas seems never to give in to this possibility, no doubt because of the enormous risks of exclusion and violence it runs.

14. To put this sentence in context, here are the lines from *Adieu* leading up to it: "This 'is necessary' . . . reintroduces us, as if by force, into places that ethics should exceed: the visibility of the face, thematization, comparison, synchrony, system, copresence 'before a court of justice.' . . . The 'birth of the question' is the third. Yes, the *birth*, for the third does not wait; it comes at the origin of the face and of the face to face. Yes, the birth of the *question as question*, for the face to face is immediately suspended, interrupted without being interrupted, *as* face to face, as the dual of two singularities. The ineluctability of the third is the law of the question" (*A*, 30–31).

15. As Derrida demonstrates, this situation becomes even more extreme in *Otherwise Than Being*, where "substitution . . . dislodges even more drastically the primacy of intentionality" so that "the word 'question' is now forced to adapt to the situation of the hostage: the subject is hostage insofar as it is less a 'question' than '*in* question.' Its accusation, its persecution, its obsession, its 'persecuting obsession' is its 'being-in-question'" (*A*, 56).

16. For the reader who does not pick up on the reference, Derrida refers explicitly to "Violence and Metaphysics" at the bottom of the page.

17. In a note in *Adieu* Derrida actually defends Levinas against himself, claiming that in an interview in the early 1980s Levinas conceded too much when he said that the themes of the third and justice were not adequately treated in *Totality and Infinity:* "The question of the third was not only present, as we see, but developed in *Totality and Infinity*. One is thus a bit surprised by the concession Levinas seems to make to one of his interlocutors during an interview" (*A*, 143 n. 62).

18. My analysis here owes much to Peter Wake, a doctoral student at DePaul University, who analyzes these two orders in Descartes and Levinas in a lucid and illuminating manner in his essay, "Phenomenology and the Ethical Relation: Levinas Interrupted," in *International Studies in Philosophy*, forthcoming.

19. Jean-François Lyotard, "Levinas's Logic," trans. Ian McLeod, in *Face to Face with Levinas*, ed. Richard A. Cohen (Albany: State University of New York Press, 1986), 117–58.

20. Derrida writes further in "Violence and Metaphysics": "I could not possibly speak of the Other, make of the Other a theme, pronounce the Other as object, in the accusative. I can only, I *must* only speak to the other; that is, I must call him in the vocative" ("VM," 103). This claim will be taken up in relation to friendship in Chapter 8.

21. "But if all justice begins with speech"—that is, with the Other *as* speech— "all speech is not just" ("VM," 106). Rhetoric, the rhetoric of theory, the political rhetoric of protecting borders, of affirming the homeland, is more often than not a violence that reduces the other to some category within the Same. This helps explain

the ambivalence of the word *justice* in Levinas, sometimes applied to the face-to-face relation, sometimes to the interruption of this relation in the figure of the third.

It is always possible to be inhospitable toward the other, even if denial, rejection, or repression are themselves forms of welcoming. In "Violence and Metaphysics" Derrida develops this logic in the context of Levinas's understanding of war: on the one hand, war is only possible when the face has been forgotten or repressed; on the other, one can make war only against a face. Something similar could be said of hospitality: on the one hand, one can offer hospitality or be hospitable only to a face; on the other hand, it is the very welcoming of the face that allows one to be hostile or to refuse hospitality to it.

22. Jacques Derrida, *Of Hospitality*, trans. Rachel Bowlby (Stanford, Calif.: Stanford University Press, 2001). Hereafter abbreviated as *H*. Translation slightly modified.

23. Levinas himself speaks of this passage from the *Sophist* in a couple of places, one of the most prominent being—curiously—the text he devotes to Derrida in *Proper Names* (trans. Michael B. Smith [Stanford, Calif.: Stanford University Press, 1996], 61): "But the Saying is not exhausted in the *Said*, and the sign did not spring from the soil of the ontology of the Said, to receive from it its paradoxical structure of relation (which astonished Plato to the point of pushing him to parricide) and make up for a self-eluding presence. The sign, like the Saying, is the extra-ordinary event (running counter to presence) of exposure to others, of subjection to others; i.e. the event of subjectivity. It is the one-for-the-other." The *Sophist* is also mentioned in an essay from 1972 in *Humanisme de l'autre homme* (Paris: Fata Morgana, 1972), 10.

CHAPTER 7

This chapter was first presented at a conference at DePaul University entitled "Drawing from Philosophy: A Symposium Around Jacques Derrida's *Memoirs of the Blind*" (February 5, 1994). The text was read in two voices, the first ostensibly male, a native English speaker, and the second female, a native French speaker. It was subsequently published in an earlier version as "To Believe: An Intransitive Verb? Translating Skepticism in Jacques Derrida's *Memoirs of the Blind*," *Paragraph* 20, no. 2 (July 1997): 105–23.

1. Jacques Derrida, *Mémoires d'aveugle: L'autoportrait et autres ruines* (Paris: Editions de la Réunion des Musées Nationaux, 1990), 9, 130. Hereafter abbreviated as *MA*. Translated as *Memoirs of the Blind: The Self-Portrait and Other Ruins*, by Pascale-Anne Brault and Michael Naas (Chicago: University of Chicago Press, 1993), 1, 129. Hereafter abbreviated as *MB*.

2. In the seventy-one drawings or paintings of *Memoirs of the Blind* the first self-portrait is that of Baudelaire, the eighteenth work in the text, and the final

self-portrait that of Jean-Marie Faverjon, the fifty-third work of the text, eighteen before the end.

3. Jacques Derrida, *The Truth in Painting*, trans. Geoffrey Bennington and Ian McLeod (Chicago: University of Chicago Press, 1987), 348. Hereafter abbreviated as *TP*.

4. James Joyce, *A Portrait of the Artist as a Young Man* (New York: Penguin, 1976), 7, 253. The following reading of Joyce owes much to a lecture by Hugh Kenner that one of the authors once had the good fortune to attend.

5. John Milton, *Paradise Lost* (New York: Norton, 1975), 1.22–26.

CHAPTER 8

An earlier version of this chapter was presented at the State University of New York at Buffalo on November 2, 1995. I would like to thank, among others, Rodolphe Gasché, Carol Jacobs, and Jill Robbins for their kind and helpful comments.

1. Jacques Derrida, *Politics of Friendship*, trans. George Collins (New York: Verso, 1997), vii. Hereafter abbreviated as *PF*.

2. Martin Heidegger, *Hölderlin's Hymn "The Ister,"* trans. William McNeill and Julia Davis (Bloomington: Indiana University Press, 1996), 142.

3. From *La trace de l'autre*, cited in Jacques Derrida, "Violence and Metaphysics," in *Writing and Difference*, 320 n. 92. Levinas writes in a similar vein in "Meaning and Sense" (in *Basic Philosophical Writings*, ed. Adriaan T. Peperzak, Simon Critchley, and Robert Bernasconi [Bloomington: Indiana University Press, 1996], 48): "The itinerary of philosophy remains that of Ulysses, whose adventure in the world was only a return to his native island—a complacency in the Same, an unrecognition of the Other."

As Don DeLillo's character Murray says in *White Noise* (New York: Viking, 1985), 258: "I don't trust anybody's nostalgia but my own. Nostalgia is a product of dissatisfaction and rage. It's a settling of grievances between the present and the past. The more powerful the nostalgia, the closer you come to violence. War is the form nostalgia takes when men are hard-pressed to say something good about their country."

4. This is more evident in the English version of *Politics of Friendship*, since the French has Derrida's essay "Heidegger's Ear (Geschlecht IV)," previously published in English but not in French, appended to it.

5. Maurice Blanchot, *Michel Foucault tel que je l'imagine* (Paris: Fata Morgana, 1986), 64; my translation.

6. Maurice Blanchot, *Friendship*, trans. Elizabeth Rottenberg (Stanford, Calif.: Stanford University Press, 1997), 289. Hereafter abbreviated as *F*.

7. Emile Benveniste, *Indo-European Language and Society*, trans. Elizabeth Palmer (Coral Gables, Fla.: University of Miami Press, 1973), 288.

8. *Philein* expresses a proximity that is founded and interrupted by a turning, a turning that is itself associated throughout the *Iliad* with relations of obedience,

persuasion, and prayer. See my *Turning: From Persuasion to Philosophy* (Atlantic Highlands, N.J.: Humanities Press, 1995), esp. chapter 3. This can be seen at the beginning of the poem when Achilles deliberates whether to slay Agamemnon. About to draw his sword on Agamemnon, Achilles senses Athena behind him and, "seized with wonder," "turned [*etrapeto*] him about, and forthwith knew Pallas Athena; and terribly did her eyes flash" (*Il.*, 1.199–200). The gods are thus just a turn away, and their gift or intervention is this turning. Achilles says to Athena: "Whoso obeys [*epipeithētai*] the gods, to him do they gladly give ear" (*Il.*, 1.218). Achilles knows that by turning toward the gods he ensures that the gods will turn toward him. Achilles thus obeys Athena and is turned away from committing an act of violence against Agamemnon.

9. Jacques Derrida, *Signsponge*, trans. Richard Rand (New York: Columbia University Press, 1984), 118. Even Patroclus's name is emblematic in this regard as well, meaning "father of renown," and it is, as scholars have noted, played on, reversed and feminized, in book 9 in the name "Cleo-patra."

10. Translated here as "bluntly," the word *sèchement*, meaning "in a dry [*sec*] manner," indicates that a reference to "Signature Event Context," or "SEC," is not very far away.

CHAPTER 9

An earlier version of this chapter was presented during an open classroom at the College Year in Athens (CYA) undergraduate foreign study program in Athens, Greece, on May 21, 1998. Other versions were given at Marshall University and Trinity College. My deep thanks and gratitude to Alexis Phyloctopoulos at CYA, Jeffrey Powell at Marshall, and Andrew Haase and Drew Hyland at Trinity for their hospitality and generous reception of this work.

1. Jacques Derrida, *Adieu to Emmanuel Levinas*, trans. Pascale-Anne Brault and Michael Naas (Stanford, Calif.: Stanford University Press, 1999); *Of Hospitality*, trans. Rachel Bowlby (Stanford, Calif.: Stanford University Press, 2000).

2. *Le Monde*, December 2, 1997, 18.

3. Immanuel Kant, *Perpetual Peace*, trans. Lewis White Beck (Indianapolis: Bobbs-Merrill, 1957), 20–21.

4. Derrida has used the word *invention* rather frequently over the last two decades, particularly in *Psyche* (Paris: Galilée, 1987), which is subtitled *Inventions of the Other*, but also in *Adieu*, where the word is analyzed in the context of Levinas's discourse on the state of Israel. Levinas asks whether Israel has tried not only to "provide a refuge for men without a homeland" but to "create on its land the concrete conditions for political *invention*" (*A*, 84; my emphasis).

CONCLUSION

To understand many of the allusions in this chapter, one needs to know its initial context. An earlier version was originally presented at a conference organized by David Goicoechea at Brock University, Ontario, November 3–4, 1995. Each participant in the conference, which went under the title "The Resurrection in Derrida's Glorious *Glas*," was asked to address a particular configuration of themes in Derrida's work. The title given to me was "The Resurrection and Castration: From the Pillar of Fire Toward the Future Perfect." My heartfelt thanks to David Goicoechea for providing this genuine chance for reflection. The earlier version of this essay was published as "Passing on the Mantle," in *Derrida's Glorious Glas* (St. Catherines, Ontario: Thought House, 1997), 163–86.

1. "A 'Madness' Must Watch Over Thinking," trans. Peggy Kamuf, in *Points . . . : Interviews, 1974–1994*, ed. Elisabeth Weber (Stanford, Calif.: Stanford University Press, 1995), 343–44.

2. All biblical passages are from the *New Revised Standard Version: The New Oxford Annotated Bible* (New York: Oxford University Press, 1991).

3. See also Mark 9:11–13; Luke 1:17.

4. Jacques Derrida, *Glas*, trans. John P. Leavey Jr. (Lincoln: University of Nebraska Press, 1986), 1a. Hereafter abbreviated as *GL*. Following John Leavey in his *Glassary* (Lincoln: University of Nebraska Press, 1986), I have indicated the English translation page number, followed by *a* to indicate the left column or *b* to indicate the right column and then *i* if the quote is in an insert within that column.

5. See Derrida's comments about *Glas* in "This Is Not an Oral Footnote," in *Annotations and Its Texts*, ed. Stephen A. Barney (Oxford: Oxford University Press, 1991), 204–5:

> 1. *Self-annotation*: it comments on itself, explains itself, interprets itself, describes itself directly and figuratively and in all ways, including typographically and physically (two columns, two bands, double binds). . . .
>
> 2. All modes of secondariness are tried and mimed and made parasitic and grafted, tattooed (inserted on the body). (Exegesis of sacred texts, commentaries, paraphrase, scientific texts, philosophical theses, farces and satires, "anatomy of criticism," Rabelais, Joyce.)
>
> 3. The text has no beginning and no end, no hierarchy, but [is] a text on religion, on proper names, on authority, law, theft, hierarchy.
>
> 4. It is an absolutely secondary text, twice secondary (Hegel and Genet, for example), secondary with respect to absolute knowledge (absolute note) and text (Hegel, for example), but it is at the same time not secondary.

5. The text is a continuous annotation on something that lies between discourse and nondiscourse: the syllable "GL": *glose, glossa, glotte,* Hegel, Genet's mother Gabrielle, the scene of *Gl*aviau, *gl*adiolus. . . .

6. The text plays on play, the fortuitous—*alea*—and necessity, mimesis (cratylism and the arbitrariness of the sign).

7. It mimes and plays on structures of the nonacademic or non-Western gloss (Rabbinical, Talmudic, Islamic; but these are also themes).

8. The two columns face each other and annotate each other, but they are both equally principal texts without any relation to each other, as if they did not belong to the same book: a deconstruction of the unity of the book.

6. "Two Words for Joyce," trans. Geoff Bennington, in *Post-Structuralist Joyce: Essays from the French*, ed. Derek Attridge and Daniel Ferrer (Cambridge, U.K.: Cambridge University Press, 1984), 150.

7. James Joyce, *Ulysses* (New York: Random House, 1961), 151. Hereafter abbreviated as *U*. According to Don Gifford in *Ulysses Annotated* (Los Angeles: University of California Press, 1988), this passage, echoing Revelation 7:14–15, "was the scriptural basis for the well-known nineteenth century revival hymn 'Holiness Desired,' or, popularly, 'Washed in the Blood of the Lamb,' by *Elisha* Hoffman" (156; my emphasis).

8. Jean Genet, *Our Lady of the Flowers*, trans. Bernard Frechtman (New York: Bantam, 1964), 246. Hereafter abbreviated as *LF*.

9. See Matthew 16:14; Mark 6:15, 8:28; Luke 9:8, 19.

10. See Matthew 11:13–14; see also John 1:21, where John the Baptist denies being Elijah.

11. "UG," 286. Derrida speaks of the "disquiet regarding familial legitimation; it is this which makes *Ulysses*, as well as *Finnegans Wake*, vibrate" (ibid., 280).

12. "If I have only recently discovered this double dolor or mourning of Eli (to be distinguished, if only by a bit, from Elijah, or Eliah, which turns out to be one of my first names), I must have read and then forgotten, at the time of my dream of elders and eyes, the dramas of Isaac and Tobit" (*MB*, 23).

13. See 1 Samuel 15:27–28 and Isaiah 3:18–23. Curiously—indeed gloriously—the Hebrew word for mantle, *adderet*, comes, according to William L. Holladay's lexicon, from *eder*, meaning "glory" or "splendor." My thanks to Dana Hollander and Arndt Wedemeyer for this reference.

14. It is the chance of French as well, for *un manteau de cheminée* is also a mantelpiece, although one tends in modern French to simply say "la cheminée."

15. This scene is analyzed in *Glas* in terms of a theory of the fetish (211b–14b).

16. Jacques Derrida, "By Force of Mourning," trans. Pascale-Anne Brault and Michael Naas, *Critical Inquiry* 22, no. 2 (winter 1996): 185. Hereafter abbreviated as "FM."

17. Jacques Derrida, "The Deaths of Roland Barthes," trans. Pascale-Anne Brault and Michael Naas, in *Continental Philosophy*, vol. 1, (1988), 264. Hereafter abbreviated as "DRB." Both this and the above text on Marin can also be found in Jacques Derrida's *The Work of Mourning* (Chicago: University of Chicago Press, 2001).

18. "A skiff, a crumpled throwaway, Elijah is coming, rode lightly down the Liffey" (*U*, 227); see also 279, 550, 676. Elijah's name also appears on a poster outside Merrion Hall (*U*, 250). Bloom feeds the gulls, inviting comparison with Elijah's retiring into the wilderness and being fed by ravens (*U*, 153). At *U*, 197 we hear the phrase "Hast thou found me, O mine enemy," spoken in 1 Kings 21 when Elijah finds Ahab, who, along with his wife Jezebel, has just taken over a vineyard whose owner was unjustly killed. In chapter 12 there is a reference to "Carmel mount [and] the children of Elijah prophet" (*U*, 339; see also *U*, 552). At *U*, 667, there is a reference to the scene in 1 Kings 18:42–44, where Elijah sees a cloud like a man's hand on Mount Carmel and portends the end of the drought. In chapter 15 a "rocket rushes up the sky and bursts. A white star falls from it, proclaiming the consummation of all things and the second *coming* of Elijah" (*U*, 507; my emphasis but Joyce's pun).

19. Matthew 17:1–4; see also Mark 9:4–5 and Luke 9:30–33.

20. John Alexander Dowie, *Zion's Holy War Against the Hosts of Hell in Chicago* (Chicago: Zion Publishing House, 1900), 224, 268–69.

21. As Derrida writes of *Glas* in "This Is Not an Oral Footnote," "The text has no beginning and no end, no hierarchy, but [is] a text on religion, on proper names, on authority, law, theft, hierarchy" (204). All this could also be said, as Geoffrey Hartman in effect argues in *Saving the Text*, of Joyce's *Finnegans Wake*, the text from which I take my last word, if it is a word—my last and its first.

Cultural Memory | *in the Present*

Gil Anidjar, *"Our Place in Al-Andalus": Kabbalah, Philosophy, Literature in Arab-Jewish Letters*

Hélène Cixous and Jacques Derrida, *Veils*

F. R. Ankersmit, *Historical Representation*

F. R. Ankersmit, *Political Representation*

Elissa Marder, *Dead Time: Temporal Disorders in the Wake of Modernity (Baudelaire and Flaubert)*

Reinhart Koselleck, *The Practice of Conceptual History: Timing History, Spacing Concepts*

Niklas Luhmann, *The Reality of the Mass Media*

Hubert Damisch, *A Childhood Memory by Piero della Francesca*

Hubert Damisch, *A Theory of /Cloud/: Toward a History of Painting*

Jean-Luc Nancy, *The Speculative Remark (One of Hegel's bon mots)*

Jean-François Lyotard, *Soundproof Room: Malraux's Anti-Aesthetics*

Jan Patočka, *Plato and Europe*

Hubert Damisch, *Skyline: The Narcissistic City*

Isabel Hoving, *In Praise of New Travelers: Reading Caribbean Migrant Women Writers*

Richard Rand, ed., *Futures: Of Derrida*

William Rasch, *Niklas Luhmann's Modernity: The Paradox of System Differentiation*

Jacques Derrida and Anne Dufourmantelle, *Of Hospitality*

Jean-François Lyotard, *The Confession of Augustine*

Kaja Silverman, *World Spectators*

Samuel Weber, *Institution and Interpretation: Expanded Edition*

Jeffrey S. Librett, *The Rhetoric of Cultural Dialogue: Jews and Germans in the Epoch of Emancipation*

Ulrich Baer, *Remnants of Song: Trauma and the Experience of Modernity in Charles Baudelaire and Paul Celan*

Samuel C. Wheeler III, *Deconstruction as Analytic Philosophy*

David S. Ferris, *Silent Urns: Romanticism, Hellenism, Modernity*

Rodolphe Gasché, *Of Minimal Things: Studies on the Notion of Relation*

Sarah Winter, *Freud and the Institution of Psychoanalytic Knowledge*

Samuel Weber, *The Legend of Freud: Expanded Edition*

Aris Fioretos, ed., *The Solid Letter: Readings of Friedrich Hölderlin*

J. Hillis Miller / Manuel Asensi, *Black Holes / J. Hillis Miller; or, Boustrophedonic Reading*

Miryam Sas, *Fault Lines: Cultural Memory and Japanese Surrealism*

Peter Schwenger, *Fantasm and Fiction: On Textual Envisioning*

Didier Maleuvre, *Museum Memories: History, Technology, Art*

Jacques Derrida, *Monolingualism of the Other; or, The Prosthesis of Origin*

Andrew Baruch Wachtel, *Making a Nation, Breaking a Nation: Literature and Cultural Politics in Yugoslavia*

Niklas Luhmann, *Love as Passion: The Codification of Intimacy*

Mieke Bal, ed., *The Practice of Cultural Analysis: Exposing Interdisciplinary Interpretation*

Jacques Derrida and Gianni Vattimo, eds., *Religion*